# BIG-10
## FOOTBALL

# BIG-10 FOOTBALL

**GREGORY B. RICHARDS** and **MELISSA H. LARSON**

Crescent Books
A Division of Crown Publishers, Inc.

A Bison Book

Copyright © 1987 Bison Books Corp.

Published 1987 by
Crescent Books, distributed by
Crown Publishers Inc.

Produced by Bison Books Corp.
15 Sherwood Place
Greenwich, CT 06830, USA

Printed in Hong Kong

ISBN 0-517-63352-3

hgfedcba

# Contents

Page 1: *Quarterback Tim Clifford (14) in action for the Indiana Hoosiers, 1979.*

Pages 2-3: *Pete Johnson (33) of the Ohio State Buckeyes spots a hole and makes his move during the 1974 OSU-Michigan game.*

Below: *Ed Tunnicliff (15) of the NU Wildcats charges toward the goal line to score the game-winning touchdown at the 1949 Rose Bowl.*

# INTRODUCTION

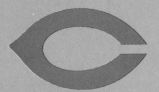

University of Chicago
*Maroons*

University of Illinois
*Fighting Illini*

Indiana University
*Hoosiers*

University of Iowa
*Hawkeyes*

University of Michigan
*Wolverines*

Michigan State University
*Spartans*

University of Minnesota
*Golden Gophers*

Northwestern University
*Wildcats*

Ohio State University
*Buckeyes*

Purdue University
*Boilermakers*

University of Wisconsin
*Badgers*

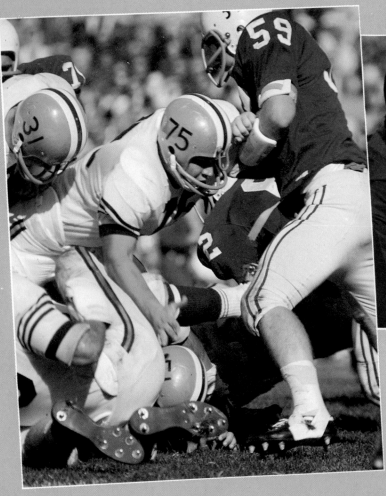

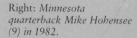

Above: *Two great rivals, two great coaches: Michigan's Bo Schembechler (left) and Ohio State's Woody Hayes, 1976.*

Left: *The Fighting Illini of Illinois meet Northwestern's Wildcats, 1964.*

Right: *Minnesota quarterback Mike Hohensee (9) in 1982.*

Far right: *Ohio State proudly proclaims its status as Big Ten Champion with this float at the 1980 Tournament of Roses Parade.*

Above: *The Wolverines get psyched up for a game at Ohio Stadium.*

Right: *The Buckeyes' drum major gives a cheer for victory.*

Far right: *The Purdue Marching Band boasts the world's largest drum.*

Top right: *MSU cheerleaders form a pyramid.*

Properly speaking, the Big Ten dates only from 1953, when the Michigan State Spartans joined the Big Nine to give the conference its present number and, incidentally, to share the 1953 championship honors with Illinois. But people had been thinking informally of Midwestern football as being represented by the Big Ten long before that, for in the nearly three-decade period between 1912 and 1940 the conference had always consisted of ten teams. To be sure, in those years it was never officially called the Big Ten and was not even officially called the Western Conference. Its real name was the ICFR, the Intercollegiate Conference of Faculty Representatives, and its origins go back to 1895.

In that year Purdue president James H Smart called a meeting of the presidents of Chicago, Illinois, Lake Forest, Minnesota, Northwestern and Wisconsin to discuss what could be done about the rising tide of violence in intercollegiate football. The result of the meeting was the creation of an organization, the ICFR, that was made up of the managers of the various teams and was charged with the responsibility of revising the rules of intercollegiate football in such a way 'as to reduce the liability of injury to a minimum.' This was soon done to everyone's satisfaction, and the next year, 1896, seven teams that had subscribed to the new rules (the same schools as those represented at the presidents' meeting, except that Lake Forest was now replaced by Michigan) became charter members of the new ICFR conference. Three years later they were joined by Indiana and Iowa, and in 1912 the addition of Ohio State brought membership to ten. Save the absence of Michigan from 1908 to 1917, the conference would remain at this level until 1940, when Chicago dropped out, and would return again to ten, in its present composition, in 1953.

Those are the facts, but they are probably less important than the perception. The *idea* of the Big Ten has been fixed in people's minds for the better part of a century, and that idea represents all that is best in college football and may even be, as the great Illinois coach, Robert Zuppke, once claimed, 'the anchor of amateur athletics in America.'

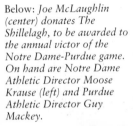

Below: *Joe McLaughlin (center) donates The Shillelagh, to be awarded to the annual victor of the Notre Dame-Purdue game. On hand are Notre Dame Athletic Director Moose Krause (left) and Purdue Athletic Director Guy Mackey.*

Bob Zuppke's name is only one of scores that the Big Ten has contributed to the lore of American sport. If no single player's name quite comes up to that of Illinois' Galloping Ghost, Red Grange, there are many that are not far behind – Bronko Nagurski, Otto Graham, Willie Heston, Tom Harmon, Archie Griffin, Alan Ameche and others too numerous to mention. The list of legendary coaches is similarly long – Fielding Yost, Bernie Bierman, Woody Hayes, Fritz Crisler, Bo Schembechler and many more, including that granddaddy of them all, the immortal Amos Alonzo Stagg, Chicago's great coach from 1892 to 1932. Lexicographers such as Stuart Berg Flexner have attributed to Stagg some of our most basic football terms and concepts – *pigskin, practice dummy, end run, shift, single wing, cheerleader, letter, huddle* and so on. His innovations lent an air of sophistication to the fledgling sport. But probably Knute Rockne summed it up best when he said simply, 'All modern football stems from Stagg.'

Anyone proposing to write a history of Big Ten football is thus confronted with an embarrassment of riches, but also with a difficult choice: Should the story be told chronologically, season by season, or should it be told school by school? There is much to be said for the season-by-season approach, which undoubtedly makes it easier for the reader to grasp how each year's contest for the conference title developed. But there is so much more to Big Ten football than just that annual horse race. The teams, the faculties, the students, the alumni and the fans of Big Ten universities may feel more keenly about football than any other people on earth. And those feelings are not the product of any single season, but of seasons out of mind. They do not relate solely – or even primarily – to statistics about wins, losses and standings, but to deeply-embedded traditions that have to do with pride in one's school, with old and honored rivalries and with perennially high expectations both of sport and of sportsmanship. A school-by-school history of Big Ten football may be able to do no more than hint at such things, but it must still be the preferred method, for in the end it is such things that make all the difference.

Below left: *Purdue Boilermakers fans gather around the Cannon in 1962. The trophy goes home with the winner of the Purdue-Illinois game each year.*

Below: *The original Floyd of Rosedale (bottom) poses with the trophy he inspired. The bronze statuette is the prize for the winner of the yearly meeting of the Iowa Hawkeyes and the Minnesota Golden Gophers.*

# UNIVERSITY
## OF
# CHICAGO

Founded: 1893

Location: Chicago

Total Enrollment: 8800

Colors: Maroon and White

Nickname: Maroons

Previous pages: *Chicago guard Ellmore Patterson, seen here in an aerial display, joined Jay Berwanger as an All-American selection in 1934.*

Even though the University of Chicago has not been part of the Big Ten since 1946, it holds fast as a pillar in the framework of conference football history. Chicago became one of the charter members of the conference which formed on 11 January 1895, just five years after the school was founded, and asserted itself as a collegiate superpower in its first three decades. A constellation of star players wore the Maroon jersey, including Clarence Herschberger, Walter Eckersall, Chuck McGuire and 'The Man in the Iron Mask,' Jay Berwanger.

Easily the most famous name connected with Chicago football, however, is not that of a player but of a coach: Amos Alonzo Stagg, a Grand Old Man of football whose 72-year continuous career in the sport is unequaled. Generally regarded as the greatest football coach of all time, 'Mr Football' held the record for the most victories won with 314. That mark was passed only recently by Paul 'Bear' Bryant of Alabama with 323 and by Eddie Robinson of Grambling with more than 320.

Stagg did not invent football, but he began so early in the game that he can be considered a true pioneer. Young Amos, a native of West Orange, New Jersey, first played with a championship Yale team in 1888 when he was a graduate student. His coach was none other

*Below: Andrew Wyant, the first player recruited to the new University of Chicago football team, arrived in 1892.*

than Walter Camp, who placed the 147-lb Stagg at right end. The team lost only one game in Stagg's two years at Yale, and he was named by Caspar Whitney to the first-ever All-America team.

After two years at Yale Stagg began coaching at the YMCA training school in Springfield, Massachusetts. In 1892 he was summoned to fledgling University of Chicago by former Yale professor William Rainey Harper. In an unprecedented move, Harper promised Stagg an associate professorship, tenure and a then-astronomical $2500 salary to head up the physical education and intercollegiate athletics programs. Stagg delightedly accepted and decided he would both play *and* coach (at the time, no rules existed to prohibit that arrangement).

Stagg helped speed the evolution of football from a contest of sheer physical strength and forward momentum to today's highly strategic, multiple-offense game. Early college matches were bloody and at times violent; players in the 1893 Chicago game at Purdue were almost indicted for assault and battery by a local district attorney. But before long, Stagg began lacing his game plans with sophisticated and sometimes deceptive ballhandling maneuvers. The handoff, cross-buck, reverse, half-spin and such tricks as the hidden ball and Statue of Liberty were all Stagg innovations. He lent some of that creativity to one of the earliest books on the sport, 1893's *Scientific and Practical Treatise on American Football for Schools and Colleges.*

Not only was Stagg imaginative, he was successful. In his first eight years – which included a ridiculously long, 21-game slate in 1894 – Stagg guided Chicago to a spectacular 83-23-8 record and its first conference championship in 1899. Stagg was also the first collegiate coach to organize an *indoor* football game. Bad weather in 1895 forced the Minnesota Golden Gophers and the Maroons into Chicago Coliseum, and a huge audience followed. The teams split a hefty $10,812 in gate receipts, a new high.

By developing halfback Clarence Herschberger into an All-American, Stagg made history by cracking the Eastern schools' monopoly of honor teams. The 158-lb fullback was a rambunctious, free-spirited player who, in spite of his success, occasionally got under Stagg's skin. On the night before the 1897 contest with Wisconsin's Badgers, for example, Herschberger is said to have challenged Maroon captain Walter Kennedy to an eating contest. Kennedy won by stuffing in nearly eight pounds of food, against Clarence's seven. The

*Above: The great Walter Camp, seen here as captain of the Yale University football team (1878-79), later coached a young Amos Alonzo Stagg at Yale during the 1888 and 1889 seasons. Stagg played right end.*

*Top right: Fullback Clarence B Herschberger became the first Chicago player to be selected All-American by Walter Camp, in 1898. He was also the first of Amos Alonzo Stagg's success stories.*

fullback decided to better his mark the next morning by plowing through half a dozen eggs – and became so ill he was unable to play in the game. Chicago sorely missed its All-American and lost 23-8, the Badgers stealing the Maroons' claim to the conference title by handing them their only defeat of the season.

In 1904 Chicago placed not one but two men on the All-America, the first Big Ten team to do so: Fred Speik, a hard-hitting end, and quarterback Walter Eckersall. Eckersall's name competes with that of Jay Berwanger whenever someone tries to name the best player in Chicago history, but Eckersall has the edge, since he was named All-American in 1904, 1905 and 1906 – compared to Berwanger's two listings – and was one of the very few college players to win that honor three times.

As a 118-pound terror on the Hyde Park (Illinois) High School team, Eckersall helped beat not only every prep school in region, but even college teams, including Stagg's squad. The coach must have been overjoyed when 'Eckie' decided to attend Chicago. Having topped out at 140 pounds, the ferocious back was smaller than many Big Ten opponents, but he was nonetheless a superb all-around player, capable of running, kicking, passing, punting and even tackling.

Stagg started Eckie at end in 1904 but put his talents to full use the next year in the quarterback spot. Eckersall, along with teammates Babe Meigs, Hugo Bezdek, Jesse Harper and All-America center Mark Catlin, responded by driving the Maroons to what Stagg always insisted was their greatest season. The squad was destined for glory: Bezdek was later a brilliant coach for Penn State, and Harper was among the first to bring fame to Notre Dame. Chicago was the only team in the Big Ten in five years to stop the Point-a-Minute machine from Michigan, and handed a 2-0 heartbreak to the Wolverines to end their record 55-game winning streak.

Little Eckersall was primarily responsible. In the final minutes of the Michigan game Walter shot a 60-yard punt into the Wolves' end

Above: *Diminutive quarterback Walter Eckersall led the Maroons to the Big Ten championship in 1905 and was voted All-American for three successive years (1904-06). His extensive talents were capped in the 1906 season when he became the first Maroon to use the forward pass.*

Above right: *Center Paul 'Shorty' Des Jardien made All-America in 1913.*

zone, where Denny Clark pulled it in for a return sprint. Clark almost made it out of the end zone but was grounded by Maroon captain Maurice Catlin just shy of the goal line. The resulting safety made for the upset of the decade – but not before Eckersall thwarted a last-ditch touchdown run by becoming the only man who ever tackled Michigan's phenomenal halfback Willie Heston from behind.

By Eckersall's final year of play, 1906, the forward pass was allowed, and Coach Stagg looked to his brilliant strategist to make use of it. 'Do you think you can throw this thing with any accuracy?' Stagg asked Walter, tossing him the oversize, balloon-shaped pigskin of the day. 'I'll throw it,' Eckersall replied. 'Just make sure you have someone who can catch it!'

Stagg did: Wally Steffen, who would later coach his way to fame at Carnegie Tech. In the fourth game of the season Stagg unleashed his aerial offense against Illinois. Eckersall, who had never thrown a forward pass in a game, hurled the ball 75 yards to Steffen for a touchdown. Walter Camp's 'greatest quarterback of all time' completed every subsequent throw in a 63-0 victory over the stunned Illini. Eckersall's foot was equally good at scoring, and Eckie kicked five field goals each against Illinois and Notre Dame during his career. The Maroons smashed all other opponents in 1905 and snared the conference championship.

Steffen's talents were showcased by the teams of 1907 and 1908, which secured back-to-back Big Ten titles. In the first of those sea-

sons another ball carrier, Harlan 'Pat' Page, helped the Maroons to a 4-1 season, defeated only by Pop Warner's Carlisle Indians. Page, a fantastic all-around athlete, became the first in the conference to win a letter nine times – in football, basketball and baseball. The team went 5-0-1 the following year, and quarterback Steffen made the All-America. Steffen also surprised the football world by use of another Stagg invention, the fake pass, to make sweeping runs, and when he did throw, star ends Page and John Schommer were usually in the right places to connect for considerable gains.

Four years went by before Chicago repeated as conference champions – in 1913 – taking both the Big Ten title and claiming national honors. Leading the Maroons was captain Nels Norgren, a fine halfback who outdid Pat Page by lettering 12 times in four sports. Center Paul 'Shorty' Des Jardien was named by Walter Camp to the All-America team, and placed Norgren on his second string.

Over the following seven years, Stagg faltered somewhat, compiling 23-23-1, and posting the only winless season of his entire career in 1918. Only one player made All-America: the bruising tackle Charles McGuire, in 1920 and 1921. But from 1921 to 1924, the great coach put on one last pyrotechnic display. In those four years his teams went for 6-1-0, 5-1-1, 7-1-0 and 4-1-3 seasons, the final one bringing the Maroons their sixth and final Big Ten championship.

One key to Chicago's success was mammoth linebacker Austin 'Five-Yards' McCarthy, who broke through the opposing line with seeming ease. Two other linemen, tackle Franklin Gowdy and guard Joe Pondelik, helped the Maroons hold an Illinois team starring Red Grange to a 21-21 tie and ultimately to pick up the conference title. Both Gowdy and Pondelik made the All-America for 1924, but McCarthy was edged out by Notre Dame's Elmer Layden of 'Four Horseman' fame. Two years prior, Chicago fullback John Thomas also had made the list.

The 1924 championship season marked the beginning of the end for Chicago, whose athletic program fell victim to a gradual de-emphasis on sports over the next several years. The football program was doomed by the appointment of Robert Hutchins as university president in 1929. Hutchins sought to purify the school's image as a strictly academic environment, and football was useless in that pursuit. By 1932 Hutchins had forced Stagg, now 70 years old, into involuntary retirement, much to the outrage of the alumni, students,

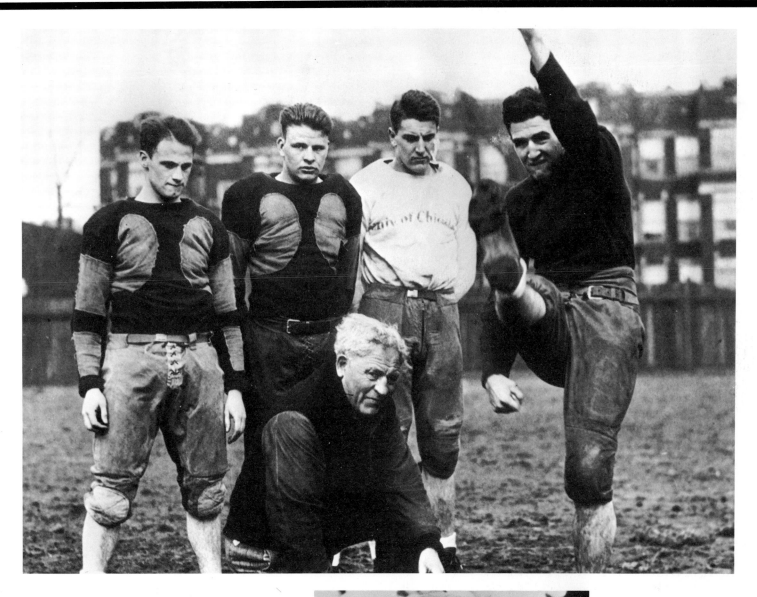

press and public. The final blow came in 1939, when Hutchins announced Chicago was giving up intercollegiate football altogether. Other sports met the same fate seven years later when the university withdrew from the Big Ten conference.

But before bowing out of the picture completely the Maroons, under coach Clark Shaughnessy, had produced another legend, John Jacob 'Jay' Berwanger. The 6-foot, 200-pound tailback started for the Maroons as a sophomore in 1933 and played a full hour in every conference contest, carrying the ball 184 times for a four-yard average gain.

Berwanger managed to see his way past opponents in spite of a combination helmet-mask he wore to protect his nose, which had never properly set after being broken in his freshman year. The contraption, made of leather-covered straps of spring steel, earned the tailback his nickname, 'The Man in the Iron Mask.'

In 1934, Berwanger's junior year, the Maroons managed to win half their conference games. Jay carried the ball 119 times with a five-yard average, completed 14 passes for 196

Above: *Coach Amos Alonzo Stagg holds the ball for team captain Don Birney for a practice kick-off. Perhaps the greatest football coach of all time, he headed the Maroons from 1892 to 1932.*

Left: *Clark Shaughnessy took over as head football coach when Stagg had to give up the position in 1932.*

yards, scored eight touchdowns and returned 18 punts for 186 yards. A phenomenal punter, Berwanger booted the ball 77 times, and 30 of his punts soared out of bounds to prevent runbacks. On top of his other skills, Jay was a rugged defensive player who terrorized opponents at cornerback. In the first half of play with Minnesota, he made 14 tackles. Both Berwanger and guard Ellmore Patterson were named to the All-America.

Berwanger repeated on the honor team in his last year, 1935, and is best remembered for his searing runs against superpower Ohio State. Berwanger frustrated Buckeye attempts by slipping past scrimmage and tearing up the slick, muddy field time and again. On one drive Berwanger took the ball at the Chicago 40-yard line, shrugged off would-be tacklers and made his way to the sideline. Then the tailback cut back to the middle and the Buckeye defense moved in for the kill. Jay seemed to hesitate for a few seconds as he backed up and looked for an opening; but then, with a sudden burst of speed, he shot through a tiny opening, made his way back to the sideline, and streaked all the way past the defenders for the Maroon's second touchdown. In the record book Berwanger is credited with a 60-yard run, but it is estimated he covered at least 100 yards on that treacherous, waterlogged turf.

Yet as was too often the case, Berwanger's efforts alone could not save the Maroons from defeat, and Ohio State won the game 20-13. But by season's end, Jay had established himself as a champion, with career totals of 1839 yards rushing on 439 carries; 50 completed passes of 146, for 920 yards; 22 touchdowns and 22 points-after for 152 total points; 223 punts, with 80 placed out of bounds; and 54 kickoff and punt returns for a 32-yard average.

The greatest tribute to Berwanger's talents came at season's end, when New York's Downtown Athletic Club gave him its very first award for the nation's most outstanding collegiate player. That this first Heisman Trophy could go to a player whose team had compiled an unspectacular 9-13-2 record over three years reflects well on both award committee and player. We can only imagine what Berwanger might have accomplished playing for one of the major forces of the era: Ohio State, Michigan or Minnesota. But the Chicago Bears were enough impressed with the feisty Maroon player to make him their first draft pick.

Former Coach Amos Alonzo Stagg also found recognition after leaving the Maroons, and at age 70 was still decades away from retirement. 'I am fit, able and willing,' he told the

press. 'I refuse to be idle and a nuisance.' Stagg found acceptance at the College of the Pacific in Stockton, California, and began coaching the Tigers in 1933 in a way that belied his age. In a few short years, he whipped the Tigers into shape and had the team meeting opponents such as UCLA, Southern California, Stanford and St Mary's. Stagg brought the small school within one victory of a Rose Bowl berth in 1942, and over his 14 seasons at Stockton won several Far Western Conference championships.

In 1946 Stagg moved on to a 10-yard contract with Susquehanna University in Sellinsgrove, Pennsylvania, as an assistant under his son, Amos Jr. He and his wife moved back to their California home in 1953, and the restless coach then guided the team at Stockton Junior College for seven years until finally retiring at age 98. The 'Grand Old Man' lived five more years and died at age 103 in March 1965, eight months after his wife of 70 years, Stella, had passed away. The traditions of excellence he left behind is perfectly in keeping with the high standards Chicago has always, and very successfully, striven to maintain. And that same great tradition would also be passed on to Chicago's successor, Michigan State, when it joined the Big Ten in 1953. So the spirit of Amos Alonzo Stagg is very much with us still.

Above: *All-American halfback John Jacob 'Jay' Berwanger was the first player ever to receive the coveted Heisman Trophy.*

Opposite: *The grand old man of football, Amos Alonzo Stagg, is credited with transforming the game from a display of brute force to a strategic contest.*

# UNIVERSITY OF ILLINOIS

Founded: 1867

Location: Champaign-Urbana

Total Enrollment: 35,997

Colors: Orange and Blue

Nickname: Fighting Illini

Page 18: *Jack Trudeau (10) of the Fighting Illini at the 1984 Rose Bowl.*

*Right: George Huff served as athletic director at the University of Illinois from 1895 to 1936.*

When the ICFR, or Western Intercollegiate Conference, later to become the Big Ten, was organized in 1896, intercollegiate football had already been played at the University of Illinois for five years, thanks to the efforts of an Illini freshman named Scott Williams, who led the fight to organize a football team. Illinois' first game took place against Illinois Wesleyan in 1890 with Williams serving not only as quarterback and captain but also as coach!

In 1895 George Huff arrived in Champaign and took over as football coach; one year later he assumed the dual duties of athletic director and baseball coach. Although coaching champion baseball Illini teams brought Huff fame, his contributions to the football program as athletic director, a post he filled until his death in 1936, were perhaps even more significant.

In 1897 Illinois secured the coaching services of a former star halfback at Princeton, Fred Smith. Illinois also had a strong fullback in Arthur Johnson, and at season's start the squad felt ready to take on Amos Alonzo Stagg's strong University of Chicago team. Illinois won the game 18-12, although Johnson had to be carried from the field with a broken collar bone. Also in that season Illinois played a game against the Carlisle Indians, at the old Chicago Coliseum, which was historic for two reasons: the contest was both held at night and indoors. Special trains carried 700 rooters up from Champaign for the game in Chicago. Although the Illini lost the game 23-6, some 10,000 people had paid admission and both

teams received about $4000 after expenses.

For the next several years Illinois football teams fared poorly against their Big Ten rivals in the new conference, largely because their coaches stayed for only one or two years. The lack of continuity particularly hurt play against conference rivals Chicago and Michigan, which enjoyed the skilled coaching of Stagg and Fielding Yost, respectively.

In 1907 Arthur Hall became coach of Illini football, and he remained until 1912, lending some badly needed stability to the program. He wasted no time in making use of the newly-legalized forward pass. Illini teams of 1907 and 1908 were built around the passing talents of 130-pound Pomery Sinnock, the Big Nine's

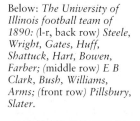

*Below: The University of Illinois football team of 1890: (l-r, back row) Steele, Wright, Gates, Huff, Shattuck, Hart, Bowen, Farber; (middle row) E B Clark, Bush, Williams, Arms; (front row) Pillsbury, Slater.*

first quarterback to throw the football. In the last game of the 1908 schedule, against rival Northwestern, Sinnock completed 25 forward passes in a 64-8 shellacking of the Purple.

It was the 1910 season, however, that provided Illini football fans with their first taste of real glory, as the team put together the Big Nine's first unbeaten, untied season. The Orange and Blue had even prevented all comers from scoring, and after romps over Millikin and Drake, it was time for the first annual Homecoming game. Two underclassmen named Elmer Ekblaw and C F 'Dab' Williams, already thinking about how much they would miss the beautiful Champaign campus after their college days were over, had conceived the idea, soon endorsed by the faculty.

The Illini played their first Homecoming game against Chicago, led by quarterback and ace kicker Otto Seiler. Seiler actually rose from the hospital bed where he had been confined all week to play in the game. His dropkicking heroics, notably a 38-yard field goal, provided the margin of victory for Illinois, which had not beaten Chicago for six long seasons. Seiler became Illinois' first Homecoming hero, and the resulting celebrations lasted well into the night.

But the following two seasons proved disappointing for Illini fans, who had to settle for a 4-2-1 record in 1911 and a 3-3-1 record in 1912. Critics wished aloud for new coaching blood to bring back the success of the golden season of 1910, and George Huff began to search for a new coach. He finally decided upon a young man who was at the time coaching the game at Oak Park (Illinois) High School. His name was Robert Zuppke. For the next 29 seasons he virtually became Illini football, and ultimately was recognized as one of the greatest football coaches in collegiate athletics history.

Born in Berlin, Germany, in 1879, Zuppke was the only Big Ten coach in history never to have played varsity football. Small of stature, weighing only 140 pounds, and a gifted painter, he had had fine art in mind as a career but fell in love with the football he saw played in the big Eastern colleges of the US. Teaching and coaching on the high school level in Muskegan, Michigan, and then at Oak Park High brought him, finally, to Illinois, where he was destined to make history.

A direct and blunt taskmaster with a heavy German accent, Zuppke was nevertheless a great and innovative football mind. While still a high school coach, he had invented the spiral snap from center, as well as the screen pass. Later he would experiment with the first huddle. Most important, Zuppke favored

intricate plays and finesse over brute strength, which allowed his Illinois teams to compete with much larger and stronger competition such as the Minnesota teams of that era.

Harold Pogue, who played halfback for 'Zup,' remembered what the new coach told the team at their first practice of the 1913 season.

*It's what you deliver yourself, boys, that counts. When a ball is snapped, remember that you're part of a machine and that the success of our team will depend on each individual giving us everything he has in his heart and body ... You must carry out your assignments. You must stretch yourself for every inch of yourself if we are to be a winner.*

That advice, as fresh today as it was in 1913, guided Zuppke's teams and molded the characters of some of football's greatest players. Compiling a 4-2-1 record in his first season, Zuppke returned in 1914 with what he later described as the greatest Illinois team of his career. Zuppke used I-formations, T-formations and punt formations that allowed for surprise kicks, making the 1914 team the most modern of its day.

Above: *Robert Zuppke, the great Illini football coach of 1913-42. A brilliant strategist and innovator, in his 29 years at Illinois he had four undefeated teams, won three national championships, won or shared seven Big Ten titles, and compiled an outstanding record of 131-81-13. He also produced some of football's greatest players, most notably the unstoppable Red Grange, who wreaked havoc for the Illini in 1923-24-25.*

Zuppke had fine players, too. At quarterback was George 'Potsy' Clark. Pogue and Bart Macomber were the halfbacks, and Gene Schobinger made a powerful fullback. Up front the line consisted of captain and guard Ralph Chapman, who became Illinois' first All-American. This splendid Illini team blanked its first four opponents and held the others to single figures to establish itself as the class of the nation.

The next three seasons saw Zuppke's Illini compile an overall record of 13-5-4, although they did not gain the conference crown again until 1918. Those three seasons, 1915 through 1917, also comprised the Illini football career of George S Halas, who would become one of the founders of the National Football League, and who returned time and again to Illinois to recruit players from his alma mater.

The 1916 season became famous for one of Zuppke's greatest upset victories. The game was played against a seemingly unbeatable Minnesota Gopher team. Chicago sportswriters suggested that Illinois should simply forfeit rather than waste the time to travel up to Minneapolis. Zuppke believed that the only chance his team had against the Gophers was for his players to be loose, relaxed and unafraid of losing. The night before the game he broke training rules for his team and they all went out together for a meal and a show. The next day, right before the contest, he gave an intentionally hilarious speech which had his players laughing as they took the field. Zuppke's preparation had not been all psychological, however. He had also outlined a game

Above: *George S Halas played for Illinois from 1915 to 1917. He later became one of the founders of the National Football League.*

Right: *Ralph (Slooie) Chapman was captain and guard on the superb 1914 Illini team. He became the first All-American at the University of Illinois.*

plan keyed on Minnesota's three best ballcarriers, and he guaranteed that if the Illini could stop those three players they would win.

It was a hard-fought game, especially for the Illini players. The original 11 men on the field played the entire game against wave after wave of fresh Minnesota Gophers. But the Illini gritted their teeth and hung on for victory, the score 14-9, one of the biggest upsets in the history of the conference. One of the stunned wit-

Right: *The 1914 Illini team, which Zuppke considered his best ever.*

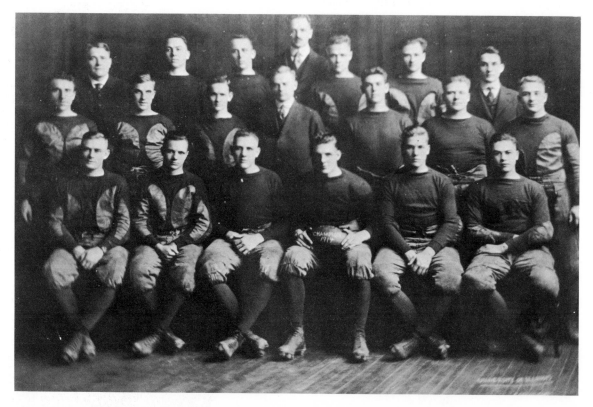

nesses was the revered Walter Camp, who had come to Minnesota to see the famous Gopher team crush Illinois. Camp honored Macomber with a spot on his All-America team, probably on the strength of what he had seen on that never-to-be-forgotten afternoon.

Halas, who had accompanied the team on the trip, even though he was hobbling on a broken leg, later described the thrill of the upset:

*I knew how well Zup prepared a team for a game like that one, but to see it all unfolding just the way he'd planned it . . . well, you almost couldn't believe it . . . I still can recall the feeling of exhilaration we all had when that game ended. And I can remember how I threw my crutches up in the air and ran out on the field when it finally was over.*

Although many Big Ten football stars had joined active military service, lowering standards somewhat, the 1918 Illini season was nevertheless memorable. Illinois was unbeaten and unscored-upon in the four conference games, although two military service teams beat the Illini, each by a score of 7-0. No Illini made All-American that year, but among outstanding players was tackle Burt Ingwerson, who later described the dual roles of football player and military trainee in the Student Army Training Corps.

*We had to drill every night outside the Armory after football practice. When we'd go to a game we'd have to wear our uniforms, and we'd march between train stations, or from the train to our hotel or dormitory.*

By the 1919 season many of the players came back from the service, ready for intense competition. The year would also see Upset King Zuppke's biggest upset – against an Ohio State team that had welcomed home famed back Charles W 'Chic' Harley for his final season. The Illini, who had lost to Wisconsin, were three-touchdown underdogs as the two teams took to field in Columbus. The afternoon proved a grinding one, and many players on both sides were injured. With two minutes left in the game, Ohio State led 7-6. Illinois launched a do-or-die passing attack that landed the ball on the Buckeye 20-yard line with seconds left.

End Chuck Carney, who would become an All-American in 1920 and today is still hailed as possibly the best end in Illinois history, later described the tension on the sidelines.

Above: *Tackle Burt Ingwerson was an outstanding Illini player during the lean 1918 season*

Above: *All-American halfback Bart Macomber was on the 1916 team which upset the Minnesota Gophers.*

Left: *Number 77, Harold 'Red' Grange, whose astounding ability as a runner earned him the nickname 'The Galloping Ghost'.*

*Ralph Fletcher, our regular kicker, was hurt. Dick Reichle also was on that team, and he'd done some kicking, but he also was hurt that day. Zuppke started looking for someone who could try to kick, and I remember Bob Fletcher running up to him and saying, 'I'll kick it.'*

And he did. Sophomore Fletcher, who had never attempted a field goal before that afternoon, sent the kick through the uprights for a 9-7 Illini win. Chic Harley reportedly broke down in tears; it was the Buckeye star's only defeat in his fabulous career.

Legend has it that as the victorious team headed back to their quarters to await the train home, an Illinois alumnus approached the curly-haired Fletcher and offered the youth $1000 – an enormous sum in those days – for the shoe with which he had kicked the winning field goal. Fletcher declined. Illinois was once more the Big Ten champion, although again no All-Americans were chosen that year.

The 1920s were a pivotal decade in the history of Illinois football. It was a period of rapid growth, during which Memorial Stadium was built and dedicated. Chief Illiniwek and his war dances first brought delight to the fans. And 'Illibuck,' the turtle trophy, was first passed between Champaign and Columbus as the winner's prize. (Later, trophies came to include the Cannon, symbolic of the Purdue-Illinois contest, and the Tomahawk trophy with Northwestern.) It was also during this period that Illinois became known as the 'Fighting Illini,' after yet another dizzying upset of Ohio State in 1921.

The years 1922 to 1925 stand out not only in the history of Illini football, but in the larger history of American popular culture. For it was in those days that Red Grange worked his magic on the football field and won the hearts of fans everywhere in the nation. There was never a player like him before, and there probably never will be again.

Harold Grange grew up in Wheaton, Illinois, and had played some football at Wheaton High School – along with basketball, baseball and track. The young Grange had supplemented the family income by delivering ice from a horse-drawn wagon, having won the job at age 14 by hoisting a 100-pound block of ice to his shoulder. When he later attained fame as 'The Wheaton Iceman' at Illinois, pictures of Grange grinning, with a cake of ice on his shoulder, appeared in newspapers all over the country.

Red Grange almost didn't play football for Illinois. After meeting Coach Zuppke, who

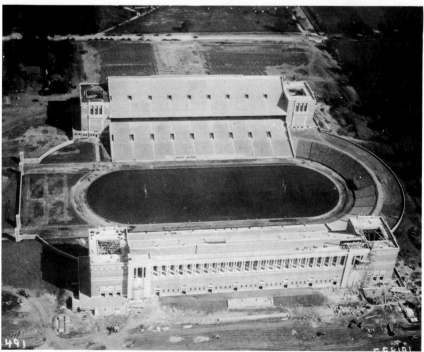

Above: *Red Grange heads toward the goal line against the Michigan Wolverines, 18 October 1924. Grange's five touchdowns led Illinois to a 39-14 upset victory.*

Left: *Memorial Stadium under construction at the University of Illinois, 1924.*

12 touchdowns in seven games and led the nation in yards gained with 1260. The Illini were unbeaten, and Walter Camp added the sophomore's name to his 1923 All-America list. Illini guard Jim McMillen was also selected. Camp said of the redhead:

*Red Grange of Illinois is not only a line-smasher of great power, but also a sterling open-field runner and has been the great factor in the offense of Illinois through the Midwest conference. He is classed as the most dangerous man in that section and probably the country over, when all kinds of running must be considered.*

Meanwhile, Grantland Rice, the dean of American sportswriters and the man who had given 'The Four Horsemen' of Notre Dame their name, sat down at his typewriter and composed a poem about Grange that began:

*A streak of fire, a breath of flame,*
*Eluding all who reach and clutch;*
*A gray ghost thrown into the game*
*That rival hands may never touch . . .*

Rice began calling Grange 'The Galloping Ghost' in print, and the name soon spread. So did Grange's fame, as he returned to Champaign for his junior year in the fall of 1924. Anticipation was running high as the day approached for the formal dedication of new Memorial Stadium – the game between Illinois and Michigan, both unbeaten in 1923.

No one could remember a more eagerly-awaited Illinois football game. Fraternity and sorority houses were gaily decorated, fans streamed in by the thousands from Chicago, and even the heated baseball pennant races were temporarily forgotten. Harry L Farrell, sportswriter for the United Press in New York, described the anticipation:

*Out here in the West, where men are men and football teams are made of them, nobody wants to discuss anything but the battle impending between Michigan and Illinois. More than 70,000 spectators are expected, and double that number of seats could have been sold if there were places for that number. There is more real enthusiasm around here than there has been in New Haven or Boston for the Harvard-Yale games.'*

In his own way, Zuppke had been preparing his players for the Michigan game for months. He had written each player several times over

had offered his characteristic mild encouragement, Grange chose to attend Illinois but arrived on campus in 1922 intending to stick to basketball and track. Fate, in the form of his new Zeta Psi fraternity brothers, intervened. The husky 170-pound freshman was ordered to go out for football or face that dreaded punishment – a paddling.

Grange trudged off to the football field, took one look at his competition, and, convinced he was simply not good enough to play for Illinois, came back to his fraternity house. But he was back the next day, possibly with a sore rear end, and within a week donned uniform number 77.

Grange made his varsity debut as a sophomore against Nebraska, romping for 208 yards against the stunned Cornhuskers and scoring every touchdown in a 24-7 victory. At the end of that 1923 season Grange had scored

the summer, telling them how lightly Michigan was taking the Illini and how easily the Wolverines and their coach, Fielding Yost, expected to win. Like his teammates, Red Grange had digested this Zuppke propaganda, and years later he recalled it:

*Zup had worked on that game from the start of the summer. He started telling us all kinds of things Yost had been saying about us all summer. It wasn't until a long time afterward that I found out that Yost had been in Europe the whole summer.*

The afternoon of 18 October 1924 was clear and unseasonably warm. Up in the stands the tension in the air could almost be cut with a knife. In the locker room, Zuppke told his players to remove the heavy woolen stockings that adorned the lower legs of all players in those days. Staring at him curiously, a few players complained that their legs would surely get cut in the contest without some sort of protection.

'Well, you're no bloomin' chorus girls,' Zuppke replied in his staccato German accent. 'Take 'em off!'

Immediately upon leaving the locker room, the Michigan team noticed the stockingless Illini and Yost ran over at once to make sure that no grease or other lubricant had been applied to the players' legs. There was none, and Zuppke's psychological trick began to work. The temperature soared into the 80s, and the Wolverine players began to feel hot and weighed down by their woolen stockings. However, their real troubles, in the person of Red Grange, hadn't even begun.

In the first 12 minutes of the game, beginning with the opening kickoff, Red Grange ran for four touchdowns. He made them on runs of 95 yards, 67 yards, 56 yards and 44 yards, and Zuppke, realizing that his star was exhausted, sat him down on the bench to rest. The din from the Memorial Stadium crowd was unlike anything heard before or since. One witness described it as 'something not heard since Caesar's return to Rome in triumph from the Wars.'

Zuppke kept Grange out of the game until the second half, when he sent him in to score his fifth touchdown and pass to Marion Leonard for Illinois' 6th and final touchdown. The Wolverines had been routed 39-14. It seemed impossible, but there it was on the scoreboard!

Later in that 1924 season Grange played another exceptional game against Stagg's University of Chicago team – Homecoming for the

Maroon. The Illini started on the wrong foot, allowing Chicago to post a 21-7 lead before the end of the first half. Grange had been double- and triple-teamed, making his end runs ineffective, though his passing had earned 177 yards.

In the third quarter Grange somehow rammed through the Maroon line for a five-yard touchdown run. The score was 21-14. Then, with the clock close to running out, Illinois took over on its own 20-yard line. The 80 yards loomed large with so little time left. So the Illini gave the ball to Red Grange. Sweep-

Above: *Red Grange gazes at his famous number 77 jersey after his last game with Illinois.*

Top: *Grange with his manager, C C Pyle (left) in 1925, shortly before The Galloping Ghost signed up with George Halas' Chicago Bears.*

ing past his interference and the defensive end, he turned the corner and streaked the whole 80 yards to a touchdown. Tie score! In the final minute of play he scored yet again on a 55-yard sprint, only to have it called back for a holding penalty. Thus the game ended in a 21-21 tie.

'That was the toughest football game I ever played in college,' Red later recalled. 'Every time I was tackled I was hit hard by two or three men. The entire Illinois team took a terrific beating.'

A mysterious loss to Minnesota late in the season dropped Illinois into a second-place tie with Iowa, with the conference crown going to Chicago – as it turned out, for the last time. Grange was again voted to the All-America team, and to this was added the first *Chicago Tribune* Big Ten MVP award.

With the 1925 team eroded by graduations and injuries, Zuppke made several player switches, and moved Grange to quarterback. The Illini lost three of their first four games, and would finish 3-5-1 overall, but Red Grange still had some running to do. His best game of the season was played at mighty Penn, in front of its hometown fans and the Eastern writers who still weren't convinced that the red-headed back was as good as the Corn Belt sportswriters had said.

Though the field was deep in mud from recent downpours, Grange rushed for 363 yards that day, scoring three touchdowns on runs of 56, 13 and 20 yards. Illinois won 24-2 before a stunned Penn crowd. Up in the press box was Lawrence Stallings, the ex-Marine who had written *What Price Glory* and had been hired to do a color story on the game. After struggling at the typewriter for an hour, he looked at what he had written and tore it up. 'I can't write it,' he sighed. 'It's too big.'

Carrying their heads a little higher after the victory over Penn, the Illini won their last three games over Chicago, Wabash and Ohio State. Grange was named All-American once more. And a few days later he belonged to George Halas' Chicago Bears. Grange's manager, Champaign theatre owner C C Pyle – many called him Cash and Carry Pyle – had taken on the enormous task of fielding endorsement offers for the Illinois wonder boy, and had met with George Halas to sign the richest football contract in the league's history until the merger between the NFL and the American Football League. Zuppke reportedly tried to talk his star out of turning pro, but without success.

In his Illinois career the Wheaton Iceman had compiled a record of 3637 yards rushing and 643 passing. And that was in only 20 games over three years.

Paul Sann, in his book *The Lawless Decade* described the impact Grange had on the fast-living generation of the Roaring Twenties:

*Red Grange, Number 77, made Jack Dempsey move over. He put college football ahead of boxing as the Golden Age picked up momentum. He also made some of the ball yards obsolete. They couldn't handle the crowds. He made people buy more radios. How could you wait until Sunday morning to find out what deeds Red Grange had performed on Saturday? He was 'The Galloping Ghost,' and he made sports historians torture their portables without mercy.*

In trying to analyze what made him the greatest player of his time – perhaps of all time – many writers spoke of Grange's great legs, the uncanny peripheral vision which allowed him to get a panoramic view of the field, and of course his great heart. But perhaps his coach, Bob Zuppke, paid him the ultimate tribute. 'I will never have another Grange,' he said (it sounded like 'Grench' in Zup's heavy accent), 'but neither will anyone else.'

Below: *Tackle Butch Nowack was an outstanding member of Bob Zuppke's last championship teams, in 1927 and 1928.*

Above: *Coach Zuppke with Charles Bennis (left) and quarterback Jack Beynon, whose 'Flying Trapeze' flea-flicker plays enlivened the 1934 season.*

Opposite top: *Paul Patterson carries the ball for an Illinois touchdown during the 1947 Rose Bowl. UCLA was toppled 45-14.*

Opposite bottom: *Illinois and UCLA in action, 1 January 1947.*

Right: *Alex Agase autographs a football for Alan Ladd while Buddy Young looks on, following the Illini victory at the 1947 Rose Bowl.*

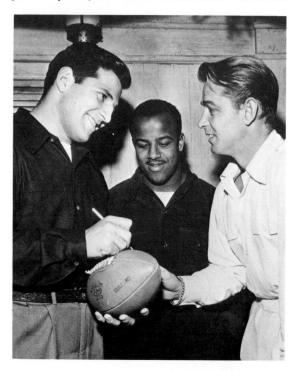

As Grange began his career with the Bears, Zuppke put together a new 1926 Illini team, winning a 6-2 record. And in 1927 and 1928 his teams won back-to-back conference championships with only two losses. Zuppke contrived to do this with players like guard Russ Crain, All-America in 1927, and tackles Butch Nowack and Lou Gordon. (Gordon was All-America in 1928). But although no one could have predicted it, these were Zuppke's last championships.

When the stock market crash came, it seemed that Illini football fortunes had crashed along with it. In the early 1930s Illinois plummeted far down in the Big Ten ratings, and Michigan and Minnesota teams dominated. The 1934 Illinois team brightened things for a while with their 'Flying Trapeze' flea-flicker plays, featuring star quarterback Jack Beynon, and the Illini finished 4-1 in the

conference that season. But then athletic director George Huff died in 1936, and the doldrums settled in again. By 1938, the alumni were growing restless, and a movement was under way to force Zuppke to resign.

The aging coach had just one more upset up his sleeve, however, and it was a big one – a win over mighty Michigan and their biggest star, Tom Harmon, in 1939. 'No one but Bob Zuppke could have done it,' wrote journalist John Dietrich in the *Cleveland Plain Dealer*. 'No one but Zuppke could reach into the hearts of his players and light the flame of emotion that sent them into a football game as into a crusade.'

Michigan had made the mistake of comparing Harmon, on his way to the Heisman Trophy, to Red Grange. Harmon was a better runner, they said, and would avenge Grange's humiliation of Michigan in 1924. Zuppke leaped on that claim and reportedly screamed at his players before the game, 'Are you going to let this upstart Harmon show up our own Red Grange?'

No, they were not. The Illini ended the first half, leading 9-7, with a 'sleeper' pass play for a touchdown by fullback George Rettinger. In the second half, wily Zuppke used a quick-count play call to surprise the Wolverines for another score, and the charged-up Illini hung on for a 16-7 win. Harmon had scored once on them, but he was no Red Grange.

A couple of mediocre seasons followed, and after the 1941 season, Zuppke resigned to pursue his suspended art career – with great success. Ray Eliot, Zuppke's assistant for four seasons and a popular choice with the players, was selected to replace the departed legend. Eliot had great respect for Zuppke but disagreed with his mentor on one point – the use of game films. Zuppke had never believed in them, but Eliot was convinced that as the game of football became more modernized and complex, films would be increasingly useful to the players. Eliot was to use films to good effect throughout his Illinois career.

In 1942, his first season as coach, Eliot was fortunate enough to field 159-pound Alex Agase. The small Assyrian, who had won only one letter in high school, told Eliot he thought he was just too small to play in the Big Ten. 'Young man,' Eliot replied, 'it's not the size of the body that counts. It's the size of your heart.' Agase, dubbed the 'wandering guard,' would go on to win acclaim as the only man in Big Ten history to win All-America honors at two schools. He was selected All-America in 1942 at Illinois, switched to Purdue the following season for naval officer training and made

All-America for the Boilermakers. He then
returned in triumph to Champaign in 1946
after his military service to once again receive
All-America honors.

In 1946 he joined a team of fired-up Illini
players, back from military service and ready
to wreak havoc on the gridiron again. In that
year Illinois cast off the reputation of also-ran
and bulldozed the Big Ten, finishing with a 6-1
conference mark, the only loss being an upset
by Indiana. The Illini, led by quarterback Perry
Moss and Agase, made a solid team in all cate-
gories, and when the invitation came to play
Pacific Coast Conference champ UCLA in the
Rose Bowl under the new contract between the
two conferences, the Illini were ready. After
Eliot made sure each Illini player had read the
belittling remarks made about them in the
West Coast papers, they whipped the Bruins

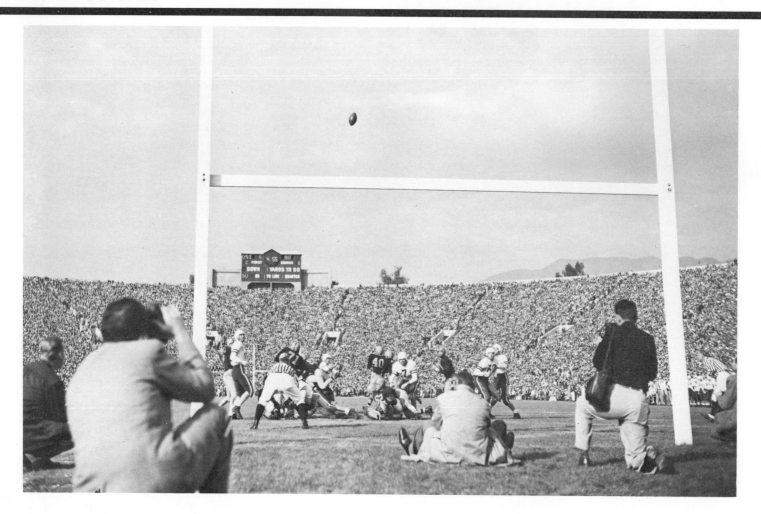

45-14. Moss, Agase and halfback Julie Rykov-ich all made their marks in Pasadena, and as Eliot was carried off the field by his happy players, the celebrating began in faraway Champaign.

In 1951 the Illini were again back in conten-tion for a Rose Bowl invitation, this time with a sharp passer in quarterback Tommy O'Con-nell and a great guard and captain in Chuck Studley. Johnny Karras made All-America halfback that year, and was joined by Al Brosky, a sensational safety. Little kicker Sam Rebecca added some glorious moments with his heartstopping field goals. Only a scoreless tie with Ohio State had muddied the Illini record, and on New Year's Day the Orange and Blue were again in Pasadena.

This time Stanford was the Illini's victim, in a 40-7 drubbing. Illinois ranked No 2 in the nation behind Kansas in the final Associated Press poll. But Grantland Rice didn't believe it. After the Rose Bowl game he wrote:

*I doubt that any other team in the country would have beaten this hard-hitting Illinois squad that Ray Eliot coached and directed so ably. Here was a hard-bitten, fast-moving squad that knew its job. I think it was a much better team than Kentucky and many other bowl winners. The weather was perfect. So was Illinois.*

All-America picks after that golden season were Johnny Karras and Al Brosky.

Although the Illini did not win the confer-ence crown for the remainder of the 1950s, they tied in 1953 with Michigan State. There were some exciting players for fans of the

Top: *Stanford University attempts a field goal versus the Number 2-ranked University of Illinois in the first quarter of the 1952 Rose Bowl. Stanford was crushed, 40-7.*

Right: *Tom O'Connell, the talented Illini quarterback who helped take his team to the 1952 Rose Bowl.*

Above: *Illinois star halfback Johnny Karras moves through a wall of Stanford players for a gain of eight yards in the early minutes of the 1952 Rose Bowl.*

Right: *J C Caroline, 'Mr Zoom' of the 1953 Illini. The talented team just missed going to the Rose Bowl when Michigan State won the honor.*

Orange and Blue to watch that year. Among them were J C Caroline and Mickey Bates, known as 'Mr Boom (Bates) and Mr Zoom (Caroline).' Known for high jinks on and off the field, they led a team which many felt should have been the Big Ten's Rose Bowl representative. Michigan State had been on probation, but was taken off in time to go to Pasadena – a disappointment to both Illinois players and fans.

Ray Eliot resigned as head coach following the 1959 season after a career of upsets, big victories and, of course, the smell of roses. Players like Bill Brown and Ray Nitschke had played for Eliot and then gone on to brilliant pro careers. The popular coach became assistant athletic director, a post he held until 1973.

Eliot's successor was Pete Elliott, brother of Bump Elliott who coached the Michigan Wolverines during the same period. In Elliott's seven seasons at Illinois he compiled a 31-34-1 overall record, and took the Illini to the Rose Bowl once again in 1963.

The 1963 squad had such talented players as Archie Sutton at tackle and Rich Callaghan at end, as well as Mike Taliaferro, a sharp quarterback. But it was center/linebacker Dick Butkus who led the team. Called the 'Mountain Man' by his teammates, Butkus played both center and linebacker under the one-platoon rules of the time, and was almost as good at

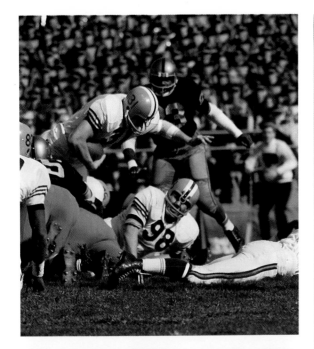

blocking as he was at tackling. Of the player who led the 5-1-1 conference champion Illini, Coach Elliott later said:

*Dick was the greatest asset to a team as anyone I've ever seen. He was the best football player I've ever been around and the greatest leader. When we recruited him, I felt he was the kind of player who could win the Heisman Trophy, and I was very disappointed when he didn't win it. I don't think anyone deserved it more. I think the Heisman would have been enriched by having a name like Dick Butkus on it.*

After a tie with Ohio State and an upset loss to a weak Michigan team, Butkus and the Illini went on to beat Michigan State in the season finale for a ticket to the Rose Bowl. Beating Washington 17-7 was the cap on a wonderful season for Illinois. Butkus once again made All-American and added conference MVP to his honors. He led the team in a lap around the Rose Bowl after the final gun sounded, perhaps as a slap in the face to the Washington team, which had made fun of the 'Big Fat Big Ten' as being out of shape.

Two of Butkus' teammates, fullback Jim Grabowski and safety George Donnelly, joined him on the All-America list in 1964. Butkus would go on to even greater fame as a member of George Halas' Chicago Bears.

In 1967 Pete Elliott, all set to step up to the athletic directorship at Illinois, resigned following a scandal about a 'slush fund,' which

*Above: Rich Weiss (17) handles the ball for the Orange and Blue during a game against OSU, 11 November 1978.*

*Top left: Fullback Jim Grabowski (31) dives for extra yardage. He joined Dick Butkus and safety George Donnelly on the 1964 All-American team.*

*Center left: Illini Larry Powell (26) in action, 1978.*

*Opposite: 'The Mountain Man', Dick Butkus, played both center and line-backer for Illinois and led his team to Rose Bowl victory on 1 January 1964.*

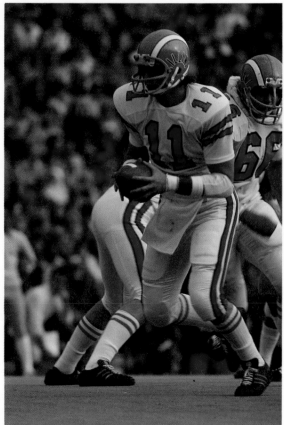

also cost basketball coach Harry Combes and his assistant Howie Braun their jobs. His successor as football coach, Jim Valek, presided over four seasons of disaster and a 8-32-0 record. Illinois' next two coaches, Bob Blackmon (1971 to 1976) and Gary Moeller (1977 to 1979), fared somewhat better, but Illinois usually found itself at the middle or bottom of the Big Ten pack, as the 'Big Two' – Ohio State and Michigan – reigned supreme. All-American Illini players during the 1970s, however, included tackle Tab Bennett, linebacker Scott Studwell and placekicker Dan Beaver.

With the hiring of Mike White in 1980, however, things began to improve. An offense-minded coach with coaching experience at Cal, Stanford and in the NFL under Bill Walsh, White brought a good record to Illinois and molded several fine quarterbacks after coming to Champaign. Among them were Tony Eason and Jack Trudeau. In 1983 Illinois again ascended to the Rose Bowl after nine victories over its conference opponents, but lost to UCLA 45-9. The 7-4 1984 season and the 6-5-1 1985 season both saw wide receiver David Williams named to All-America; and though the 1986 season, with its 4-7 record, was a disappointment, it was nevertheless clear that the Illini were again turning out outstanding players, hosting huge crowds and enjoying their conference rivalries. In short, they were again a force to be reckoned with in the Big Ten.

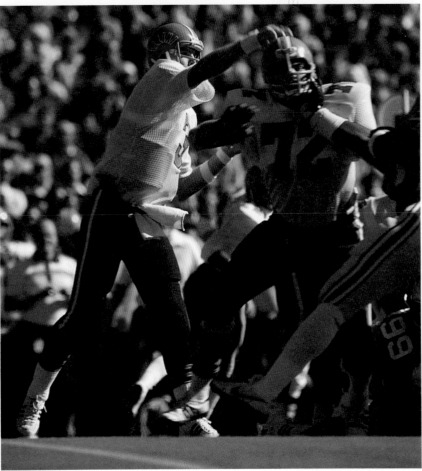

Opposite top left: *Parker (69), Sullivan (97) and Young (83) in 1975.*

Opposite top right: *Steger (11) and Jurczyk (66) in action, 1976.*

Opposite bottom: *Big Paul Moore (99), November 1976.*

Above: *Mike White, Illinois coach, in September 1985.*

Right: *Quarterback Tony Eason (3) in October 1981.*

Top: *Lee Boeke (80) snags the ball versus OSU, 1980.*

Above: *Jack Trudeau (10) heaves a pass during the 1984 Rose Bowl. Illinois lost to UCLA, 45-9.*

Right: *Illinois in action versus UCLA in the 1984 Rose Bowl.*

Far right: *A pretty Illini cheerleader does her bit to urge her team to victory.*

Left: *Chief Illiniwek is a colorful figure at Illinois games.*

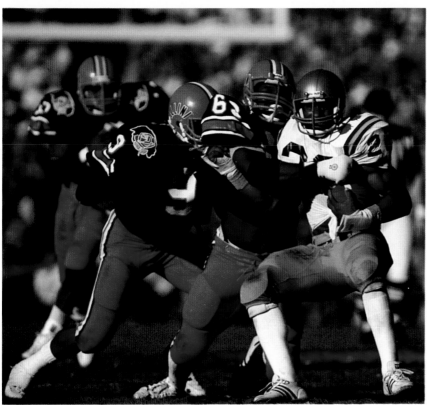

# INDIANA UNIVERSITY

Indiana

Founded: 1820

Location: Bloomington

Total Enrollment: 30,579

Colors: Cream and Crimson

Nickname: Hoosiers

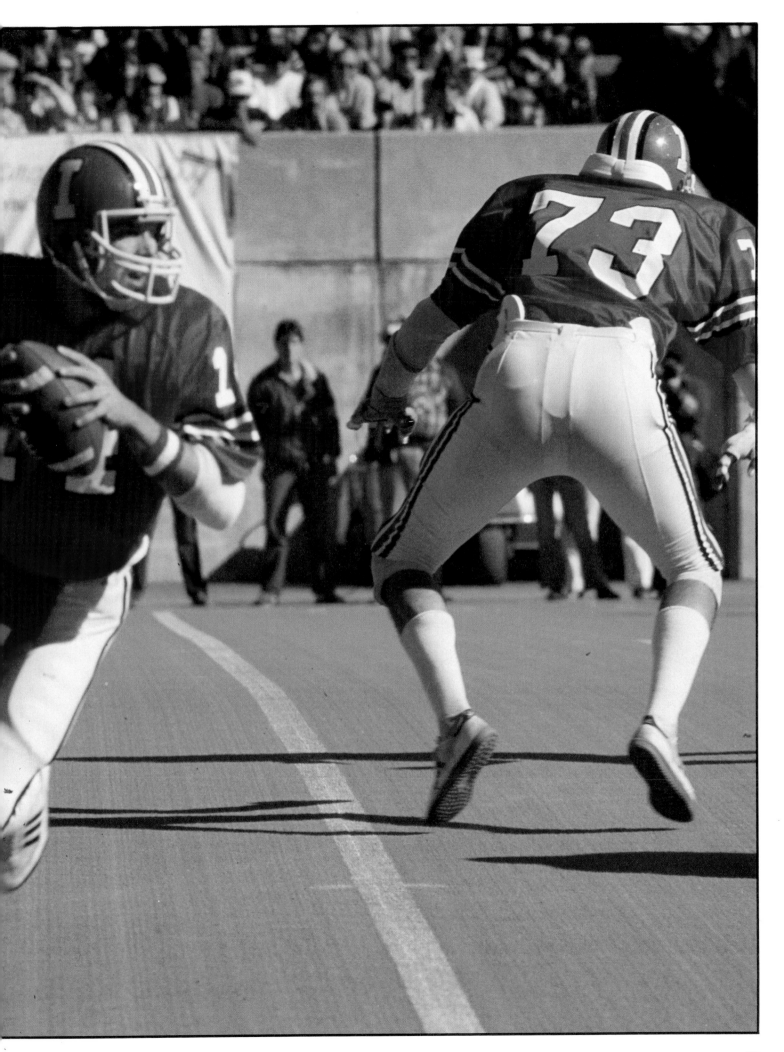

Above: *An 1887 engraving by Frederic Remington entitled 'A tackle and a ball-down.'*

Right: *The Old Oaken Bucket symbolizes the rivalry between Indiana and Purdue.*

Opposite left: *One of the greatest all-round athletes of all time, Jim Thorpe was assistant coach at Indiana in 1915. Here he is seen as Carlisle's star halfback in 1912.*

Opposite right: *Mickey Erehart played right halfback for the Hoosiers in the 1920s.*

Previous pages: *Quarterback Tim Clifford (14) looks for an opening in a game versus Michigan, 1980.*

The word 'Hoosier' is not, by any means, as synonymous with college football as it is with basketball. Indiana University's cage teams have all but eclipsed Indiana football in national recognition; yet few colleges can boast of a fan population as patient and as devoted as Hoosier gridiron boosters.

That has been the case since 1885, when Indiana first initiated a series of intramural football games. The next year, Indiana added outside competitors, including Butler, Hanover, Wabash and Franklin colleges. All games were played by the old 'Harvard' rules at a field in Indianapolis.

But the first official team wasn't assembled until 1887. The primitive-looking eleven, coached by Professor Arthur B Woodford, played but one game – a loss – with Franklin. A tie with DePauw and a 40-2 loss to Wabash came in the one-game seasons to follow, and no team was fielded in 1890.

The early 1890s were rife with the same sort of controversy that would plague amateur athletics in the decades to come: charges of financial offers made to outstanding players and captains, the violent and sometimes fatal nature of play, rowdyism among rooters and so on. The University took matters in its own hands by making management of the team, including finances and the hiring of respectable coaches, a faculty responsibility. As if in response to such reforms, the 1895 team posted its very first winning season with a 4-3-1 record.

The first faculty-hired Indiana coach, Madison G Gonterman, hired away from Harvard, coached his teams to 6-2 and 6-1-1 seasons. He was replaced by James H Horne – the second most successful coach in Indiana history – who accomplished a winning 33-21-5 record over seven seasons. Horne was popular for his victories over Purdue, the first for Indiana, which came three in a row.

The Purdue game had already become the central focus of the football year, and later grew into an intense intrastate rivalry symbolized by its own trophy, the 'Old Oaken Bucket.' This ancient, monstrous container, goes the fable, was used by Morgan's Raiders during the Civil War during their invasion of Indiana's Yankee territory. Hoosier alumni thought it would be an ideal war trophy, and added a commemorative plaque. Over the years, a chain of bronze block letters, 'I' and 'P', has been added, the links recording each year's victor.

The bucket has been through more than its share of youthful pranks. Once the bucket disappeared for several months and was pre-

sumed gone for good when an anonymous tipster called Indiana University. A search party ended up digging the bucket out of the dirt in the library basement. Another time, after Indiana had upset Purdue, the bucket disappeared shortly after arrival in Indianapolis. A railroad station agent had placed the bucket in the hands of students dressed in IU sweaters, who had claimed to be an 'honor guard' dispatched to take the bucket to Bloomington. Of course the Old Oaken Bucket never arrived on campus, and did not resurface for some time.

Besides perpetuating a hotly contested rivalry, Coach Horne developed a few good players during his term. Among them was a 140-pound terror from Muncie who would become Indiana's first All-American and a Hoosier athletics legend. Wiry, trim Zora G Clevenger appeared on the gridiron as a feisty halfback and contributed to a solid 18-14-2 Hoosier record over his four years on the squad from 1900 to 1904.

Clevenger distinguished himself as an athlete of remarkable versatility, starring not only in football but also in baseball and basketball. Upon graduation in 1905, the popular 'Mr Clev' coached baseball for two seasons. He

moved on to serve as varsity coach at Tennessee, where he led the Volunteers through their first undefeated season, and later was athletic director for Missouri and Kansas State. Clevenger returned to Indiana in 1923 and put in 23 years as one of the country's most dedicated and respected athletics directors and Big Ten Conference representatives.

Clevenger had a part in a 1901 victory margin over Franklin that is still in the Indiana record books: 76-0. And he was on campus in 1905 to see Indiana post its greatest season since football's inception at Bloomington. Coach Horne had retired in 1904, the victim of a nervous breakdown that put him in bed for more than a year. The new coach, James M Sheldon, helped the Hoosiers to shut out six opponents, tie arch-rival Purdue 11-11 and lose only to Amos Stagg's unbeaten Chicago team. Outweighed by 20 pounds a man, the Hoosiers nevertheless dominated the first half of play and ended up holding the Maroons to a relatively small 15-6 win.

In two decades remembered largely for the successes of others – mostly Minnesota, Illinois and Ohio State through 1920, and Michigan and Illinois during the 1920s and '30s – the Hoosiers produced a few exciting moments of their own. The team of 1910, for instance, managed a 6-1 slate including five shutouts and allowed only three points during the entire season, a field goal by Wisconsin. Ironically, Indiana missed out on its first national title by a field goal in its only loss, 3-0, to Illinois, a championship team that had held all its opponents scoreless. The Hoosier team, considered by some to be Indiana's finest ever, was captained by end Arthur 'Cotton' Berndt, who became an assistant coach and in later years was familiar to most IU students as the long-standing mayor of Bloomington.

Indiana enjoyed an even more famous public figure for one year, 1915, when Coach Clarence Childs hired his former Olympic teammate and Carlisle star halfback Jim Thorpe to assist him with football and baseball duties. Considered even today as probably the century's greatest all-around athlete, Thorpe was welcomed into Bloomington by a wildly enthusiastic crowd, including, said the Indiana yearbook, a throng of schoolboys 'more in their glory than when a circus comes to town.' The quiet, amiable Thorpe thrilled game audiences with his trademark drop-kick exhibitions. 'It was nothing for him to dodge a dozen tacklers, or to punt 75 yards with an easy nonchalance that seemed almost uncanny,' the yearbook noted.

Childs himself drew national attention with his unique training methods, which included use of a phonograph at the sidelines to prop up morale and of whippet hounds to egg on men training for the dash. Childs was known to tie a chain-gang of football players to his Ford Model T and putter across the landscape, beckoning his men to run faster.

In 1917 Indiana produced another fine crew, which recorded a 5-2 season. Under Coach Ewald O 'Jumbo' Stiehm the wartime team

Top: *Triple-threat halfback Chuck Bennett was conference MVP of the 1928 season.*

Right: *Fullback Corby Davis was All-American and conference MVP in 1936.*

held opponents scoreless in its victories and was sacked only by the mighty Minnesota Gophers and Ohio State's Chic Harley. Purdue was squashed 37-0, the largest margin ever over that arch rival. Stiehm's 1920 team, starring guards William McCaw and Elliott Risley, also went for 5-2, losing only to Iowa by three points and to an unbeaten Notre Dame squad.

Old Jordan Field, a wooden stadium with seating for 4000, was replaced in 1922 by a new Memorial Stadium. The new stadium, constructed at a cost of $250,000, originally seated 20,000 and later was expanded to a capacity of 33,000.

A long-awaited 'first' for Indiana came in 1928 when triple-threat halfback Chuck Bennett became the Hoosiers' premier All-American. Bennett's streaking runs and fierce style of play made him the conference's choice for most valuable player of the year, even though the 1928 team won only two Big Ten games.

Indiana's football fortunes took a big turn in 1934 with the hiring of a new leader, Alvin Nugent McMillin, who would become Indiana's most successful coach. Bo McMillin came from the coaching post at Kansas State and had starred in his college days with tiny Centre College of Danville, Kentucky. The scrawny quarterback was selected as an All-American by Walter Camp in 1919, and in 1921 he passed up a fat, $10,000-a-year pro baseball contract to lead the 'Praying Colonels' to a stunning upset of Harvard, unbeaten for 25 straight games.

'I didn't take the coaching job at Indiana to be sexton at a cemetery,' the drawling Texan announced upon his arrival in Bloomington. He proved that with a 3-3-2 record in his first year, including a 17-6 upset of Purdue, and fielded only the third team in 14 years to at least break even. McMillin's next three teams produced winning slates and walked away with the Old Oaken Bucket again in 1935. In all, Bo would take nine and tie once in his 14 battles with the Boilermakers, creating feverish loyalty among his supporters in Bloomington, and he would develop a string of some of the greatest players in Indiana football history.

Among them was Vern Huffman, who not only served as an All-American basketball player but also starred as an All-Big Ten halfback on the gridiron, good enough to make conference MVP in 1936. The same year, versatile fullback Corby Davis made All-America and followed Huffman as MVP. This brilliant kicker, blocker and defensive player was given most of the credit for knocking powerful Ohio

State out of title contention in a 10-0 Hoosier win, the first victory over OSU in 13 years.

Halfback Billy Hillenbrand captured national attention in 1942 with the same brand of versatility, and helped to usher in Hoosier football's Golden Era. The 190-pound wonder galloped with blinding speed and terrorized the enemy with surprise touchdown runs. He was equally adroit as a passer and punter, and was a hard-hitting defensive lineman. Often named as the greatest triple-threat back in Hoosier history, Hillenbrand earned Indiana's first consensus All-America honors in 1942. Billy contributed to a 7-3 season, the best since 1910.

Upholding that excellence in the next year were halfback Bob 'Hunchy' Hoernschmeyer and famous end Pete Pihos. Hunchy, a freshman made eligible under special wartime rules, dominated headlines in 1943 by leading the nation in conference offensive yardage, with 277 rushing and 596 passing for a total of 873. His national total hit 2669 yards, surpassing both the legendary Tom Harmon of Michigan and Northwestern's Otto Graham. Pihos

Above: *Halfback Billy Hillenbrand was a skillful runner, passer, punter and defensive lineman. These talents earned him consensus All-American honors in 1942, a first for Indiana.*

43

*Opposite: End Pete Pihos, voted best Hoosier player ever.*

*Below: Halfback Bob 'Hunchy' Hoernschmeyer in 1943.*

snared All-America selection in the same year, making for IU's first back-to-back All-America choices, and was voted Indiana's most outstanding player of all time in 1969.

In 1944 McMillin's eleven ran up 292 points, a new high, and posted a 7-3 season that included five shutouts, all in spite of Pihos' departure for the military. John Tavener, a tough center and a great team leader, was chosen All-American that year, and Hoernschmeyer, playing his last season before joining the Navy, topped the Big Nine in passing and set a school record for punt returns, running back 28 of them for 635 yards.

Pihos returned after the war ended in 1945,

along with guard Howard Brown, to join up with freshman halfback George Taliaferro and help create Indiana's greatest football squad ever. With the running of ends Bob Ravensberg and the gigantic Ted Kluszewski, and smart passing by quarterback Ben Raimondi, the Hoosier squad smashed powerhouse Michigan on the opening day of the season, causing a great stir among football followers. Could the perennial doormat of the conference be making a bid for greatness?

The team answered that question with a phenomenal 9-0-1 season, the tie coming in a 7-7 game with Northwestern. Minnesota was dumped 49-0; Nebraska by 54-14; and Iowa by 52-20. It ended with a 29-0 shellacking of Purdue and confirmation of the impossible: The Hoosiers were undefeated. Coach McMillin was carried off the field on the shoulders of his men and was given an equally enthusiastic hand by his peers, who voted him national Coach of the Year. Ravensberg shared in the limelight as an All-American; and Pihos and Taliaferro would one day be voted into the Football Hall of Fame.

*Right: Halfback George Taliaferro in 1945.*

Above: *The undefeated Indiana Hoosiers of 1945.*

Left: *A N (Bo) McMillin, Indiana coach from 1934 to 1945. His teams were among the most successful in Hoosier history.*

It was a glorious finish to the McMillin era. The genial coach was named athletic director in 1946, but he stepped down from his post at the end of the 1947 season to coach and manage a professional team, the Detroit Lions. Sadly, his career in professional football was cut short by his death soon thereafter. McMillin had brought the Hoosiers to national respectability, compiling a record of 63-48-11 in his 14 years at Indiana. He had given the school its longest ever winning streak – 12 games in 1945-46 – and the only three consensus All-America selections.

His passing marked the start of a drought for Hoosier football which would last for the next twenty years. The period was marked by some outstanding players, but none was able to bring his team to dominance in either the conference or the public eye. Indiana had already gone through 17 coaches; now the revolving door would continue to spin as Indiana searched for a measure of consistency and success in its football program. Five more men crossed the threshold before that search was fulfilled.

One of them, Phil Dickens, actually did the Indiana image more harm than good. Dickens was cited by the conference for recruiting violations in his first year on the job, 1957, and ended up getting himself suspended for his first season. Dickens never quite cleared matters up; based on evidence that athletes had been given illegal aid payments, without regard to need, in 1957 and 1959, the NCAA in 1960 placed IU on a four-year probation. The Big

Ten conference added its own one-year probation for the violations, and Coach Dickens ultimately lost his job.

Amidst all the negative press, however, there was some good. The 1958 team, in particular, drew attention as a pack of upstarts who relied on the old single-wing offense to confuse their thoroughly modern competition. In a streak of wins over Minnesota, Miami, Michigan State and Michigan, the team mustered 12 consecutive quarters of shutout defense. A nine-year string of losses to Purdue was finally cut with a 15-15 tie, contributing to a season record of 5-3-1. Among standout players was the gigantic end Earl Faison, who figured heavily in victories the following season over Illinois, Nebraska and Michigan, and a 0-0 match with Ohio State. Faison made All-America in 1960.

Before bowing out of the picture, Dickens developed two more All-Americans, fullback Tom Nowatzke and guard Don Croftchek. Both made the list in 1964. Nowatzke may have had an even better season in his junior year, 1965, when he led the conference in rushing with 98 carries for 486 yards, a five-yard

Left: *End Earl Faison, All-American in 1960.*

Above: *Quarterback Harry Gonso (16) in 1967.*

average. Proving his virtuosity at all tasks, Nowatzke set new Indiana season records of 756 yards rushing, 58 points scored, five field goals, five fumble recoveries and four interceptions.

Dickens' replacement, John Pont, came to Indiana in 1964 from successful stints at Miami of Ohio and Yale. After stumbling through two disastrous seasons, Coach Pont succeeded in installing his quarterback-option offense, implemented by the famous BIG combination, an acronym representing flanker Jade Butcher, tailback John Isenbarger and quarterback Harry Gonso.

Gonso, who led the Pont attack, was a sharp-minded passer and an equally great runner who tallied 1443 yards total offense in 1967. When he did throw, it was usually to the sure-handed Butcher, whose record of 30 TDs makes him the all-time scoring leader for Indiana. Isenbarger, a free spirit who had originally been drafted as a quarterback, possessed talents in both running and punting. His last-

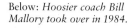
Above: *The sensational 1967 Hoosier team, who earned the nickname 'The Cardiac Kids' with their unpredictable plays and last-minute victories.*

Below: *Hoosier coach Bill Mallory took over in 1984.*

minute unplanned runs from punt formation were heartstopping but effective; no one, especially not Pont, ever knew if John would kick or run. Antics like those gave the 1967 team its nickname, 'The Cardiac Kids.'

So inexperienced was this backfield that it simply didn't know that the things it routinely did couldn't be done. Behind a rugged defense formed by Doug Crusan, Jim Sniadecki and Ken Kaczmarek, the Hoosiers began their season by winning – and winning – 'in such wildly implausible fashion that they soon captured the imagination of the nation.' IU sports information director Tom Miller later wrote about the team: 'Suddenly they were the darlings of the football world. All but one game was a cliff-hanger.'

In the opener second-half scoring overcame a strong halftime Kentucky lead for a 12-10 victory. Against Kansas a field goal in the final moments downed the Jayhawks 18-15. Two turnarounds helped the Hoosiers pull out a 20-7 decision over Illinois, and a quick underhand pass in the final seconds against Iowa by Gonso to Butcher ended a 21-17 squeaker. A touchdown in the last moments of the Michigan game left Indiana ahead 27-20. 'I wish this were a movie,' an exhausted but elated Coach Pont told the press, 'so I'd know how it comes out.' More last-minute victories over Wisconsin and Michigan State, a solitary breezer over Arizona 42-7, and a satisfying crunch of Purdue, 19-14, brought a happy conclusion: Indiana's first share of a conference title since 1945, and a trip to Pasadena, California for the Rose Bowl classic.

A tough Southern California eleven snatched further glory from the Hoosiers in a hard-fought 14-3 game, but Pont's feat of bringing Indiana from Number 9 to Number 1 in Big Ten standings won him a much-deserved Coach of the Year Award. Isenbarger and bruising guard Gary Cassels made it into the All-America for 1967, and Isenbarger repeated in 1969, joined by Butcher.

Each of the BIG Trio made it into the record books, as well. By career's end, Butcher had nabbed 118 passes for 1876 yards; Gonso completed 250 of 513 for 3376 yards and 32 TDs, rolling up 4448 yards in total offense; and Isenbarger rushed for a total of 2465 yards, with 1217 of them run in 1969 alone.

Indiana never quite was able to repeat the glory days of the late 1960s, although Chris Gartner was chosen for All-America in 1972. Pont ended up leaving the school to coach at Northwestern, ending his tenure with a string of less than successful seasons. Replacing him was Lee Corso of Louisville, who had had luck in transforming a lackluster football program into a winning game.

Corso had a colorful, humorous and at times irreverent approach to football which

Above: *Coach John Pont, who brought the Hoosiers to the Big Ten Co-Championship in 1967.*

Top: *Coach Lee Corso provided side-line entertainment, if not victory, from 1970 to 1980.*

Right: *Flanker Jade Butcher, part of the 1967 BIG offense.*

Top right: *Tailback John Isenbarger was All-American in 1967 and again in 1969.*

endeared him to many. During his 10-year term – the second longest in Hoosier football history – Corso chalked up a 41-68-2 record, showing enough wins after his first three years to keep the Hoosiers out of the basement.

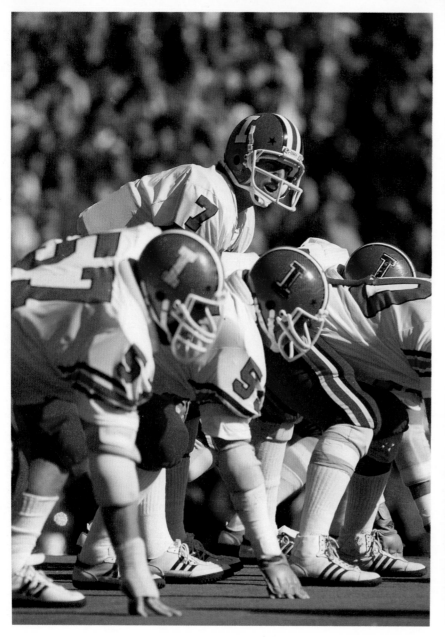

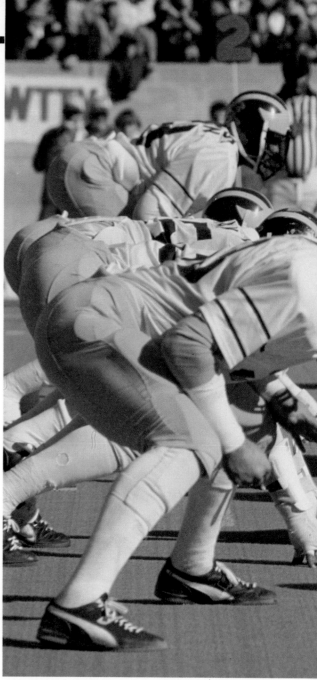

Above: *Quarterback Babe Laufenberg (7) in action, October 1981.*

Top right: *Quarterback Tim Clifford (14) helped his team to a relatively successful 8-4 season in 1979 and was awarded Big Ten MVP honors.*

Boosters got a taste of victory in the 1976 and 1977 seasons, with records of 5-6 and 5-5-1 respectively, both featuring wins over rival Purdue. Star quarterback Tim Clifford helped bring his team to an 8-4 season in 1979 and a first-ever New Year's victory over unbeaten Brigham Young, 38-37, in the Holiday Bowl. Clifford became only the fourth player in Hoosier history to win Big Ten MVP honors.

If not always entertained by wins, Corso's audiences were nevertheless often amused by the coach's wit on and off the field. In his first year on the job, Corso dutifully attended every local football banquet offered him to see if he could drum up interest – and recruits – at Indiana's high schools. 'I've attended 150 banquets this winter,' he told the press on one occasion, 'and have been served chicken all 150 times. I don't get a haircut anymore: I get *plucked*.'

Corso provided plenty of dramatics at game time. He was often seen wandering down the sidelines with ammonia capsules in one hand

and a Saint Christopher medallion in the other. During one slaughter at the hands of his alma mater Louisville, whose coach persisted in keeping his battering first string in play, Corso trotted onto the field waving a white towel.

Corso closed out his Indiana years with a 6-5 showing in 1980, and victories over Purdue in the following two years. He was replaced by Sam Wyche, coach of the professional San Francisco 49ers, who lasted for just one 3-8 season. Bill Mallory, a no-nonsense, pro-defense coach with plenty of collegiate experience and a 99-52-1 record from Miami, Colorado and Northern Illinois, took the reins in 1984.

Not unlike his predecessors, Mallory got off to a slow start with a dismal 0-11 record in his first year, but rose to 4-7 in 1985 and 6-6 in 1986. Indiana students, alumni and fans have given Mallory the same benefit of the doubt accorded all Indiana coaches and hope realistically for greater moments in years ahead.

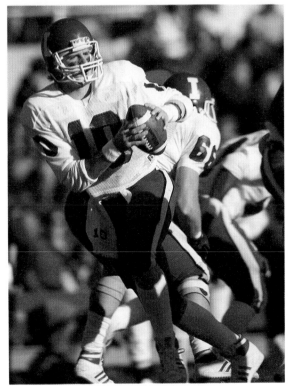

Far left: *Quarterback Steve Bradley (18) in action, November 1984.*

Left: *Wide receiver Duane Gunn (89) in action, October 1981.*

# UNIVERSITY OF IOWA

Iowa

Founded: 1847

Location: Iowa City

Total Enrollment: 29,651

Colors: Gold and Black

Nickname: Hawkeyes

Page 52: *Star Quarterback Chuck Long (16) led the Iowa Hawkeyes to the 1986 Rose Bowl. He was Heisman Trophy runner-up, College Player of the Year, and All-American.*

The University of Iowa is a 'newcomer' to the Big Ten Conference, having joined the organization in 1899 along with Indiana University (the league was then informally called the Big Nine, since Ohio State University did not join until 1912). Since then, the history of football Hawkeye-style has been one of great rivalries, scrappy players and colorful coaches.

Nearly half a century has passed since Hawkeye fans thrilled to the heroics of scholar-athlete Nile Kinnick, Iowa's only Heisman Trophy winner and the man for whom the university's Kinnick Stadium is named. And other honored names such as Duke Slater, Aubrey Devine, Calvin Jones and Alex Karras conjure up memories of past Iowa achievements.

Yet Hawkeye fans of the future may well look back on the 1980s as the decade of the Glory Years. Under the inspired leadership of head coach Hayden Fry, the Iowa Hawkeyes enjoyed a conference record of 31-10-1 in the 1981-86 seasons, earning a bowl berth in each of those years. At last Iowa fans knew that their school had regained its place in the Big Ten and the right to be mentioned along with such perennial conference powerhouses as

Ohio State and Michigan.

When the University of Iowa joined the conference that would become the Big Ten college football was still a young sport. The first of Walter Camp's 'official' All-America teams had been published just one year before in *Collier's* magazine. Only two years earlier the point value of a touchdown had been set at five points, with the goal after reduced to one point. Five yards equaled a first down, and seven more seasons would go by before the advent of the forward pass in 1906 ushered in football's modern era.

Iowa thrived during the sport's infancy. The school's football team, coached by Alden Knipe, won nine games and tied one to go undefeated in both the 1899 and 1900 seasons, and players named to the All-Conference team in 1900 included quarterback Clyde Williams and tackle Joe Warner. But capable as Knipe was, Iowa's first truly great coach was Howard Harding Jones, a former Yale end who led the Hawkeyes from 1916 to 1923. Along the way he compiled a record of 42 Iowa wins, 17 losses and a single tie. Under Jones Iowa tackle Fred Becker became the school's first All-American in 1916, followed by end Lester Belding in

Below: *Kinnick Stadium, home of the Iowa Hawkeyes.*

Above: *Coach Howard Harding Jones, who manned the Hawkeyes from 1916 to 1923. His superstar 1921 team went undefeated to win their first Big Ten title. In 1922 they were again undefeated, but had to share the Big Ten title with Michigan and Chicago.*

Above right: *Legendary tackle Fred 'Duke' Slater's lightning speed and tremendous strength contributed to the Hawkeye's awesome 1921 season.*

1919. Coach Jones was assembling and developing the players who would form the backbone of one of the school's greatest teams.

Among them was Fred 'Duke' Slater, son of a Clinton, Iowa minister. Before his Hawkeye career was over he would be among the first black men to achieve All-America status and would become one of Iowa's legendary tackles. At the age of 15 young Slater quit high school to work, taking a job as an ice-cutter on the Mississippi River near his hometown. The job was arranged by his father, who apparently wanted his son to attend college and hoped that the hard work in subzero cold would make school look better by comparison. It did.

Slater made the Iowa varsity as a freshman in 1918, impressing Jones with his size,

strength and tenacity. He was a big man for those days – standing 6 feet 2 inches and weighing in at 210 pounds. A quiet boy, he called attention to himself only by his immense talent – and his bare head, for Slater never bothered to wear a helmet. Although Slater was most often double- or even triple-teamed, he had such strength that he was able to toss blockers out of his path like rag dolls and close in on the unfortunate ballcarrier. To add further to opponents' misfortunes, the speedy Slater was often the first man downfield after a punt, ready to wreak havoc.

'He almost never made a mistake,' Coach Jones later said of Slater. 'He was simply never out of position, never fooled by a fake, never mistaken on where the opposing ballcarrier was going, never late on his offensive charge.' Slater went on to play professional football with the Chicago Cardinals, then returned to the Iowa campus for a law degree. He became a judge of the Cook County Superior Court and served until his death in 1966. In 1968 a newly-built dormitory, not far from the Iowa football stadium, was named Slater Hall in his honor.

In 1919 another answer to a coach's prayer came in the form of Aubrey Devine, a 5-foot 10-inch 175-pound triple-threat quarterback whose skill at the running forward pass helped make him Iowa's first nationally-acclaimed

Above: *Duke Slater's refusal to wear a helmet did not hinder his future as a professional football player with the Chicago Cardinals and later as a judge of the Cook County Superior Court.*

Above right: *Triple-threat quarterback Aubrey Devine was also a major factor in that unforgettable 1921 season.*

hero. Also adept at basketball and track, he would go on to win nine major letters at Iowa. Devine led in passing, rushing and scoring in both the 1919 and 1920 seasons, but that proved to be only a preview of 1921.

The 1919 and 1920 campaigns had been fairly successful, with the Hawkeyes establishing records of 5-2-0 in both years. Coach Jones must have sensed that he had the nucleus of a great team. Along with Slater and Devine, he now had Gordon Locke, a line-smashing fullback with remarkable speed. There was also blocking back Glenn Devine, Aubrey's brother, and Craven Shuttleworth, a talented sophomore who played as the other halfback. Up front on the line with Slater was Les Belding, the great pass-receiving end. But how to best utilize their talents? Jones devised an offensive shift which called for halfbacks Glenn Devine and Shuttleworth to drop off into the backfield and block for Aubrey Devine and Locke, who now did most of the ball-carrying. The innovation confused Iowa's Big Ten and non-conference opponents alike.

After dispatching Knox College 52-14, the 1921 Hawkeyes were ready for a big hurdle, Notre Dame. And Iowa scored an unforgettable 10-7 win over the Irish, with the edge coming on Devine's 38-yard drop-kicked field goal after he called a perfect game at quarterback. Duke Slater spent the day blocking, tackling and harassing Irish safety Frank Thomas on punt returns, 'doing the work of three men in the line,' as Jones put it.

Handing the Irish what was to be the only defeat in their sparkling 11-game season was a high point of that glorious year for Jones, who

called it 'the biggest moment of my coaching career.' But Aubrey Devine's greatest afternoons were yet to come. After his touchdown pass to Les Belding and a 33-yard punt return beat Purdue 13-6, Devine ruined Minnesota's homecoming in the following game, and in the process established himself as a real star.

What Aubrey Devine accomplished that afternoon was to score four touchdowns himself, pass to Belding for two more, and drop-kick five extra points. He carried the pigskin 34 times for 162 yards, returned seven punts and kickoffs for another 180, and passed for 122 yards. His touchdown passes to Belding were for 43 and 25 yards. Devine also did all of the punting. His game total of 454 yards caused shaken Gopher coach Henry L Williams to call him 'the greatest football player who ever stepped on Northrup Field.' The final score: Iowa 47, Minnesota 7.

Iowa's next opponent, Indiana, fared no better. Devine and the Hawkeyes shut them out 41-0, with the star quarterback galloping for four touchdowns, kicking four extra points, running for 183 yards, and passing for 102 in the first three quarters before being taken out for a replacement by a merciful Coach Jones.

And so it went in that long-ago autumn of 1921 as Iowa finished the season undefeated and unequaled for its first Big Ten title and first claim to national honors. Aubrey Devine was unanimously voted an All-American, and Duke Slater made every All-America team except Walter Camp's. Gordon Locke, whose best season was still to come, also earned All-America honors. And that fighting 1921

Hawkeye team won a special place in the hearts of their fans that it still occupies today.

The Big Ten had voted in June 1921 to ban post-season games. Ohio State had been trounced by the California Bears the year before, and some believed the Big Ten was trying to avoid being embarrassed again in the Rose Bowl. In any event, the unbeaten 1921 Hawkeyes had to turn down the Rose Bowl invitation, and fans across the state of Iowa were sorely disappointed.

However, the 1922 season provided plenty of consolation. The Hawkeyes sailed through another undefeated campaign, captained by the durable Gordon Locke in his senior year. In a sense, Locke came into his own after the departure of Aubrey Devine. He scored four touchdowns in each of two games, against Knox College in the season opener and against Northwestern to clinch the league title. To top that, Locke scored three times in a 28-14 win over Minnesota. Against Ohio State in a 12-9 win Locke scored both Iowa touchdowns. His 72 points in five games set a Big Ten record which lasted until 1943. The 1922 Hawkeyes finished with another 7-0 record and a winning streak of 17 straight games.

Although considered by most to be the best team in the conference and perhaps in the nation, Iowa was forced to share the Big Ten title with unbeaten Michigan and once-tied University of Chicago. But Iowa had convinced even cynical Eastern sportswriters of its prowess with a win over mighty Yale in its New Haven backyard, and Gordon Locke attained unanimous All-America status, Camp's list included.

Above: *Perhaps the greatest Hawkeye victory of 1921 was the upset of the Fighting Irish of Notre Dame, 10-7. Iowa handed the team its only defeat of the season.*

Left: *Fullback Gordon Locke, who did most of the ball-carrying in both 1921 and 1922, made All-America in both years and Walter Camp's list in 1922.*

*Above: The 1922 Hawkeyes went undefeated (7-0) and won an incredible 17 games in a row.*

As Iowa's team matured, so did the rest of college football. At the University of Illinois, Coach Bob Zuppke was experimenting with the modern huddle and welcoming a freshman by the name of Red Grange. In 1926 the first electronic scoreboard was installed by the University of Wisconsin and was first used in its 20-10 victory over Iowa. And in 1928 the Big Six conference was formed by charter schools Kansas, Kansas State, Missouri, Nebraska, Oklahoma, and Iowa State. It would later become the Big Eight.

At the end of the 1923 season, during which the Hawkeyes suffered three losses, Coach Howard Jones left Iowa to coach at Duke University. After a year there, he went on to coach Southern California to seven Pacific Coast Conference titles, two national championships and five Rose Bowl victories between 1925 and 1940. He died suddenly of a heart attack near the end of the 1940 season.

With Jones' passing, Iowa football fortunes deteriorated. Coach Burton Ingwerson led the Hawkeyes from 1924 to 1931, during which time the team's conference record was never better than 3-1-1. These were Red Grange's years at the University of Illinois, and also the era of Fielding Yost's excellent Michigan teams which won Big Ten titles in 1925 and 1926. Yet Iowa produced some outstanding players along the way. Halfback Willis Glassgow, and tackles Emerson Nelson and Peter Westra were standouts, each winning All-America mentions.

The University of Iowa campus grew steadily, meanwhile, and in 1929 a new stadium was dedicated, during the same construction frenzy that produced the main wing of the Memorial Union and the Field House. Built at a cost of nearly half a million dollars, Iowa Stadium seated 53,000 spectators. Iowa now had a place for its football heroes to display their magic. All that was needed were the heroes. They would arrive in good time.

In 1932 O M 'Ossie' Solem took over the football coaching duties, and in 1934 a spark of hope arrived in the form of a young sophomore speedster named Ozzie Simmons, who before long proved himself a budding star at halfback. He drew attention as the first black college back with his breakaway speed, stunning ability to change directions and the 'swivel hips' that many sportswriters were to mention.

But Hawkeye football had not improved much under Solem, and Simmons' exploits were the exception in a mediocre team. In 1935, however, Simmons benefited from the hard-nosed tackling of Dick Crayne, who had been the team's leading runner but unselfishly toiled to open holes for his new teammate. In only his second game as a Hawkeye, against Northwestern in 1934, Simmons gained 166 yards from scrimmage and another 124 on punt returns in a 20-7 Iowa romp.

Ralph Cannon of the *Chicago Daily News* attempted this description of Simmons' great running ability:

*This slithery, rubbery, oozy flier with his gyrating balance, cool, masterful mental poise, sleek, smooth weaving hips and the most perfect open field pivot probably in the game today, can make his legs talk more languages than even Red Grange's when he was a sophomore . . . He is a master, a finished big league runner . . . who knows all the tricks of open field progress.*

High praise for a sophomore, but Simmons was to prove he was no fluke. In his three seasons at Iowa, from 1934-36, he gained more than 1500 yards rushing and eight times ran for touchdowns of 50 yards or more. Coach Solem later said of him, 'He was one of the two or three greatest backs I've ever coached and the best halfback I've ever seen.'

Coach Solem departed under fire after the 1936 season and Irl Tubbs took over as coach, following a stint at the University of Miami in Florida. Tubbs' two seasons were undistinguished in every way except one – the remarkable play of a tow-headed young man named Nile Kinnick.

The stocky 5-foot 9-inch, 170-pounder had come from Benson High School in Omaha to save Iowa football – or so Hawkeye fans and sportswriters began to think as Kinnick's feats glittered against the dull background of a 2-13-1 record for the 1937 and 1938 seasons. The youngster ran, passed, kicked and defended like no one Iowa fans had ever seen, winning national attention as the nation's leading punter in his sophomore year, 1937, with 70 kicks and a 43-yard average. He received honorable mentions for All--Conference and All-America status.

In fairness to Irl Tubbs, the disagreement that precipitated his departure proved that he was somewhat ahead of his time in the Big Ten conference. At the end of the 1938 season he informed the athletic board that, in order to become competitive, Iowa needed to institute a training table and a dormitory for its football players. Both items are taken for granted today, but in 1938 conference regulations prohibited both, and Tubbs objected by handing in his resignation.

The Iowa administration then began efforts to lure Dr Eddie Anderson from Holy Cross back to his native Iowa to coach the Hawkeyes. A schoolboy star, Anderson had left the state to play for Knute Rockne at Notre Dame. He had been a winner everywhere he went, had picked up an MD degree and was now the doctor Iowa fans knew the ailing team needed. The administration signed him to a three-year

*Above: Halfback Willis Glassgow won All-America honors in 1929, during a series of otherwise unspectacular seasons for the Hawkeyes in the 1920s.*

*Left: Halfback Ozzie Simmons' stunning speed and poise on the field earned him over 1500 yards rushing in his three seasons at Iowa, from 1934-36.*

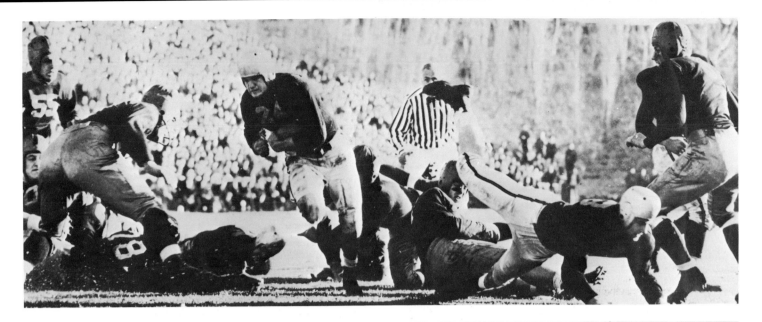

contract at $10,000 per year – quite a figure for a head coach in those days – and the good doctor went to work.

As he watched drills prior to the 1939 season Anderson must have instinctively realized that Nile Kinnick, now a brilliant but largely unrecognized senior, was not only a great player but a true leader. Anderson had only a few quality players on that Hawkeye team, and in that sparkling season of 1939 Iowa would rely on only 13 or 14 players to labor for virtually the entire game. Led by Nile Kinnick, they soon became known as 'The Iron Men.' The Hawkeyes charged into the 1939 season opener with South Dakota with Kinnick operating as a tailback out of Anderson's single wing formation. Kinnick scored three touchdowns and kicked five extra points, helping to shellack the opposition 41-0.

Next came a home game against Indiana, whom Iowa had not beaten since the glory days of 1921. For that matter, the Hawkeyes had not won a conference contest at home since 1933. On this afternoon Kinnick was to justify Anderson's faith in him as a leader. The strong Indiana team, led by passing sensation Hal Hursch, was leading 29-26 midway in the fourth quarter, and Iowa was on its fourth down with three yards to go. Knowing they were well within field goal range, the Iron Men looked to their deadly drop-kicker, Kinnick, to tie the game. But he had other ideas. 'Forget the tie,' he barked as they huddled. 'We're going all the way!'

Taking the snap from center, he evaded three charging Hoosiers as his eyes calmly searched downfield. Spotting end Erwin Prasse, Kinnick shot him a bullet pass. The speedy end galloped into the end zone and Kinnick's gutsy call had turned a sure tie into a 32-29 win for the Hawkeyes.

Yet even Kinnick could not hold off Tom Harmon and the Michigan Wolverines the following week. Although he fired a 69-yard scoring pass, it was Iowa's only touchdown, and the Hawkeyes lost 27-7. Harmon scored all four Michigan touchdowns and later described it, not immodestly, as his finest day in football.

But then the Hawkeyes got back on track with a 19-13 victory over Wisconsin's Badgers, gained on the strength of Kinnick's three soaring passes. Next, two blocked kicks led to a 4-0 win over Purdue. Against Notre Dame, late-game heroics by the determined Kinnick included a 60-yard punt which went out on the

*Above, top and opposite: Number 24, Nile Kinnick, headed the 1939 Hawkeye squad known as 'The Iron Men'. Kinnick almost singlehandedly accounted for the success of that season, scoring and passing for 16 of the 19 touchdowns for the team and leading them to five fourth-quarter victories.*

opponent's 5-yard line to preserve a 7-6 upset of the previously unbeaten Irish.

In the next Iowa game Minnesota's Golden Gophers, defending conference champions, got off to a 9-0 lead, but then Kinnick put on a passing exhibition for Hawkeye fans. First he threw 45 yards to Prasse for one touchdown, then heaved a last-ditch pass to Bill Green as Gopher tacklers brought him down in the final minutes of play. Kinnick couldn't watch from under the pileup, but Green scored the winning touchdown as time ran down. In this, as in most other games, Number 24 and many of his linemen had played the full 60 minutes. The score, as a Chicago sportswriter put it, was 'Nile Kinnick 13, Minnesota 9. Tersely, that tells the story of the most spectacular football game in modern Big Ten history.'

Dr Eddie Anderson afterwards described Kinnick's leadership on those thrilling afternoons:

*He was a perfectionist. Never satisfied unless he could come as close as he could to absolute perfection in any move he made. He could never feel convinced there was no room for further improvements, and his spirit was transmitted to his teammates. More often than not, as a result of his inspiration, we had as many as seven or eight players who'd go the full 60 minutes with him in a particular game. And they knew Nile was never wasting himself; when Kinnick wasn't running the ball, or passing it, he was blocking for somebody else. There was no such thing as using Nile Kinnick on a fake.*

Then came disaster. In the season's final game against Northwestern, Kinnick's relentless style of play caught up with him. Having played virtually every minute of seven full games, Kinnick suffered a shoulder separation and watched helplessly as the Hawkeyes, without his last-minute magic, struggled to a 7-7 tie with the Wildcats. A win would have given them the conference title, because on the same day, at Ann Arbor, Michigan, the Wolverines were upsetting the Ohio State Buckeyes. Thus the Buckeyes, with one loss, backed into the Big Ten title over the Iron Men, who had achieved a better overall record until the tie with Northwestern.

At the end of the 1939 season Kinnick's statistics were counted up. Of 19 Hawkeye touchdowns that season, he passed for 11 and scored five himself. Kinnick dropkicked 11 points-after to personally account for 107 of 130 points scored. He passed for 684 yards and 33

completions, ran for 374, returned 35 punts and kickoffs for 616 yards, and averaged 39 yards on 73 punts. He led the nation in kickoff returns with 377 yards and interceptions, having nabbed eight. But one statistic revealed the intangible, almost mystical quality Kinnick's leadership brought to the Hawkeyes. Five times in 1939 he brought them victory in the fourth quarter.

Soon the honors rolled in. The Heisman Trophy, Maxwell and Walter Camp Awards, all given to the top college player, were Kinnick's. He was a consensus All-American, topping the ballot on every team, and was named honorary captain of the team picked by the All-American Football Board, the only honor team that designated a leader. He was also made the Big Ten's Most Valuable Player. Perhaps the greatest national honor was his selection as Associated Press Athlete of the Year, beating out even baseball great Joe DiMaggio.

The University, too, showered Kinnick with honors. Graduating from the College of Commerce, he was elected to Phi Beta Kappa and the Order of Artus, the honorary commerce society. Presented to him was the Iowa Athletic Board Cup for excellence in scholarship and athletics. Dr Eddie Anderson, who had seen that 'special something' in Nile Kinnick one year prior, was selected Coach of the Year.

The professional football scouts came sniffing around, inevitably, but they were disappointed. Iowa's star wanted to attend law school and felt that pro football would conflict with his goal. There was a whole wide world waiting outside of football.

*Opposite page: Nile Kinnick's incredible performance in 1939 earned him the Heisman Trophy (top two), the Maxwell and Walter Camp Awards, Big Ten MVP honors and a place on the 1940 All-Star team (bottom).*

*Left: Kinnick became a fighter pilot during World War II, and was tragically lost at sea on 2 June 1943. He remains the greatest Hawkeye of all time.*

At his acceptance of the Heisman Trophy in the closing days of 1939 Kinnick said: 'I thank God that I was born to the gridirons of the Middle West and not to the battlefields of Europe. I can speak confidently and positively that the football players of this country would rather fight for the Heisman Trophy than for the Croix de Guerre.' Ensign Nile Kinnick, scholar and athlete, was lost at sea on 2 June 1943 when his Navy fighter crashed into the Gulf of Paria, only four miles from his aircraft carrier. In 1972 Iowa Stadium was renamed Kinnick Stadium in honor of Iowa's hero.

America's war years were dark ones for Iowa football. The general shortage of players due to the war effort was no doubt responsible for much of the trouble. A succession of coaches came and went, and Iowa finished no higher than fourth in the conference standings and mustered only one victory in the three seasons spanning 1943 through 1945.

Dr Eddie Anderson left Iowa after the 1942 season for military service, returning after E P Madigan coached the 1943 and 1944 teams and Clem Crowe had labored for the 1945 campaign. Anderson coached for four more seasons at Iowa before packing his bags for good in 1949, just as Iowa football was nearing another turning point.

Along the way, two animals had become part of Iowa football and endeared themselves to Hawkeye fans – a bird and a pig. During the 1935 season, Governor Floyd B Olson of Minnesota and Governor Clyde Herring of Iowa made a wager on the game between the Hawkeyes and Gophers in an effort to ease the tension of an intense rivalry. After Iowa lost the game 13-6 Herring presented Olson with 'Floyd of Rosedale.' Floyd was a full-blooded champion pig, brother to 'Blue Boy' who appeared in the movie *State Fair*. Floyd later made his home in Minnesota, but a bronze replica created by St Paul sculptor Charles Brioscho travels back and forth between the two schools as a prize for the winner. Floyd, measuring 21 inches long and 15 inches high, holds a special place in the hearts of Hawkeye fans. Cries of 'Bring Floyd home!' helped provide the inspiration for the Iowa team to beat the Gophers in 1985.

The Hawkeye nickname has an even older tradition. First attached to the people of the Iowa territory in honor of a white scout in James Fenimore Cooper's novel *The Last of the Mohicans*, the name was borrowed by the school shortly after its founding. But not until 1948 did Iowa fans gain a tangible symbol of the name. A journalism instructor, Richard Spencer III, first drew the lively hawk after

Above: *Lineman Calvin Jones was All-American in 1954 and 1955 and, as one of Coach Evashevski's most talented players, saw his Number 62 jersey retired.*

studying some stuffed birds in the natural history museum. The mischievous-looking hawk was an immediate hit and acquired the name Herky from alumnus John Franklin after a statewide contest. Herky has symbolized Iowa athletics ever since, and cheerleaders in Herky outfits help stir up the crowds at athletic events.

The 1950s were to prove important years for Iowa and for the Big Ten conference. The conference had bid goodbye to the University of Chicago and welcomed Michigan State University in 1949, bringing the group to its present membership. College football had become big business as television coverage began to make an impact. Perhaps as a consequence, recruitment violations among the teams of the Big Ten began to surface, sometimes necessitating temporary suspensions of guilty schools. For good or ill, the Big Ten had taken its place as the most famous, and most successful, college football conference.

Iowa's teams of the free-wheeling 1950s, which included such players as Alex Karras, Calvin Jones and Randy Duncan, were

Above: *Herky the Hawk became the Iowa mascot in 1948.*

Top: *The bronze statue of Floyd of Rosedale.*

Top right: *All-American center Jerry Hilgenberg.*

Center right: *Forrest Evashevski of Iowa (third from left) meets with Big Ten coaches Woody Hayes, Milt Bruhn and Ara Parseghian.*

coached almost entirely by one man, Forrest Evashevski. From 1952 to 1960 he compiled a record of 52 wins, 27 losses and four ties. Evashevski, or 'Evy,' as he was often called, had first gained prominence at the University of Michigan, where he had been the chief blocking back for Tom Harmon, the legendary Wolverine hero of the 1938, 1939 and 1940 seasons. Early on, he became known as a man who spoke his mind and never backed away from difficult situations.

Evashevski arrived in Iowa City in 1952, amid much fanfare, having served as head football coach at Washington State. By that time Hawkeye football fortunes had slipped considerably. The Iron Men of the 1930s were

a fading memory, and Iowa alumni and other fans were sure that the tough-talking Evy would lend the team respectability. Early in that first season, he made this promise to the alumni: 'We will work hard and we will guarantee you interesting football. If that isn't enough, you'd better get yourself a new football coach.'

Soon, Iowa was again boasting outstanding players. Evashevski developed Jerry Hilgenberg, the first Hawkeye to achieve All-America status at center and the first in a long and illustrious line of Hilgenbergs to play for Iowa. Then came Calvin Jones, a two-time All-American in 1954 and 1955 and perhaps the best lineman in Iowa football history. A mighty blocker and tackler, Jones had planned to attend college elsewhere but decided to join the Hawkeyes after visiting two high school teammates at the school. At the end of the 1955 season Jones not only repeated as All-American but collected the Outland Award as the nation's best interior lineman. Evashevski paid Cal Jones the supreme honor of retiring his Number 62 jersey, making him only the second Iowa player so honored. The other uniform was, of course, Nile Kinnick's Number 24. In a tragic coincidence, Jones also met his death in a plane crash less than a year after he graduated.

In spite of Evy's solid coaching and a host of strong individual players, until the 1956 season Iowa remained mired in the middle of the Big Ten standings every season. But the 1956 season featured a dramatic turnaround as the Hawkeyes celebrated a 5-1-0 conference season, losing only to Michigan. Evashevski's wing-T formation, borrowed from former teammate and Delaware head coach Dave Nelson, gave the Hawk attack real punch. Quarterback Kenny Ploen, a fine passer, was joined by two brilliant ends, Jim Gibbons and Frank Gilliam. And Iowa's potent tackling force was led by a fierce competitor named Alex Karras.

The Hawkeyes entered the season finale with the Minnesota Gophers. Before the game Evashevski told his team, 'You have only 60 minutes to play football, and the rest of your life to remember it!' An inspired Iowa team, after a scoreless first half, capped a 63-yard scoring drive with a 16-yard touchdown pass from Ploen to Gilliam. The game ended 7-0, and the Hawkeyes snatched the Big Ten title. They finished the season by drubbing Notre Dame 48-0 and became the first Hawkeye team to beat the Irish in 16 years – and the first in 51 years to win more than eight games. Ranked third in the nation, this tough, brash Iowa team then went on to beat Oregon State 35-19 in their first Rose Bowl.

Alex Karras and Kenny Ploen gained All-America honors that year, and Ploen was named Conference MVP. Gilliam and center Don Suchy also received mention. In 1957 Karras again was honored as All-American and added another Outland Award to Iowa's fame. However, that season ended with disappointment as Evy's Hawkeyes failed to turn back the tide of the Ohio State Buckeyes under Woody Hayes, who upset Iowa to take the conference title that year.

In 1958 came Randy Duncan, who had taken over the quarterbacking chores from Kenny Ploen the year before. The most talked-about Iowa player in two decades, the

Above: *End Frank Gilliam's dexterity helped take the 1956 Hawkeyes all the way to a Rose Bowl victory.*

Left: *Tough tackle Alex Karras, one of the stars of the heady 1956 season, was All-America in both 1956 and 1957 and won the Outland Award in 1957.*

Opposite top: *Kenny Ploen (11), a skillful passer, won conference MVP and All-America honors for his superb performance in 1956. Here he finds an opening in a game against Wisconsin, 1956.*

Opposite bottom: *Bill Happel (40) of Iowa goes over the top for seven yards as Aurelius Thomas (64) of Ohio State comes in to stop him. Woody Hayes' Buckeyes upset the Hawks to win the Big Ten title in this game on 16 November 1957.*

180-pound Duncan was highly intelligent and personable. He was also an extraordinary passer, and proved it during the Hawkeye's stunning season. Joined by Suchy, who repeated at center, and some talented ends, including Curt Merz, Iowa zipped through the Indiana, Wisconsin, Northwestern and Michigan teams.

Then came the fateful home game against Woody Hayes' Buckeyes. Iowa had already clinched the conference title and Rose Bowl berth, and was favored over Ohio State, which had suffered a loss to Northwestern and scored ties with Wisconsin and Purdue. The game, which Hayes later described as 'the greatest offensive contest I've ever been in,' was tied 7-7 at the end of the first quarter, 21-21 at the half, and 28-28 heading into the final quarter. But Iowa came out on the short end of the offensive fireworks, and the Buckeyes struck for a 10-point fourth quarter to win 38-28. The Hawkeyes had gained 249 yards in the air, 178

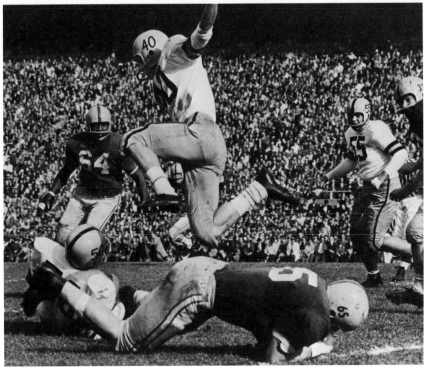

*Above: End Curt Merz was on the great 1958 team which won the Rose Bowl and the Grantland Rice Trophy, reserved for the best team in the country. He received All-America honors along with star quarterback Randy Duncan.*

*Top right: Linebacker Mike Reilly was one of the bright spots in an otherwise undistinguished string of seasons in the 1960s. He was All-American in 1963.*

on the ground and had scored four touchdowns, but it wasn't enough. Ohio State had won mainly on the strength of repeated short rushing bursts, or the 'three yards and a cloud of dust' for which Woody Hayes' teams became famous.

Happily, Iowa ended its season by romping past Notre Dame 31-21 on two sharp touchdown passes by Duncan. The 1958 Hawkeyes saved perhaps their best performance of the season for the Rose Bowl, routing the California Bears 38-12, and rolling up 516 offensive yards (429 rushing and 87 passing) in the process. It was perhaps this brilliant game that led the Football Writers of America to boost the Iowa team from second place in the nation to first and to award the Hawkeyes the Grantland Rice Trophy, symbolic of the nation's best team. The honor was well deserved; Iowa

had led the Big Ten in scoring, rushing, passing and pass-completion average. They had also set new conference records for first downs, 22, and total yards gained, 416.7, per game.

Perhaps Ike Armstrong, athletic director at Minnesota, best summed up the competition's esteem for Iowa when he called them 'the best team I've ever seen in the Big Ten.' Randy Duncan was voted Conference MVP and a unanimous All-American, and was runner-up to Pete Dawkins of Army in the Heisman Trophy voting. He won the Walter Camp Award as Back-of-the-Year and was named the Helms Foundation Player of the Year. Curt Merz also achieved All-America status. Many people were predicting that the Hawkeyes were about to become the Big Ten's next football dynasty. But it was not to be.

After an undistinguished 1959 season, during which Iowa's conference record was 3-3-0, the Hawkeyes bounced back in 1960 with a 5-1-0 record and a share of the Big Ten title. Halfback Larry Ferguson and guard Mark Manders, both All-Americans, were standouts, and quarterback Wilburn Hollis also received All-America mention. Yet Hawkeye fans remembered 1960 chiefly as 'the year we lost Evy.'

Evashevski had constantly feuded with Iowa athletic director Paul Brechler. Eventually Brechler was ousted, thanks mainly to the tremendous popularity of Iowa's head coach with fans, faculty and alumni. Evashevski was then named to replace Brechler as athletic director,

but Iowa officials drew the line at having the same man hold the jobs of coach and athletic director. So the 1960 season was Evy's last as head coach.

There followed ten years of futility for Iowa football, as Jerry Burns and then Ray Nagel coached the Hawkeyes, producing only one winning season between them. Evashevski fired both, and then resigned as athletic director in 1970. Many observers felt that if Evy had gotten along with Brechler he might have remained Iowa's head coach for 20 or 30 years. But Forrest Evashevski left Iowa, and the dynasties were left to Woody Hayes and Michigan's Bo Schembechler.

Dismal though it was, the story of the 1960s would be incomplete without mention of Iowa players who received All-America honors: linebacker Mike Reilly in 1963, guard John Niland and end Karl Noonan in 1964 and Niland again in 1965. Such fine individual performances made the other chagrins of the 1960s all that much harder to bear for Hawkeye fans.

In 1972 Iowa Stadium was renamed Kinnick Stadium in honor of Nile Kinnick. AstroTurf was installed, and seating capacity was steadily increased, a process that has continued up until the present. But the fans who thronged the stadium were obliged to continue suffering throughout the 1970s as head coaches Frank Lauterburg (1971-73) and Bob Commings (1974-78) led Iowa's football effort, finishing no better than 3-5-0 in the conference in the decade and finishing last in 1971 and 1973. Although individual Hawkeye players won acclaim, including offensive tackle Rod Walters and offensive guard Joe Devlin, Iowa football fortunes were nearly at their nadir.

On 9 December 1978 Hayden Fry became Iowa's head coach, following a distinguished head coaching career at Southern Methodist

*Above: Hayden Fry took over coaching duties for the Hawkeyes in 1978, and by 1981 the team had arrived once again at the Rose Bowl.*

*Top: Quarterback Tom McLaughlin looks to make a short pass for the touchdown as Bruce Davis (63) provides protection in a 1975 game versus OSU.*

Above: *Gales (12) and Mosley (18) in action versus the Ohio State Buckeyes, 21 October 1978.*

Right: *Station (36), Spitzig (38) and Pryor (99) down a Buckeye, 22 September 1984.*

Left: *Tailback Ronnie Harmon (31) zips downfield for a Hawkeye touchdown.*

Top left: *Great tackle Larry Station (36) in action for the Hawkeyes.*

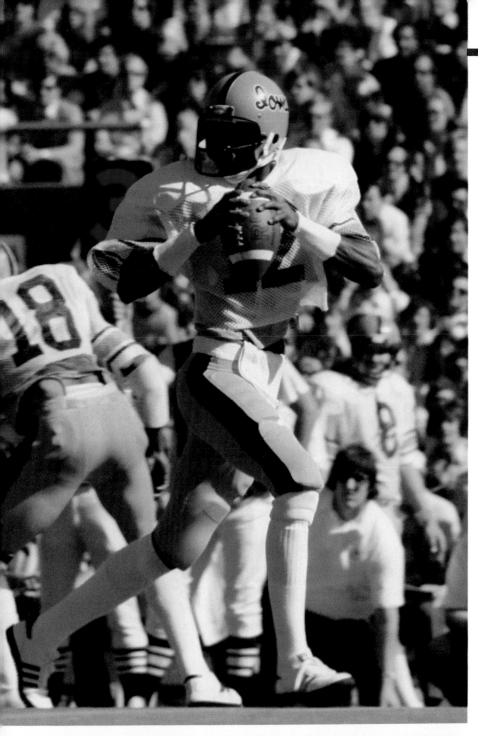

(1962-1972) and North Texas State (1973-1978). 'He had turned around two struggling programs,' remarked Chalmers 'Bump' Elliott, Iowa's popular athletic director. 'When we went looking for a coach, I immediately thought of Hayden.' Fry quickly got the approval of alumni and fans the following fall with near-upsets of Oklahoma and Nebraska, and four conference wins.

The 1981 season shone with the results of Fry's steady hand at the helm and brought fans what some thought they might never see again, a Big Ten co-championship and Rose Bowl berth. Even a 28-9 loss to Washington did little to dim the new spirit of hope in Iowa, and the next four seasons brought a combined Big Ten record of 25-8-1 and berths in the Peach Bowl, Gator Bowl, Freedom Bowl and, in 1985, the Rose Bowl.

Along the way, players such as Andre Tippett, Reggie Roby, Jay Hilgenberg (the latest in the Hilgenberg line of Hawkeye centers) and Mark Bortz enjoyed distinguished Iowa careers and went on to the professional ranks – Hilgenberg and Bortz to Super Bowl competition with the Chicago Bears. Hayden Fry's fame spread. In his tenure at Iowa the colorful Texan, always sporting sunglasses and cowboy boots, did more than spiff up the Hawkeye uniforms and institute the 'Tiger Hawk' football logo; he had turned the program completely around, just as Elliott had predicted.

The 1985 Hawkeyes compiled a conference record of 7-1-0, losing only to Ohio State in an upset, and won a Rose Bowl berth. Although they lost to UCLA, a host of honors were showered on Hawkeye players, led by quarterback Chuck Long. Besides finishing as Heisman Trophy runner-up, Long was named college Player of the Year and was, of course, a first All-American. He had completed 231 of 351 passes for 2978 yards and 26 touchdowns – all school records. He also became the first quarterback in the history of the Big Ten to go over 10,000 yards passing for a career totalling 10,142 from 1981 to 1985. Among the other All-Americans to emerge from that great 1985 season were tailback Ronnie Harmon (Iowa's all-time leading receiver) and tackle Larry Station.

By mid-decade Hawkeye fans had a new spring in their step, and much credit was due to Hayden Fry. Iowa's first victory of the 1986 season put Fry past Forrest Evashevski as Iowa's winningest coach, and the season ended with a fine 9-3 record. With football fortunes on the rise, Iowa had once again joined the elite of both the conference and the nation, and their future is very bright indeed.

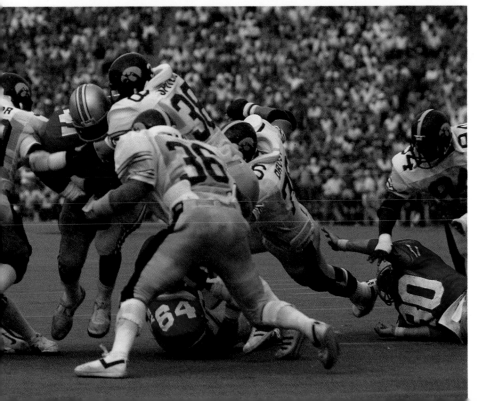

71

# UNIVERSITY OF MICHIGAN

Founded: 1817

Location: Ann Arbor

Total Enrollment: 34,340

Colors: Maize and Blue

Nickname: Wolverines

College football was only ten years old at the University of Michigan, and still consisted entirely of campus games between lower and upperclassmen, when students decided it was time to take on one of the prestigious Eastern schools. They struck a deal with Cornell students to play at a neutral site, Cleveland, and wrote Cornell President Andrew White to secure permission.

White's reply was anything but conciliatory. 'No, I will not permit thirty men to travel 400 miles to merely agitate a bag of wind,' he wrote to. Michigan President James Angell.

Cornell would have to wait 14 more years before playing its first intercollegiate game, but Michigan became the first Midwestern school to do so when it took on Racine College on 30 May 1879 at Chicago's White Stocking Park. Michigan beat the small Wisconsin school by one touchdown and one field goal, the only scores in the game. Thus the Midwest's most powerful football dynasty was born.

Michigan added many new, more powerful rivals in the years that followed, sometimes accepting more challenges than it could handle. In 1881 they played Harvard, Yale and Princeton *in the same week*, losing all three contests. After the faculty cut the schedule back to a reasonable level the Wolverines established a steady record of wins in the 1880s, concentrating mostly on Midwestern competition.

By the 1890s Michigan football had begun to take on the character of modern amateur athletics. The faculty responded to evidence of professionalism by taking control of the program in 1893 and advocated membership in the ICFR, or Intercollegiate Conference of Faculty Representatives, in 1896. But Michigan's first official seasons made for little glory, featuring losses to Amos Stagg's all-powerful Chicago eleven. In 1898, however, the Wolverines asserted their potential by edging undefeated Chicago 12-11 and winning their first conference title. Louis Elbel was inspired to write Michigan's well-known fight song, 'The Victors,' at the end of that historic season, and the team contributed its first All-American, William Cunningham, to Walter Camp's annual write-up.

The real turning point came two years later, in 1901, when athletic director Charles Baird hired 30-year-old Fielding Harris Yost as head football coach. Baird knew of Yost's reputation of success at Ohio Wesleyan, Nebraska, Kansas and Stanford, all of which had gone on to conference championships, and he decided that this winning coach was just the man to help beat dreaded Chicago. Yost brought with

him an innovative approach to offense based on speed, rather than bulk. He admonished players during practice to scramble into scrimmage formation quickly between plays. 'Are you just a spectator? Hurry up! Hurry up!' His urgent chiding earned him the nickname 'Hurry Up' Yost.

Following Yost from San Jose Normal college in California – one of five schools Yost coached in 1900, all to championships – was freshman Willie Heston. The two of them would bowl over collegiate football in the next four years, creating the famous 'Point-a-Minute' Wolverine teams that would score a record 55 straight undefeated games.

Heston, the nation's first college athletics star, was an unstoppable halfback – he was tackled by a single man only once in his career. He helped the 1901 team steamroll 8000 yards for 550 points – virtually one for every minute of play – and 11 victories for a perfect season. The Wolverines racked up typical scores of 107 points over Iowa, 86 over Ohio State and 128 over Buffalo.

Michigan capped that season by gaining an invitation to the first New Year's Day game intended as the grand finale to the Pasadena, California, Festival of Roses. The Wolverines smothered undefeated Stanford 49-0 and allowed their exhausted opponent to resign the game with eight minutes still left to play. The

*Above: Fielding 'Hurry Up' Yost, Michigan's coach from 1901 to 1926, produced eight undefeated teams and presided over the legendary 'Point-A-Minute' teams of 1901-04 which produced an incredible 55-game winning streak.*

*Opposite top two: Halfback Willie Heston scored an awesome total of 72 touchdowns in his four years with Michigan (1901-05). His running skill made him the first nationally famous college sports hero, and legend has it that the unstoppable Heston was brought down by a lone tackler only once in his brilliant career.*

*Opposite bottom: The Little Brown Jug has been given to the winner of the annual Wolverine-Gopher game since 1903.*

*Page 72: Michigan's Jim Harbaugh in 1986.*

the most physically punishing games ever staged. Dr Henry Williams' Gophers held the Wolverines to a 6-6 tie, and even held on to Yost's team's brown water jug. Yost later asked for it back, only to be told 'Come and win it back.' Thus the famous Little Brown Jug trophy was established.

By the end of the 1905 season the Wolverines had racked up four straight Big Ten titles and scored 2821 points to their opponents' 42, all with no forward passing and a touchdown value of just five points. Heston alone scored

Pasadena ceremony officials were so appalled by the defeat that the 'Rose Bowl' game, as it would eventually be called, was laid to rest for the next 16 years, replaced by unusual spectator events such as chariot racing.

In 1903 the Point-a-Minute machine stalled only once entering into a deadlock with Minnesota. Minnesota played a revolutionary seven-man line/four-man secondary defense, designed specifically to stop Heston, in one of

72 touchdowns during his four years and was selected a consensus All-American 1903-04. Neil Snow made the lists in 1901.

The stubborn Chicago Maroons put the only serious blemish on the near-perfect four-year campaign. In the final minutes of a grueling stalemate, the last game of the 1905 season, Chicago's Walter Eckersall booted a 60-yard punt into the Michigan end zone. Wolverine Denny Clark nabbed the ball and started out of the end zone, only to be stopped short by Maurice Catlin, Chicago's captain. The Maroons thereby picked up a safety for a 2-0 win and snatched away the conference title to bring the Point-a-Minute express to a grinding halt.

Yost lost much of that phenomenal team to graduations the next year, but he built a new super-squad around Adolph Schulz. 'Germany' had arrived in 1904 to take his place in history as football's first behind-the-line center. The player at first irritated Yost by dropping back behind the line as each scrimmage began, but the better view accorded Schulz improved his play, especially when the forward pass was made legal two years later in an attempt to make football less brutal.

Schulz contributed to a 4-1 season in 1906, leading to a share of the Big Ten title. In 1907 the team blanked all its competitors, scoring 107 points in five shutouts before losing the season finale to Penn 6-0. Schulz was named to the All-America team that year.

The following season was the first in 12 years that Michigan played outside the Big Ten conference. A set of new regulations which would have restricted Michigan's play with Eastern teams impelled the university to drop its membership in the conference. Michigan continued to play some Big Ten teams, including rivals Minnesota and Ohio State, until the conference passed a rule in 1910 prohibiting Big Ten schools from playing former members.

Yost produced successful teams even without the incentive of a conference crown. In 1909 the Wolverines lost only to Notre Dame 11-3, and they upset Penn to make Michigan the first Midwestern school to defeat the 'Big Four' of Yale, Harvard, Princeton and Pennsylvania. Gigantic guard Al Benbrook won All-America honors in 1909 and in 1910 was instrumental in bringing the Little Brown Jug home with a 6-0 win over Minnesota.

'Hurry Up' Yost brought the forward pass to life in that game. To counter the supposedly unbeatable 'Minnesota Shift' offense tactic he used some of the first spiral passes (thrown by quarterback Neil 'Shorty' McMillan) to confuse the Gophers' defense and secure victory. Benbrook and end Stanfield Wells led a defense

Left: *Paul Goebel was a key member of Michigan's undefeated 1922 and 1923 squads. He was All-American in 1923.*

Right: *Triple-threat Harry Kipke sparked the resurgence of the Michigan team in 1922 and 1923. He returned to his alma mater as coach in 1929, leading the Wolverines to four straight conference titles and two national championships starting in 1930.*

Top right: *Michigan Stadium, home of the Wolverines.*

that gave up a maximum three points per game in a 3-0-3 season, and both were named All-Americans.

Though banished from all conference competition, Michigan held its own in the next six years, winning 33, losing 12 and tying three games. All-American stars included tackle Miller Pontius and halfback James Craig, who led the Wolverines to a 6-1 season in 1913, and the amazing Johnny Maulbetsch, who scored 12 TDs to contribute to a 6-3 season in 1914. Yost's teams continued to perfect an aerial offensive style, identified by the press as a strategy relying on 'a pass, a punt and a prayer.'

Meanwhile, the Michigan athletics board, under chairman Ralph Aigler, urged the Regents to reapply for membership in the Big Ten conference. They did so and were accepted in time for Michigan to play a game with Northwestern on 20 November 1917. This was in fact the first point at which the Big Ten actually consisted of ten teams. Michigan lost the game but chalked up eight subsequent victories behind fullback Cedric Smith, who was chosen an All-American along with Ernest Allmendinger and Frank Culver.

The next year, Michigan went undefeated and picked up a share of the conference title in an abbreviated wartime season of five games, and freshman fullback Frank Steketee made the All-America team. But Yost didn't have the same luck in 1919 and posted his worst-ever Michigan record of 3-7. He rebounded the next year, however, to begin a domination of the conference that would last through the 1920s.

The 1921 team was bursting with talent, including center Ernie Vick, Paul Goebel and

the triple-threat, pint-sized halfback Harry Kipke. Though weighing only 158 pounds, Kipke had already created a sensation in his career at Lansing High School. In 1921 he and the team shut out five opponents, drubbing Minnesota 38-0 and losing only to Ohio State.

Kipke and friends were determined not to offer the Buckeyes a fourth straight doormat the following season, and they fought a spectacular battle in OSU's newly-dedicated stadium before a crowd of 72,500. In the second quarter, already leading 3-0 on a Goebel field goal, Yost decided it was time to dust off 'Old 83,' a neat reverse pass play that had scored dozens of touchdowns for Michigan during his reign. It began when Irving Uteritz, the quarterback, took the snap from center and rode along with the line of scrimmage to the right. Uteritz then faked a handoff to the end coming around to the right. Kipke, in the tailback position, scooted to the right as well, but spun smartly to left in time to receive a pitch from Uteritz. Arcing back around left, Kipke caught the eyes of two OSU defenders, but they shifted too late. The back stormed around the left end, seconds ahead of the Buckeyes, and zipped 34 yards for a touchdown. Kipke is said to have tossed the ball to an official and quipped, 'Well, the place is really dedicated, now.'

Kipke nabbed an OSU pass in the third quarter for a 45-yard scoring run, and after another interception booted a 37-yard field goal for a 19-0 Wolverine victory. He had punted eleven times for an average 47 yards, prompting the post-game comment by Walter Camp, 'Kipke, you're the greatest punter in football history.' By season's end Michigan returned to title status with a 6-0-1 record, outscoring foes 183-13. Goebel and Kipke were named All-Americans, as teammate Ernie Vick had the year prior.

Above: *Quarterback Benny Friedman, who joined end Bennie Oosterbaan to form the famous 'Benny to Bennie' combination of the mid 1920s.*

Yost was named athletic director at the retirement of Phil Bartelme, and he volunteered to go on coaching the football team without pay, an arrangement which lasted through 1926. Even with more responsibilities to handle, Yost continued to top himself, and in 1923 he produced his eighth undefeated team at Michigan. The injury-ridden Wolverine eleven often had to depend on Jack Blott, who became known as 'The Michigan Line,' and on the final performances of Kipke and Goebel. But the team finished 8-0 and tied for the conference title with Illinois.

'Hurry Up' Yost contemplated retirement in 1924, and just before the season began he announced the hiring of a new coach, George Little, of Ohio football power Miami U. Yet in his first season (6-2), Little complained that Yost could not stay out of the football picture, and Little left for Wisconsin's coaching post in 1925. Among Yost's 'meddling' influences was the introduction of bench-warmer sophomore Benny Friedman, who joined with some other sophomores to create Yost's best remembered team. Among the new players was a big, blond end named Bennie Oosterbaan, who would team with quarterback Friedman to create Michigan's renowned 'Benny to Bennie' aerial duo. With former playing stars Harry Kipke, Jack Blott and 'Cappie' Cappon on his coaching staff, Yost had immeasurable talent along the sidelines as well.

The Wolverines started the 1925 season by blowing away Michigan State 39-0, and Michigan rolled over its next four opponents with shutouts: Indiana, 63-0; Wisconsin, 21-0; Illinois, 3-0; and Navy, 54-0. On an impossibly slick, rain-soaked field, the Wolverines literally slipped to a 3-2 loss to Northwestern, but the team recovered to stomp Ohio State and Minnesota 10-0 and 35-0, respectively, taking the Big Ten title and being called by most sportswriters the national champion.

Both Benny and Bennie were named All-Americans, along with guard Harry Hawkins, linebacker Bob Brown and Tom Edwards — part of a defense that had even held the immortal Red Grange back in a 3-0 loss to Illinois. For the season, Friedman had passed for 760 yards and 14 TDs, contributing to a Michigan point total of 227, against the three points Northwestern scored.

He would star again in his final season, 1926, beginning in the opener against Oklahoma A & M with three touchdown passes to back Bo Molenda and one to Oosterbaan that stitched up a 42-3 victory. The two Bennies took on MSU next, connecting on a 21-yard touchdown pass to help bring MSU down finally 55-3.

Only Navy put a damper on the pair's antics, sinking the Wolverines 10-0 in Baltimore. Friedman shot off one pass after the next to Oosterbaan, but to no avail. 'Each should have gone for a touchdown,' the quarterback said later. 'Those big Navy tackles, Wickhorst and Eddy, were murdering me.' At one point in the game Friedman turned to his lumbering partner, Oosterbaan, and suggested *he* try passing the ball. But Wickhorst and Eddy gave the big end the same treatment, piling all over him. 'When we pried him loose,' Friedman recalled, 'Oosterbaan looked at me and said, "Benny, if it's all the same to you, I'd rather catch passes than throw them."'

But in the following week's comeback game against Ohio State the pair glittered. Ohio State was leading in the first half, 10-0, when the Bennies fired up. Friedman hurled a pass to Oosterbaan on the OSU 21, and on the next play Friedman faked a place-kick formation and threw a handy 30-yard pass to Oosterbaan, who had slipped artfully into a corner of the end zone. Just before the first half ended Friedman decided on a real field-goal attempt. As the Wolverines gathered at scrimmage, the Buckeyes yelled to each other, 'Fake! Fake! It's another pass!' As the enemy fanned out to cover the ends, Friedman had plenty of time to kick a perfect 44-yard field goal. In the final

quarter Michigan stole a Buckeye fumble, and moments later Friedman fired a pass to Leo Hoffman for a touchdown, locking in a 17-16 win over OSU.

Oosterbaan's best moment came the following week against Minnesota, when the Wolverines trailed 6-0 on a snow-covered Minneapolis field. In the fourth period the Gophers had driven to their 40-yard line when they fumbled the ball in the backfield. Oosterbaan plowed through the line to scoop up the ball, and without looking behind him charged 60 yards for a touchdown. 'Every step I took,' Bennie later said, 'I kept thinking, "Won't I look a chump if somebody catches me from behind?" . . . I guess that made me run faster.'

The Wolverines finished with a 7-1 season and shared the conference crown with Northwestern. The Bennies became the only passing duo in history to win consecutive All-America honors. But the 1926 season also ended an era in Michigan football. Not only was Friedman graduated, going on to a spectacular pro career with the New York Giants and several college coaching spots, but Yost announced that he had coached his last season and would henceforth devote all of his time to his numerous other duties as athletic director of the nation's largest university.

Yost named as a replacement his top aide,

Above: *Fritz Crisler (left), Michigan coach from 1938 to 1947, and Elton E 'Tad' Wieman (right), Michigan coach in 1927-28, with former Chicago coach and football legend Amos Alonzo Stagg in 1952.*

Elton E 'Tad' Wieman, who led the Wolverines in 1927 to a 6-2 season that included five shut-outs and a single loss to national champion Illinois. Oosterbaan closed his brilliant career with a third All-America selection, becoming the only Wolverine athlete accorded that honor. He had also starred in basketball as an All-American, and after graduation stayed at Michigan to help coach both sports. Louie Gilbert also put on an unforgettable offensive display in a lambasting of Yost's old school, Ohio Wesleyan. The backfield wonder passed 28 yards to LaVerne Taylor for a touchdown; scored with a 25-yard punt return; passed 47 yards to Bennie Oosterbaan and 24 yards to Leo Hoffman for two more TDs; and finally streaked 90 yards himself for a score. Gilbert and Oosterbaan repeated such pyrotechnics throughout the season, bringing an era to a stirring finish.

Coach Wieman slipped to a dismal 3-4-1 record the following year, 1928, and although he produced All-American tackle Otto Pommerening, he was pushed out to make room for Harry Kipke, the one-time star halfback. A no-nonsense coach who insisted that kicking, passing and defense all be practiced to perfection, Kipke pulled Michigan back onto its feet, garnering a 5-3-0 record in 1929. But his finest accomplishment lay ahead: Kipke would lead Michigan to consecutive conference titles and two national championships over the next four years, 1930-33, and would suffer just one defeat.

Coach Kipke benefited from another swift passing combo, quarterback Harry Newman and end Ivy Williamson. Newman gained stardom in 1930, outpassing eight opponents including mighty Harvard, for an 8-0-1 season. The defense also did its part, holding the competition to only two touchdowns and two field goals the entire season. Newman suffered an ankle injury in 1931, limiting his performance but not stopping the Wolverines from pushing to a 7-1-1 mark, a share of a three-way conference title and the contribution of center Maynard Morrison to the All-America. The benched Newman nearly threw in the towel at season's end, but decided he'd put in one more year on the gridiron.

He, and the Wolverines, were not to regret it. In 1932 Michigan tromped over eight opponents in a row, holding six scoreless and winning the conference title and a national championship, largely on the passing brilliance of Newman. The crafty quarterback threw constantly for touchdowns, and ran several amazing plays himself, including a quarterback sneak TD against Indiana and, against Chi-

cago, scores from a 78-yard punt return and a 27-yard run from scrimmage that totaled 12 points against a Maroon blank. Newman snagged the Douglas Fairbanks Award, something of a Heisman predecessor, and was named an All-American along with stalwart junior tackle Chuck Bernard and end Ted Petoskey.

Both linemen repeated in 1933, along with outstanding senior tackle Francis 'Whitey' Wistert, and Michigan made a repeat of the 1932 performance, this time chalking up a 7-0-1 record for its second national championship in a row, along with the Big Ten title. The only tie was with a tough Minnesota team, whose strong defense had held the Wolverines to only three points the year prior. Kipke had assembled 22 straight wins, and his four-year record now stood at 31-1-3.

But the coach lost most of his 'punt-pass-prayer' stalwarts in 1934, and his teams plunged into a grim losing slump. The 'Golden Years' were definitely over: Michigan posted 1-7, 4-4, 1-7 and 4-4 seasons from 1934 to 1937. No players made All-American, although one feisty center, Jerry Ford, won MVP honors from his teammates in 1934 before starting his path to the White House.

Always one obsessed by winning, athletic director Yost finally lost patience and brought in a replacement for Kipke, none other than Princeton's star coach, Herbert Orrin 'Fritz' Crisler. Fritz had first served as an assistant to the great Amos Alonzo Stagg of Chicago, and he had moved on to pull Minnesota out of a slump by recruiting talent for its greatest teams of the 1930s. Drafted by a desperate Princeton in 1932 to help a program that had seen only nine wins in five years, Crisler turned the tables, losing only nine in the following five years and winning 35. That was more than enough to interest Yost and the athletic board, and, with the promise that Crisler would be named athletic director when Yost retired, the young coach made his move to Ann Arbor.

It was the beginning of a highly productive, 30-year relationship. Crisler demanded and got not only the largest salary of any Midwestern coach, but also unprecedented power. He asked that the physical education and athletic

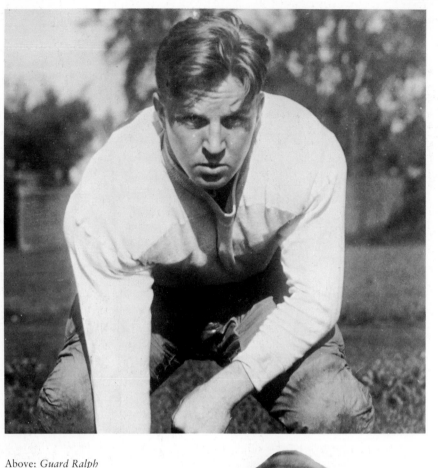

Above: *Guard Ralph Heikkinen, who was joined on the 1937 Wolverines by young backs Forrest Evashevski and Tom Harmon to achieve a 6-1-1 record for the season. Heikkinen was named All-American that year.*

programs be placed under control of one man, who would also serve as chairman on the athletic board. He inherited even more. Kipke had developed by 1937 an incredible pool of freshman talent. Starting as sophomores in 1938 were backs Forrest Evashevski and Tom Harmon, who joined such veterans as guard Ralph Heikkinen to turn the football world on end. The team plowed its way through a 6-1-1 season, losing only to Minnesota 7-6. Heikkinen was named to the All-America teams, but the youngsters gained plenty of glory of their own. Harmon's starting debut against Chicago allowed him a 59-yard touchdown sprint, and he threw two touchdown setups in a 15-13 victory over Yale. Against Illinois Harmon scored on a 13-yard run, and passed 23 yards to Evashevski for another touchdown. In the season wrap against OSU, Harmon ran for a touchdown and threw the ball to end Ed Frutig for a score.

Young Tom had arrived at Michigan already a star, having earned 14 letters in four sports at his school in Gary, Indiana. During his four years at Michigan he grew from a spindly, 145-pound frosh into a strapping 195-pound halfback who would break most Midwest scoring records. When Crisler arrived at Michigan he thought he might have to keep Harmon from developing a star complex by putting him on blocking during spring drills. But one look at the halfback ripping through scrimmage quickly smothered that idea, and it turned out that Harmon, with the

Left: *All-American Chuck Bernard played on the championship Wolverine teams of 1932 and 1933.*

help of teammate and close friend 'Evy' Evashevski, always was able to keep a level head while national media were feverishly promoting him to superstar status.

Harmon took his Michigan squad to even greater heights in his junior year, 1939, with 14 touchdowns, 130 ball carries and 37 pass completions for 1372 yards and the scoring of 102 points, including 15 extra points and one field goal. The team finished the season 6-2. Yet despite Harmon's individual brilliance, his Wolverine teams never took a conference title because of three straight losses to brick-wall Minnesota teams. Even so, Harmon was recognized with All-America honors, and certainly the respect of his fellow team members.

Perhaps former Big Ten commissioner Kenneth 'Tug' Wilson best summarized Harmon's phenomenal talents:

*"A kick off return against Penn just might have been the longest run, unofficially, in the history of college football. Taking the ball on the Michigan 17 he ripped down the right side of the field where he was*

*hemmed in by three Penn tacklers. He spun out of their clutches, reversed his field all the way to the opposite side and raced down to the Penn 20 only to be pinched in by two more desperate Quaker defenders. Again he reversed his field to*

*Right: Senior tackle Francis 'Whitey' Wistert contributed to 1933's undefeated season for the Wolverines.*

*Below: Jerry Ford was a solid center for an otherwise uninspired 1934 Wolverine team. He would later become the 38th President of the United States.*

*the original sideline, tore loose from another clutching Quaker and crossed the goal standing up. It was estimated later that he had gone close to 175 yards, around, through, between and over Red and Blue jerseys.'*

Evy, Harmon's most effective blocker, kept locker-room morale high when it appeared that Harmon's fame might eclipse the rest of the team. He used poker-faced ridicule to combat newspaper headlines such as 'Harmon Greater than Grange' and 'Harmon a One-Man Team.'

'We really laid it on,' Evashevski said later. 'We'd be getting dressed for practice and Tom would come in and somebody would say, "Here comes the team, men. We can practice now!" ' The clever and witty quarterback once

went through the locker room loudly soliciting members for the 'I-Block-For-Tom-Harmon Club.'

That club did pretty well for itself in 1940, Harmon's senior year, if the halfback's record is any indication. The Wolverines opened the season with a 41-0 slam of the California Golden Bears. It happened to be Harmon's 21st birthday, and Evy told his friend just

Above: *Stellar back Tom Harmon was the first Wolverine to win the Heisman Trophy. His remarkable running, passing and kicking expertise made him a legend in his own time, and many of his records still stand today. His career touchdown total of 33 exceeded that of the immortal Red Grange by two.*

*Above: Tom Harmon takes to the air in the 1940 season opener versus the University of California. The Wolverines walloped them, 41-0.*

*Opposite left: Backs Tom Harmon (top) and Forrest Evashevski formed the core of the Wolverine team from 1938-40. Evy provided the blocking while Harmon ran rings around the opposition.*

before kickoff, 'Let's celebrate it in a big way. If you get the kickoff, run like a thief and we'll knock a lot of guys down for you!' Evy and his pals did just that, clearing the path so that Harmon could streak 94 yards for a touchdown, the first of his four that day. The others came on a 72-yard punt return, an 86-yard twister through the entire Bear eleven, and an off-tackle/run-pass combo to Dave Nelson. On the 86-yarder, an exasperated California fan tore out of the stands and onto field to tackle Harmon himself. He missed.

The rest of the season went much the same way. Harmon scored all 21 points in a 21-14 rout of Michigan State; three touchdowns, a TD pass and all the passing and kicking in a trouncing of Harvard; a run and a pass for two touchdowns and a field goal over Illinois; and all 14 points to smash Penn. Harmon led the nation for a second straight season in both scoring, with 117 points, and running, with

1312 yards, and became the first Wolverine to win the Heisman Trophy. He was selected All-American once again, joined by Ed Frutig.

Perhaps Harmon's greatest moment came in the final game of his college career against arch-rival Ohio State. More than 75,000 football fans squeezed into Ohio Stadium to see if Harmon would break Red Grange's career touchdown record of 31. In the first quarter, Harmon dodged eight yards and slipped over the goal line to tie Red's record. He pitched the ball to Evy for a TD in the second quarter, and returned the Ohio State second-half kickoff 70 yards to set up his scoring pass to Frutig. Finally, in the third quarter, Michigan intercepted an OSU pass, and Harmon took the ball on the Ohio 18 for a rollicking run toward the end zone. He tore wide, slashed back over tackle, stiff-armed a Buckeye and outraced the rest to make football history. As a garnish of sorts, Harmon scored again in the final period

Above: *Unstoppable Number 98, Tom Harmon, in a characteristic drive while teammates provide effective blocking.*

to place his career touchdown total at 33.

Over his three years with Michigan Harmon carried the ball 398 times for 2338 yards. He completed 101 of 233 passes for another 1359 yards and 16 TDs. He scored 237 points himself, 33 points-after and two field goals. Harmon's scoring and all-purpose running records still stand today, a remarkable statement considering the specialized nature of today's pass receivers.

The Wolverine's record for 1940 was 7-1-0, but it would not be as sweet for another few years. Though Coach Crisler could barely put together successful teams using the hodge-podge of talent that shifted about from school to school during World War II, he did far better than many of his colleagues. In 1941, the Wolverines compiled a 6-1-1 record, losing only to unbeaten national champ Minnesota and tying Ohio State 20-20. Fullback Bob Westfall ran for 688 yards for a career total of 1864, just 270 less than Harmon's, and made All-America.

Another Wistert — Francis' younger brother, Albert, who wore the same Number 11 jersey — plied the line of scrimmage in 1942, and the tackle joined speeding guard Julius Franks to help clear the way for a 7-3 season. Wistert and Franks were among a stalwart line known as 'The Seven Oak Posts,' key players in a monumental 32-20 defeat of Notre Dame, and both were named to All-America teams. From 1943's grab-bag of military trainees, Crisler drew Bill Daley, Minnesota's big fullback, Wisconsin's running star Elroy 'Crazy Legs' Hirsch and teammate Jack Wink.

That melting pot team contributed to an 8-1

slate for the season, scoring 302 points behind Daley, and took Michigan's first Big Ten championship in 10 years. Daley rushed for 817 yards in six games, and sprinted for spectacular 37- and 64-yard touchdown runs in an upset of a strong Northwestern eleven. The only loss came from Notre Dame, the national champion, 35-12, as Hirsch was benched with injuries. All-America selections included Daley and defensive leader Mervin Pregulman at tackle, both of whom left Ann Arbor for the service after six games. By the end of the academic year Hirsch would letter in four sports, the only Wolverine to do so.

Without Hirsch and the two All-Americans, Crisler had more trouble mustering manpower in 1944. Among promising freshmen, though, was Dick Rifenberg, who pulled in two touchdown passes from Bill Culligan in the season opener against Iowa Pre-Flight for a 12-7 win. The Wolverines won eight but lost two — to unbeaten Ohio State and an unusually strong Indiana team featuring 'Hunchy' Hoernschmeyer, released early from service. The following season was much the same, with a fuzzy-cheeked team of 17-year old freshmen holding up a respectable 7-3 season.

The game with Army, a much older and more experienced team, led Coach Crisler to experiment with wartime's new, more liberal substitution rule. He divided his players between those strong in passing and kicking and those strong on defense, and he amazed opponents by trotting out a fresh line with each switch in ball possession. Without really intending to do so, Crisler had created double-platoon football and sparked what was to

become a nationwide boom in specialization of offensive and defensive units.

The talent pool was suddenly flooded at the end of the war, and in 1946 Fritz Crisler was picking and choosing. At least 125 varsity candidates crowded the practice field. Outstanding among them was halfback Bob Chappius, who had returned a hero of 22 European bombing missions after being shot down over enemy territory; wingback Chalmers 'Bump' Elliott, who had starred as a halfback on the undefeated Purdue team of 1943; Bump's little brother, Pete, starting quarterback the year prior; Elmer Madar, once one of Michigan's 'Seven Oak Posts'; and ends Dick Rifenberg and the towering Len Ford.

That stellar collection of talent smashed its way to a 6-2-1 season, falling only to unbeaten Army 20-13 and Illinois 13-9. Chappius ran and passed for 1265 yards, scoring twice to pull out a tough 14-7 decision over Iowa, and he scored twice again in a 14-14 standoff with Northwestern. For all its talent, though, the team had its share of difficulty getting psyched up and confident for each match. The Wolverines' high-strung, intricate offense fell apart against Illinois, fumbling the ball twelve times and letting the game slip 13-9. But Crisler tried to be patient and to be considerate of men who

*Above: All-American halfback Bob Chappius.*

*Right: Bob Chappius (49) finds himself balanced on the shoulders of Lynn Chandnois (14) of the Michigan State Spartans after snagging a pass from Bump Elliott for a first down, 9 November 1946.*

*Top: Gene Derricotte (41), leaps to toss a pass to Bump Elliott (18) for an 18-yard gain against Illinois, 4 November 1947. The Wolves won, 44-7.*

Above: *Tom Peterson intercepts a pass meant for Illinois' Dwight Eddleman. Wolverine Leo Koceski offers protection as he lunges over Peterson. Michigan scored its twentieth straight victory on 31 October 1948 by beating Illinois 28-20.*

Above: *Bennie Oosterbaan ably coached the Wolverines from 1948 to 1958, and was named Coach of the Year in 1948.*

had seen far more nerve-wracking battle and were fighting now to regain some balance.

Crisler's patience was rewarded. The team's varied emotions and energies came together brilliantly in the game against Minnesota, a 21-point shutout that kicked off a winning streak that would last three years. Chappius scored three times in a 55-7 drowning of Michigan State, and Bob Mann scored twice each in victories over Wisconsin and Ohio State. Madar was named to the All-America, and MVP Chappius broke Otto Graham's season offense record with a 1038-yard total.

In 1947 the Wolverine defense simply exploded, outscoring foes 394-53 and winning ten straight games, including post-season contests. Crisler gave a dazzling performance in coaching. He perfected his offense with a broad repertoire of buck-lateral, full spin and reverse plays and taught master strategist Howard Yerges, the quarterback, the ball-handling permutations offered by each. Each of the team's platoons responded with breathtakingly precise execution.

Chappius opened the season by scoring three touchdowns in a 55-0 whitewash of the MSC Spartans, and against Stanford he began with a 60-yard scoring shot to Bob Mann. In the first eight minutes of play the Wolverines spun off four touchdowns, leaving the bewildered Californians reeling. The same attack was mounted against Pitt, which fell 69-0, still the Wolverines' largest margin of victory in the post-war period, and against Northwestern, which was stomped 49-21. By now, the press

and fans began to speculate on a Michigan bid for the Tournament of Roses game on New Year's Day. But the superstitious Crisler forbade his team even to utter the words, 'Rose Bowl.'

Also worried that the men might be getting a little too confident, captain Bruce Hilkene held a meeting before the big Minnesota game to gain control of the team's nervous energy. After a somber speech about self-control and humility, the captain asked if there were any other problems. "I'm not getting enough publicity,' Rifenberg announced with a straight face. "The reporter from *Time* was out to interview Chappius and never even asked for my material!' The humor helped relieve the Wolves of some of their tension, and they plowed through an intimidating Gopher defense to win 13-6. Chappius, predictably enough, wound up on the cover of *Time* and was credited with, among other things, a 40-yard pass to Bump Elliott that helped win the Minnesota game.

The Wolverines stung Illinois 14-7 the following week, and followed up with 35-0 and 40-6 dumps of Indiana and Wisconsin. In the latter Chappius passed for three touchdowns, two of them to quarterback Yerges. When the Wolverines had pushed to the 40-point mark, Rifenberg gleefully asked his huddled teammates, 'Do you think it's okay now to mention R-O-S-E-B-O-W-L?'

All that stood in the way was old rival Ohio State, sorely in need of a win, having only two victories under its belt for the season. But nothing could stop Michigan, which blanked Wes Fesler's Buckeyes 21-0. So the Wolverines loaded themselves on to the Santa Fe *Super Chief* to California for a contest with the Southern California Trojans.

The California audience sat spellbound as Jack Weisenberger, the Wolverines' powerhouse fullback, charged for the first of his three touchdowns. Chappius ignored a wounded leg to throw a scoring pass to Bump Elliott, and later in the game Yerges and little Hank Fonde took turns at TDs to pile up 49 points against the hapless Trojans. Michigan had cranked out an unbelievable 491 yards total offense for a new Bowl record, and was voted national champion by a post-season Associated Press poll. Coincidentally, the 49-0 score was precisely the same as that tallied by Yost's Wolverines in the first Rose Bowl game in 1902.

By the end of the regular season, Michigan led the nation in offense with 1625 total yards. Scoring was shared by many, including Elliott, who led with ten touchdowns, Chappius, Weisenberger, Yerges and ends Mann and Rifen-

berg. Both Chappius and Elliott were named All-Americans. Crisler later called his expert backfield 'The greatest group of ball-handlers I ever saw.'

The old coach saddened his many admirers when he announced his retirement early in 1948, not long after his peers voted him the Coach of the Year. Fritz said he wanted to devote all his energies to building the Michigan athletics empire and to secure a replacement who could fulfill the promise of his single-wing offense. The man best suited to assume that honor, naturally, was Bennie Oosterbaan, former star halfback and loyal assistant to Crisler.

Although dismayed by Crisler's retirement as coach, Michigan football boosters were also pleased with the choice of Oosterbaan. They were even more pleased by his repeat of Crisler's 1947 success. Bennie preserved the single-wing attack, replacing the graduating backfield with the aerial fireworks of quarterback Pete Elliot and end Rifenberg and installing a blistering line, starring Alvin Wistert. Alvin was the third of the famous Wistert brothers from Chicago to wear jersey Number 11 while playing tackle for Michigan.

Just as Crisler had hoped, the Wolverines went 9-0 once again, and a 13-7 opener with Michigan State was the most competition they got all season. Only the non-repeat rule, which barred a consecutive Rose Bowl appearance, prevented a complete duplication of Crisler's final accomplishments. But the Wolverines were named the national champions nonetheless, and Oosterbaan followed Crisler as Coach of the Year. Listed on All-America teams were Pete Elliott, Rifenberg and, like his brothers before him, Wistert.

Oosterbaan lost most of the talent of the history-making 1947-48 teams the following year, but he produced a 6-2-1 season and lost only to undefeated Army 21-7 and Northwestern 21-20. The Army game spelled the end of a 25-game winning streak started in 1946, second only to the victory strings of 29 and 26 produced by the Point-a-Minute teams of 1901 to 1905. But Michigan still took a share of the Big Ten title for its third straight conference championship. Chuck Ortmann led the conference in total offense, and Wistert repeated

Above: *George Taliaferro of Indiana is stopped by Dan Dworsky of Michigan as Dick Kempthorn (left) and Al Wistert (11) come in to make sure the job is completed. Michigan rolled to a 54-0 win, 15 November 1948.*

Top: *Wolverine fullback Don Dufek is brought down on the one-yard line by Wisconsin tacklers John Simcic (65) and Jerome Smith (73). Michigan handed Wisconsin its first loss of the season, 26-13, on 23 October 1950.*

at All-American, joined by fellow tackle Allen Wahl.

A fourth straight title was added in 1950, but it would have to last Wolverine fans for the next 15 years. In fact, it was not a strong season, for the Wolverines failed to lead the Big Ten in a single statistic. The primary assets were Wahl at tackle, who repeated as an All-American, and halfback Don Dufek. But this 5-3-1 season did provide Midwestern football with one truly unforgettable contest. In the most bizarre Big Ten game ever played, the infamous Ohio State 'Blizzard Bowl' of 1950, played in a blinding snowstorm, Michigan won a crack at the Big Ten title and a trip to Pasadena, where the Wolves upset favored California to take their third Rose Bowl 14-6. Don Dufek scored both touchdowns and was named MVP in the game, and Ortmann completed 15 of 19 pass attempts for an impressive 146 yards.

Ortmann, Wahl, Dufek and most of the talent of the 1940s was gone by the next season, and Oosterbaan found himself entering a period where honest college recruiting practices, while morally correct, proved painfully ineffective. Crisler had warned of the coming crisis, in which colleges would be seeking the boys, and not vice versa. Devoid of any true 'star' talent, Oosterbaan's eleven posted the first losing season for Michigan since 1936. Thus began a string of unspectacular years for the Wolverines. Oosterbaan posted a record of 42-28-2 in his last eight years, from 1951 to 1958, which, while successful, did little to satisfy the appetite of an Ann Arbor public accustomed to conference and national titles.

Not that the period was without talented Wolverine football players; they merely failed to gather on the same teams. In 1951, end Lowell Perry took All-America honors, and a season later set a school record by catching 31 passes for 492 yards. The 1954 team seemed inches away from a trip to the Rose Bowl, defeated only by Indiana in its conference schedule, only to have its hopes dashed by Woody Hayes' OSU Buckeyes, featuring sensational Hopalong Cassady. The Wolverines were heavy with talent, led by back Lou Baldacci, Terry Barr and Tony Branoff in the backfield, and a line featuring Tom Maentz and spectacular Ron Kramer at the ends, tackle Art Walker and center Jim Bates. And Oosterbaan aggressively redesigned the offensive strategy to include 'I' formations that would capitalize on Kramer's abilities. But still no championship, though Walker, at least, was named to the All-America teams.

The conference title remained just as elusive

the next year, in spite of a 7-2 record and the outstanding play of All-America end Ron Kramer. Once again, Ohio State barricaded Michigan from Rose Bowl contention. Oosterbaan's eleven repeated the 7-2 record in 1956, as did Kramer on the All-America, but losses to Michigan State and Minnesota ruled out end-of-season honors for the team. The next two seasons, at 5-3-1 and 2-6-1, did little to quell speculation that Pete Elliott, the 30-year-old head coach at Nebraska, would come to Michigan to replace Oosterbaan, who had begun to mention retirement. Only the All-America selection of stand-out halfback Jim Pace, who led the Big Ten in rushing and was MVP for both his team and the conference, brightened the 1957 season.

As matters turned out, it was Pete Elliott's older brother, Bump, who was hired away from Forrest Evashevski's coaching staff at Iowa to become Oosterbaan's new backfield coach. Just before the Indiana game in the 1958 season Oosterbaan made his intention to retire public and confirmed that Bump Elliott would replace him, effective at the end of what became an injury-plagued, 2-6-1 season.

Bennie left with a 63-33-4 career record, one that would have benefited from a few less injuries and a few luckier bounces of the ball in his

*Above: All-American end Ron Kramer played for the 1954-56 Wolverines, frustrating seasons for the competent Michigan squads.*

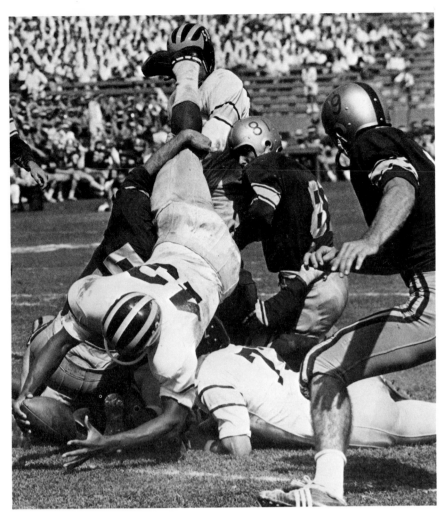

leader, but he brought with him the maturity and realistic mind-set of his predecessors. 'It will take three to five years to rebuild and win a championship,' the young blond told the football public. He wasn't far off. Over his first five seasons Elliott established an unexciting 20-23-2 record, but his sixth year, 1964, would be worth the wait.

Along the way, the Michigan-Illinois game of 1960 provided fans with particular excitement. For the first time in Big Ten history two head coach brothers took on one another, Pete Elliott heading the Fighting Illini. The coaches' mother didn't know whom to root for and decided not to go to the game. But curiosity finally got the better of her, and she showed up with a Michigan banner in one hand and an Illinois banner in the other and prayed for a tie. It was, almost, but Bump's squad narrowly edged Pete's 8-7.

1961's team also held promise for the future, offering a 6-3 record, but its star, Bill Freehan, left school early to sign a bonus contract to pitch with the Detroit Tigers baseball club. Sadly, two other promising talents, tackle Phil Garrison and center Joe Sligay, were killed in accidents. In spite of Elliott's conscientious recruiting, talent kept slipping away from Michigan in 1962 and 1963. Although he con-

*Above: Terry Barr, part of the outstanding backfield of the 1954 Wolverines.*

*Above left: Michigan's Jim Pace (43) is downed by USC's Jim Kubas (82), Jim Conroy (19) and Don Douglas (81) with one foot to go for a touchdown. He scored on the next play of this 1957 game.*

*Left: Chalmers 'Bump' Elliott took over as Michigan's coach in 1959. By 1964 the Wolverines would again be Rose Bowl-bound.*

last eight years. But Oosterbaan's gentle coaching style and insistence on a forthright, hard-working approach to athletics were winners with his players, who carried him off the field on their shoulders after the last game.

Chalmers 'Bump' Elliott, at 33, entered Big Ten coaching as the conference's youngest

tinued to beat brother Pete, Elliott's Wolverines managed only 2-7 and 3-4-2 records, and in 1962 finished at the bottom of the conference for the first time in nearly 30 years. One star, though, halfback Dave Raimey, finished a three-year career with 19 touchdowns for the season, a mark topped only by Tom Harmon.

Bump was finally redeemed in 1964 when he pulled together a collection of strong players who could work with his 'winged-T' formation. Big Bob Timberlake, a bright, versatile quarterback, led an offense featuring quick halfbacks Carl Ward and Jim Detwiler and fullback Mel Anthony. Up front were linebackers Tom Cecchini and Frank Nunley, tackles Bill Yearby and Tom Mack, and fast-footed ends Jim Conley, Bill Laskey and John Henderson. Quarterback Rick Volk backed up the defensive backfield to round out a well-balanced, hard-driven eleven.

The defense alone was so formidable that Air Force and Navy took mostly to the air in their bouts with the Wolves, throwing 75 passes between them but losing miserably. Against Michigan State Rick Sygar was the hero, catching a five-yard Timberlake scoring pass, and throwing 31 yards to Henderson for another fourth period touchdown. The 17-0 victory boosted Michigan to the number-five spot on national polls, but Purdue handed the Wolves a 21-20 setback before they could live up to that accolade.

Fighting back with a vengeance, Bump's eleven romped through the rest of its season

delivering defeats: Minnesota, downed for the first time in five years, 19-12; Northwestern, 35-0, thanks to two touchdown passes by Timberlake and a third from Volk; Illinois, 21-6; and Iowa, 34-20. All that remained between the driving Wolverines and a Rose Bowl berth was long-time nemesis Ohio State.

Both teams had tough, fast-moving defensive squads, and for the first half of play it appeared neither team would crack. Finally, late in the second period, OSU's Bo Rein fumbled a punt return and John Henderson scrambled to scoop up the ball on the OSU 20-yard line. A moment later, on the OSU 17, Elliott unveiled his 'trailer play' devised especially for the Ohio State defense. End Ben Farabee tore straight downfield, trailed by Detwiler, and drew the Buckeye defense toward him. Suddenly Farabee cut toward the middle, and the OSU defenders followed, leaving Detwiler clear. The halfback pulled in Timberlake's dart-like pass on the four and skipped over the goal line. An extra point by Timberlake put the score at 7-0; he added a field goal in the final quarter to lock in a 10-0 win and the first Big Ten championship in 14 years. Said Coach Elliott after being carted off the field, 'This is my happiest moment in football.'

Bump might have held that judgment in reserve, if only to see how the New Year's game with Oregon State at Pasadena, California, would make him feel. But as it turned out, the Ducks' defense was no match for the fast-pitching Wolverines, and Elliott soon held the ball that had won a 34-7 victory in his lap. Key

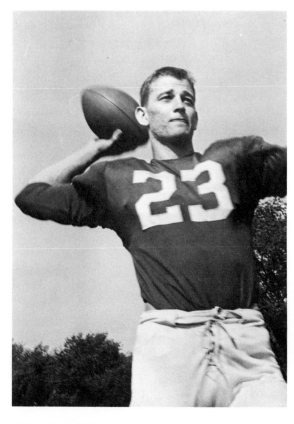

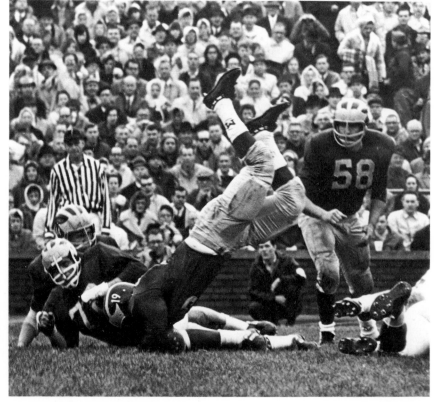

to the victory was an 87-yard touchdown run by fullback Mel Anthony, sparked by a fast Timberlake lateral. Officials marked it as the longest scoring run in Rose Bowl annals. Anthony had scored twice more in the game, joined by halfback Carl Ward. Before the season was closed, Timberlake and Yearby were named to All-America teams, and Anthony was named Rose Bowl MVP.

The Wolves were favored to repeat their success in 1965, but the team was crippled by injuries and mustered only a 4-6 season. Yearby repeated as an All-American, and the following year backs Rick Volk and John Clancy were similarly honored, yet their individual talents could not push Michigan's records any higher. Clancy did set school records for pass receiving, making 132 receptions during his career for 1919 yards. His passing partner, quarterback Dick Vidmer, also set Michigan records by throwing 117 completions for 1611 yards.

Coach Elliott could only put together 6-4

and 4-6 seasons in 1966 and 1967, but for his final year Bump had one last surprise in store: sturdy Ron Johnson, a halfback who would break a variety of school and conference marks, including a couple of Tom Harmon's. Johnson had patiently slogged through his sophomore year, 1966, carrying the ball just 12 times. His junior year would be different.

Elliott started Johnson slowly, allowing him 82 yards rushing in a season-opener with Duke and 48 yards against California, both games ending in victory. But against Navy, the 192-pound dodging halfback was unleashed. In spite of a 26-21 defeat, Johnson amazed fans with score-producing runs of 51, 62 and 72 yards. He ran the ball an unprecedented 270 yards on 26 carries and made the opposition sweat all 60 minutes of play. 'We have never faced a back like Ron Johnson,' said the Middies' coach, Bill Elias, 'and hope we do not see one like him again for a long, long time.'

Teamed with sharp-shooting Dennis Brown, Johnson gained 96 yards against Ohio

Above: *Quarterback Dennis Brown (22) in action, November 1968.*

Above left: *Brilliant halfback Ron Johnson dodges Buckeyes in the 1968 game versus OSU. Despite his two touchdowns, the Wolverines were blasted 50-14.*

Left: *Michigan halfback Carl Ward (19) is tripped up after making a short gain during the first quarter of the game versus Michigan State in Ann Arbor on 9 October 1965. Also shown is Michigan's Joe Dayton (58).*

Far left: *Fine quarterback Bob Timberlake led the Wolverines to an undefeated season and a Rose Bowl victory in 1964.*

State, became the first Michigan runner to break 1000 yards and was voted Michigan MVP. In 1968, Johnson's peers elected him the first black team captain in Wolverine history, and the modest halfback returned the honor with an outstanding year of leadership.

Only a lackluster defense kept the 1968 Wolverines from repeating Elliott's 1964 glory. After getting stung by California in the starting game, Michigan went on an eight-game victory rampage. Johnson gained 205 yards in a 31-10 dump of Duke, and scored twice against Navy. Indiana, Minnesota and Northwestern fell in succession; only Wisconsin and Ohio State lay ahead.

Against the Badgers, Johnson charged for score-producing 35-, 67- and 60-yard runs. Finally pulled from the game after his fifth touchdown – good for a Big Ten record – Johnson received a standing ovation. The halfback gained 347 yards from scrimmage, more than any runner in college ball history, and broke Harmon's career rushing record in the 34-9 rout of Wisconsin.

The Buckeyes were favored to smash Michigan the following week. Johnson tore loose for two touchdowns, but there wasn't enough power in the Wolverine defense to prevent a 50-14 loss. Michigan nevertheless clung to the second-place spot in conference standings. Johnson had gained 1391 yards and 19 TDs that season, and teammate Brown passed for 1777. Ron's three-year total hit 2440, and the senior surpassed seven Big Ten records. In addition to his All-America selection, the *Chicago Tribune* and Michigan bestowed MVP honors upon Johnson. Said Coach Elliott, 'He was the best football player and best captain I had during my coaching career.'

Bump would have no other captain; weeks later, the coach was offered a spot as assistant athletic director by Fritz Crisler's successor, Don Canham. Elliott accepted and asked the coach of Ohio's Miami University if he might be interested in replacing him. 'They don't call you every day of the week and talk to you about the Michigan coaching job,' Glenn E 'Bo' Schembechler later recalled. 'I hoped at the time Bump didn't notice the excitement in my voice.'

But Canham noticed it the first time he met with Schembechler and knew within 15 minutes that the Wolverines had found their man. A career rich in the spoils of victory was begun. Bo brought with him a solid background in gridiron coaching, having begun his career as an assistant to Woody Hayes at Ohio State. He went on to stints at Bowling Green, Northwestern and Miami, the last of which pro-

Above: *Quarterback Don Moorhead (27) in action, 1970.*

Right: *Halfback Tom Curtis made an impressive 25 interceptions during his career at Michigan.*

duced two championships, a 40-17-3 record and two elections to Coach of the Year. He also brought a unique five-man angle defense and a guarantee that he would make it work within five years. Most important, Bo brought a quick-tempered, perfectionist coaching style familiar in places like Columbus, Ohio, but never before seen at Ann Arbor.

Wolverine boosters didn't have to wait five years for anything. In his first season, 1969, Schembechler went for 8-2 to snare his first Big Ten title. In this he was greatly helped by the legacy of Bump Elliott's talent pool: junior quarterback Don Moorhead, who ran and passed for 1886 yards total offense; tight end Jim Mandich, who caught 50 passes for 676 yards; and halfback Tom Curtis, who would pull in 25 interceptions while at Michigan.

Also on Bo's first team were two impressive offensive linemen, Reggie McKenzie and Paul Seymour, and versatile backs Glenn Doughty and Billy Taylor. In 1969 Curtis and Mandich were named All-Americans; the following year, Michigan contributed Marty Huff, Dan Dierdorf and Henry Hill – five All-Americans in the coach's first two years! To top off his inaugural season Schembechler's Wolverines qualified for a trip to the Rose Bowl. The players lost to Southern California 10-3, though, just one day after their coach was hospitalized with a mild heart attack.

Schembechler soon recovered and filled the next ten years with more than his fair share of victories. The Wolverines went for a near-perfect 9-1 season in 1970, marred only by a loss to Woody Hayes' undefeated national cham-

*Above: Glenn 'Bo' Schembechler arrived on the Michigan scene in 1968 and has become the winningest football coach in the school's history. With 13 bowl appearances so far and more victories under his belt than any other active coach in the nation, he is proof of his own famous phrase, 'Those who stay will be champions.'*

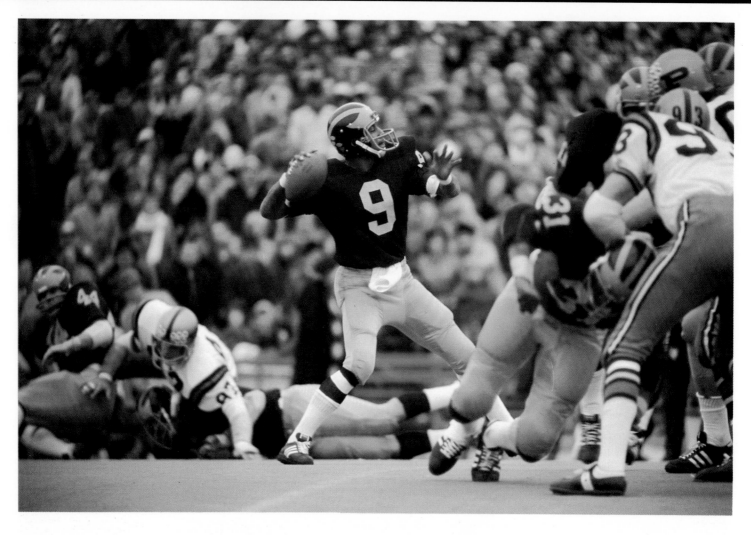

Above: *Dennis Franklin (9) finds his mark in the 1972 game versus Purdue. His fine passing took the Wolverines almost all the way to the Rose Bowl, but a tough OSU team robbed them of the opportunity with a 14-11 defeat.*

Opposite top: *Quarterback Rick Leach with Coach Schembechler in 1978.*

Opposite bottom: *Rick Leach (7) makes the handoff to Lawrence Reid (23) versus OSU, 1976. Wolverines fans celebrated wildly as they finally tromped on the Buckeyes in Columbus, 22-0.*

pion Buckeyes. Moorhead closed a career that shattered most of the school's passing records set by Dennis Brown just a few years before. Don completed 200 of 425 passes for 2550 yards and set the total offensive yardage mark at 3641.

From 1971 to 1974 Coach Bo entered his own Golden Age – not that his 17-3 record thus far was by any means shabby – and wound up posting four consecutive championships, one exclusively Michigan's and the others shared. In 1972 the Wolverines posted a perfect 11-0 conference record on a newly expanded game slate and bought a ticket to Pasadena for a crack at Stanford. The team suffered a heartbreak 13-12 loss on a fourth-quarter Stanford field goal.

During the season an enormously talented backfield – seniors Billy and Mike Taylor and Doughty and younger quarterback Tom Slade – exploded against all comers and pitched often to guard McKenzie, whose touchdown runs won several games, including a 10-7 rout of Ohio State. Named to All-America teams were Billy Taylor, who rushed for 1297 yards and achieved a new career record of 3072; Mike Taylor; the amazing McKenzie; and safety Tom Darden.

The 1972 season was almost as sweet, and

though the Big Ten had repealed the 'no repeat' rule concerning the Rose Bowl, a 14-11 loss to Ohio State kept the Wolverines at 10-1 for the season and at home on New Year's Day. Helping the Wolves share the conference title were All-Americans Randy Logan, defensive halfback, and 250-pound tackle Paul Seymour.

The Wolverines shared the Big Ten championship for the next two years, and in each season won ten games. In 1973 a tie with Ohio State prompted a conference vote on whether to send the Buckeyes or the Wolves to Pasadena. The Buckeyes won the bid, sorely disappointing Schembechler and a group of seniors who had brought him fame since they joined the squad four years earlier.

The only loss in actual battle came in 1974, to Ohio State, but with Schembechler's five-year record resting at 58-7, there were few malcontents in Ann Arbor. The undefeated 1973 team contributed All-American defensive tackle Dave Gallagher, and both years' teams added safety Dave Brown to the lists.

Schembechler continued to amass winning seasons until 1984, when he finally broke even with a 6-6 season, his 'worst' so far at Michigan. He immediately bounced back to his familiar ten victory format in 1985, with 10-1-1

for the season, and continued that trend in 1986 with an 11-2 season, climaxed by a hair-raising 26-24 victory over Ohio State to win the conference title. The battle at the Rose Bowl was hard-found, but Arizona State came out on top, 22-15.

But what a fantastic journey it had been getting there! Between 1975 and 1986 the coach had produced no fewer than six conference titles and trips to numerous Bowl games: Rose, Orange, Sugar, Gator and Bluebonnet. Unfortunately, those games rarely demonstrated the Wolves' regular-season brilliance.

In 1975, for instance, after a 8-1-2 season, Michigan stumbled before the Oklahoma Sooners in a 14-6 Orange Bowl defeat. Don Dufek Jr, son of the famous Wolverine of the 1940s, made All-America, however, and was succeeded the following year by Calvin O'Neal, Jim Smith and Mark Donahue.

Runners of note included Gordon Bell, who ran for 1048 yards and 11 touchdowns in 1974, and the next year for 1388 yards and 14 TDs; Rob Lytle, who ran for 1469 yards and 16 TDs in 1975 to help Michigan lead the nation in total offense, rushing, scoring average and

scoring defense; and Rick Leach, who totalled 1723 and 1894 yards of total offense in 1977 and 1978, respectively. All-Americans in 1977 included repeater Mark Donahue, John Anderson and Walt Downing. All that talent led to spectacular championship seasons from 1976 to 1978, but also to three gut-wrenching defeats in the Rose Bowl.

Perhaps Coach Schembechler reached his pinnacle in 1980, when the Wolves pulled out a 9-2 season and won their last eight to take Michigan's 30th conference title. Butch Wool-folk, who set the current school record for rushing, moved the ball 1042 yards; Anthony Carter, who holds the mark for passes caught, nabbed 51 that year for 818 yards and 14 touchdowns. And at long last, the Wolverines won the coveted Rose Bowl trophy, smashing Washington 23-6 in its first New Year's Day victory since 1964.

In the years following, the venerable Bo maintained a steady course, racking up 9-3, 8-4 and 9-3 seasons before his 'downfall,' 6-6 in 1984. Among All-Americans produced were Ron Simpkins in 1979; Anthony Carter, Bubba Paris, Ed Muranski and Kurt Becker in

Above: *Alumnus Gerald Ford throws out the ball to start the 1977 Rose Bowl game vs Washington.*

Left: *Butch Woolfolk (24), who holds the Michigan record for yards rushing, is seen here letting loose in 1980.*

Top: *John Anderson (86) punts to OSU, 20 November 1976.*

Opposite: *Anthony Carter holds the school record for pass receptions.*

1981; and a repeat selection for the phenomenal Carter in 1982.

Quarterback Jim Harbaugh broke his arm playing against Michigan State in 1984, limiting the strength of Michigan's offense. But the arm healed and Harbaugh was back the next year in top form. He broke not appendages but Michigan season records for passing yards, completions and touchdowns, thanks in part to tailback Jamie Morris, who gained 1054 yards. Particularly good in the crunch, Harbaugh threw his last 124 passes free of interceptions. To cap 1985, defensive back Brad Cochran and tackle Mike Hammerstein gained the honor of being named to the All-America teams.

Harbaugh in 1986 was voted All-American and was chosen Big Ten MVP. He continued to make and break records, becoming the first Michigan quarterback to throw for 2000 yards in one season. He also became Michigan's all-time leader in career pass completions with 365, and ranks third offensively, having run and passed for a magnificent career total of 5429 yards.

Above: *Anthony Carter.*

Left: *Butch Woolfolk (24) scrambles for a short gain against the Iowa Hawkeyes.*

Top: *Tailback Jamie Morris (23) tiptoes through an impending pileup at the 1987 Rose Bowl. Michigan was defeated, 22-15.*

Right: *Coach Schembechler (center) rides high on his Wolverine's shoulders after winning Fiesta Bowl XV 27-23 over the Nebraska Cornhuskers.*

Top right: *Jim Harbaugh (4) scores a touchdown in the 1985 game versus Purdue.*

# MICHIGAN STATE UNIVERSITY

Founded: 1855

Location: East Lansing

Total Enrollment: 41,032

Colors: Green and White

Nickname: Spartans

Three years after Chicago finally dropped out of the Big Ten a new and vibrant presence was ready to take its place. Michigan State University's Spartans, under coach Clarence 'Biggie' Munn, had been voted into the conference in May 1949, and though their first full conference season would not come until 1953, they wasted no time in proving their mettle. Munn, formerly an aide to Bernie Bierman at Minnesota and to Fritz Crisler at Michigan, was determined to put the small, one-time agricultural school on the map.

Michigan State had played football since 1896, engaging and often beating some of the nation's best teams, including Ivy League schools. Prior to 1950 five players – Neno DaPrato, Sidney Wagner, John Pingel, Lynn Chandnois and Edward Bagdon – had been named to All-America teams. Before long, however, MSU would set a Big Ten record for the number of All-Americans produced in one decade.

Two were chosen from a 1950 squad that lost only to Maryland in a 8-1-0 season. Halfback hero Everett 'Sonny' Grandelius ran for 1023 yards, and, along with versatile end Dorne Dibble, helped the Spartans score an average of 30 points per game. The following year Munn's intricate multiple offense, led by quarterback Albert Dorow, came alive to score 270 points over its rivals and help the Spartans march to their first perfect season in 38 years. The lightest regular tackle in the league, 190-pound Don Coleman, was pronounced 'the finest lineman in Michigan State history,' and he had the honor of seeing his jersey number retired at season's end.

Captain Bob Carey and his twin brother Bill starred as offensive ends, leading a magnificent trio of halfbacks: Don McAuliffe, Leroy Bolden and Vince Pisano. Leading a bruising defense were guards Frank Kush and Dick Kuh, complemented by linebacker Dick Tamburo and safety Jim Ellis, the national star in punt returns. MSU equaled Ohio State's season record of four All-Americans by adding Carey, Coleman, Dorow and Ellis.

The entire offense was gone the next year, along with much of the defense, and sports fans wondered if Munn could possibly follow with as good an act in 1952. But Munn wasn't about to let MSU's new image slip, and somehow his cadre of assistant coaches, a well-tuned recruiting machine, pulled together the talent needed to score 312 points for a second straight 9-0 slate. Victims included Syracuse, Penn State, Notre Dame, Texas A & M, Marquette and great rival Michigan – all of which fell by substantial margins.

Above: *Fullback Everett 'Sonny' Grandelius (24), 9 October 1950.*

Top left: *Coach Clarence 'Biggie' Munn in 1951.*

Right: *End Don Dahoney (80) upends Purdue quarterback Curtis Jones (18), 1 November 1952. Michigan State won, 14-7.*

Top right: *Hugh 'Duffy' Daugherty took over as the Spartans' coach in 1954.*

Page 102: *Quarterback Dave Yarema looks to make a handoff, 1985.*

Former tailback Tommy Yewcic was converted to quarterback, and with a running attack led by McAuliffe and a line anchored by the returning Kush and Tamburo, the Green and White rolled over all opponents on the way to its first national championship and a 24-game winning streak. Munn's dedication earned him his peers' recognition, and he became 1952's Coach of the Year. Kush, Tamburo and McAuliffe were honored with All-America selection.

Biggie had big ideas for his team's conference debut in 1953, as well. The Big Ten had voted away double-platoon football, but Munn's players somehow managed to learn defensive/offensive combinations. Captain Don Dohoney, a fine defensive lineman the year prior, led the offense's forward wall at one end with Ellis Ducket at the other. Behind was a small but smart and lightning-quick backfield featuring Yewcic, Bolden, Billy Wells and Evan Slonac. The squad pushed its win-

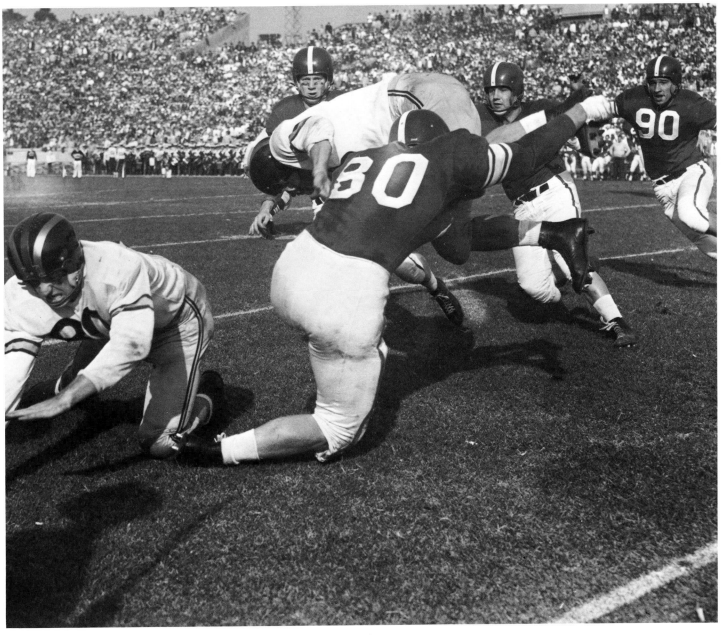

Above: *All-American halfback Walt Kowalczyk (14) made a major contribution to the success of the 1957 season. The Spartans finished 8-1.*

Right: *Earl Morrall's passing brilliance helped see the Spartans to an 8-1-0 season in 1955 and a shot at the Rose Bowl. A last-second field goal gave the Spartans the national championship over UCLA, 17-14.*

ning streak to 28 before losing at last to Purdue, 6-0, but it had trounced all other enemies to tie with Illinois to take the conference championship.

As if winning the title in its first year of membership wasn't enough, the conference handed the Spartans a Rose Bowl berth, since Illinois had been in Pasadena the year prior, and rules of the day forbade back-to-back appearances. A powerful UCLA team had MSU pinned 14-0 before the Spartans struggled back to claim a dramatic 28-20 victory. At season's end, Dohoney's efforts were rewarded by an All-America selection.

Munn decided to step out of coaching while a victor and, with a shining 54-9-2 coaching record in hand, entered the administrative world as MSU's athletic director. His hand-picked successor, Hugh 'Duffy' Daugherty, had served him eight years as line coach, both at Michigan State and Syracuse, yet he was very different from Munn in style and demeanor. Where Munn was grimly serious about football, Duffy brought a cheerful, self-deprecating and often irreverent attitude to his job that made him popular with the press and his players.

Yet Daugherty was as committed to winning as Munn. By the 1955 season he had assembled a crack team that produced an 8-1-0 season. The Spartans had bashed the Wolverines for four years straight, but Michigan handed MSU its only defeat of the year in the opening game. Champion Ohio State had been to Pasadena in 1954, so once again Daugherty's team made a trip to the Rose Bowl. And once again UCLA fell to MSU, this time by a close 17-14 score. Four players won All-America honors, including passing star Earl Morrall, all-purpose guard Carl Nystrom, Norm Masters at tackle and fullback Gerry Planutis. Daugherty himself was voted Coach of the Year.

Morrall's greatest strength, both as a college and pro player, was passing, but he also broke records as a punter, setting school marks for the longest punt, at 71 yards, and the best season average, at 42.9 yards per kick. He also set a record for the longest return of a fumble, 90 yards, which resulted in a touchdown against Purdue.

The following years were full of ups and downs for Daugherty, but his squads were always respectable. On the up side, his 1956 team went 7-2, and in 1957 the club posted 8-1 with the help of star center Dan Currie and halfback Walt Kowalczyk, both All-America choices. Daugherty's teams in 1960, 1961 and 1963 lost only two games apiece, and All-American contributions through 1963 includ-

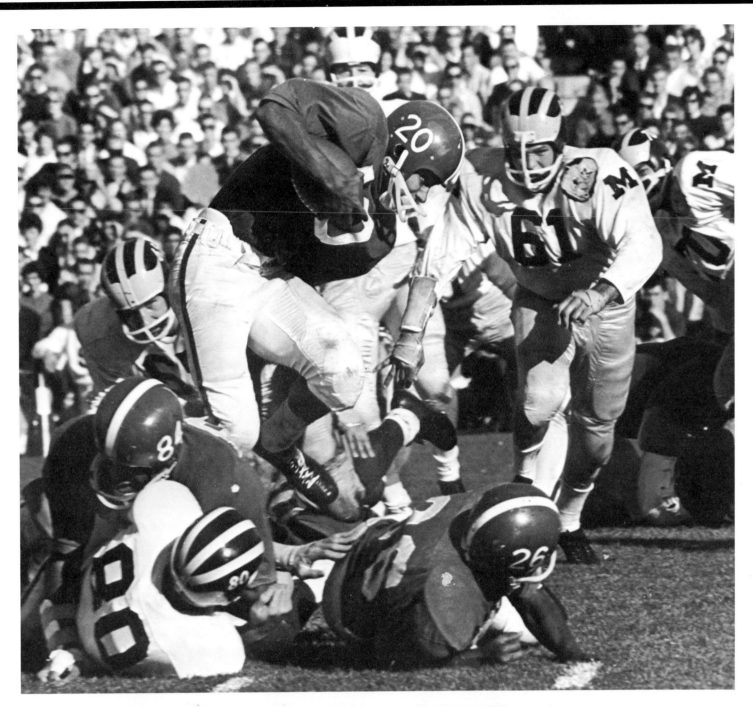

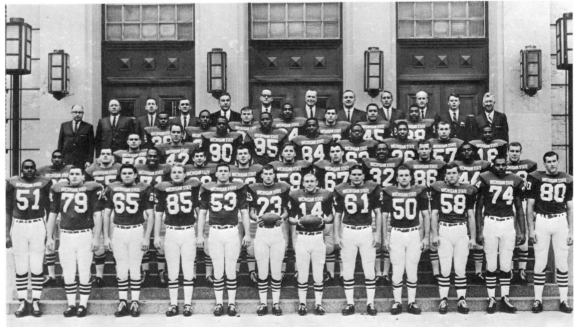

Above: *Halfback Sherman Lewis (20) stumbles through for a first down versus the Michigan Wolverines, 1963.*

Left: *The 1965 Michigan State Spartans became Big Ten champs with a perfect 10-0 season but were edged out of the national championship by UCLA, 14-12.*

Above: *Halfback Eric Allen (14) scores a touchdown against the Minnesota Gophers in 1971.*

ed hard-hitting flanker Sam Williams in 1958; quarterback Dean Look, who rushed as well as he passed, in 1959; guard Dave Behrman in 1961; explosive fullback George Saimes in 1962; and Sherman Lewis, MSU's speedy halfback, in 1963.

Lewis in particular brought some spectacular moments. The pint-sized back was a blinding runner and pass receiver who seemed cut out for breathtaking long runs. In 1963 he raced 87 yards for a goal against Northwestern, and 85 yards for a touchdown against Notre Dame. As a catcher, he pulled in two record-length passes by Steve Juday, an 88-yard bomb in a USC game and a 87-yarder thrown in a game against Wisconsin.

Even when passes fell incomplete and seasons dipped below the .500 mark Duffy remained cheerful. 'I've been an optimist since I was a kid,' he said. 'I can still remember the Christmas morning I ran down to my stocking and found it full of horse manure. I yelled, "Hey, I got a pony around here somewhere!"'

Daugherty and his squads were back in the limelight by 1965, when a 'young, inexperienced' Spartan eleven rolled over all opponents for a perfect 10-0 season. Quarterback Juday was a brilliant passer and roll-out artist, and when he combined with breakaway backs Clint Jones, Dwight Lee and Bob Apisa, the backfield was almost perfectly balanced.

Poking holes up front were tackles Don Bie-

Right: *Amazing receiver Gene Washington pulls down a pass. Such acrobatics made for thrilling viewing for Spartans fans during the superlative 1965 season.*

Top right: *Back Clinton Jones (26) goes for a gallop as Norman Jenkins (63) makes room, 1965.*

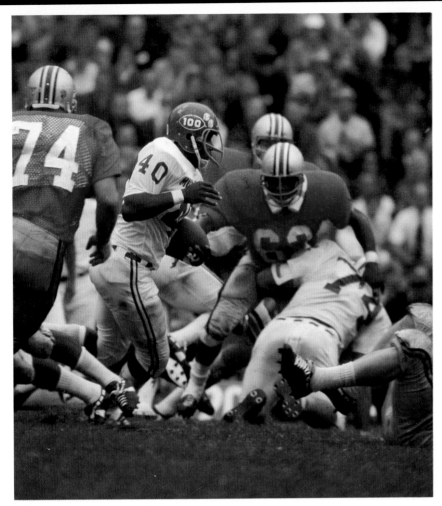

rowicz, Buddy Owens and Jerry West, and guards John Karpinski and Dave Techlin. Gene Washington, the Big Ten hurdles champion in track, dazzled spectators as a receiver, along with end Bob Viney. On defense, a 280-pound end named Bubba Smith, joined by guard Harold Lucas, effectively discouraged runs through the Spartan line, and anyone who did make it through had to contend with linebackers Ron Goovert and Charley Thornhill, or worse, 218-pound cornerback George Webster, who wreaked havoc on even the best-laid running plans.

That Superteam won two Big Ten championships in a row and in 1965 shared national honors, with only a 14-12 defeat to UCLA in the Rose Bowl marring the season. In those two years the Spartans – considered by many members of the press and a number of sports awards committees to be the best college team of the modern era — offered un unprecedented 12 All-America team members. Two-time selections included Jones, Smith, Washington and Webster. Goovert, Juday and West were honored once. And Daugherty snared Coach of the Year honors for the second time.

Only Number 1-ranked Notre Dame kept the Number 2 Spartans from a second national championship in 1966. The two undefeated teams had fought bitterly to a 10-10 deadlock

in the final quarter, when Irish coach Ara Parseghian ordered his players to run out the clock and preserve the tie. Parseghian realized his team would maintain its Number 1 standing and the national championship. For the Spartans and sports fans in general, his order changed a football game into a calculated business transaction.

Living up to the stellar moments of those two seasons would be a nearly impossible task for any coach, though Daugherty played out his last six seasons in a respectable, but hardly phenomenal, fashion. He produced several more All-America team players, including Allen Brenner, safety and pass-receiver, in 1968; guard Ronald Saul in 1969; and halfback Eric Allen, safety Brad Van Pelt and tackle Ronald Curl in 1971. The following year, Van Pelt repeated and was joined by guard Joe DeLammielleure.

The smallish Allen gained notoriety as 'The Flea,' so-named for his ability to flit about and through enemy defenses for substantial yardage. Once in the open, he demonstrated amazing speed. As a senior in 1971, Allen enjoyed Daugherty's triple-option offense, which gave him all the more opportunities to run with the ball. He broke the Big Ten's single-season rushing record with 1494 yards, and scored 18 touchdowns and 110 points.

Above: *Defense man Jim Morrissey (40) in action, 1983.*

Above left: *All-American halfback Eric Allen makes his way through a pack of Buckeyes in the 1969 Michigan State-Ohio State game.*

Opposite: *Back Dwight Lee (14) tries to shake a persistent Boilermaker, 1966.*

Totally the opposite of Allen in size was Van Pelt, who stood well over six feet and weighed in at 221 pounds. At safety, his height frustrated countless enemy pass receivers. It also made him ideal for basketball and added leverage to his stand-out baseball pitching. Upon graduation, in fact, Van Pelt almost turned to professional baseball, rather than football, as his career choice.

Coach Duffy had won two of the first seven games in the 1972 season when he told his team he would not be back the following year. Rallying to make their coach's last season a good one, the Spartans went on to upset Purdue, unbeaten Ohio State and Northwestern for a 5-5-1 season, putting Duffy's MSU record at 109-69-5. The man who had helped net two national championships, two conference titles and two Rose Bowl trips was honored during the Purdue game by a small biplane, which flew over Spartan Stadium trailing a 'We Love Duffy and the Spartans!' banner.

Daugherty settled into a faculty position while one of his assistants, Dennis Stolz, took over the command post. Under Stolz, two Spartans garnered two more spots on the All-America: William Simpson and end Billy Joe DuPree. Stolz produced a 7-3-1 in 1974, but was booted out in 1975 after MSU was placed on probation for recruiting violations.

Darryl Rogers, former head coach at San Jose State, coached for the following four years and in 1978 guided the Spartans to a 8-3 season. Quarterback Ed Smith passed for 2226 yards and 20 touchdowns, connecting with the likes of receiver Kirk Gibson, who caught 42 passes for 806 yards. All told, the team scored 411 points against its foes, and won its last seven games to take a share of the Big Ten title.

After a three-year stint by Frank Waters, George Perles took over the head coaching position in 1983 and went to work re-establishing a winning record for the Spartans. Perles, who for 10 years helped shape the Pittsburgh Steelers' defense, was seen as a cure for the football program's ailments. In his first four seasons Perles managed only a 23-22-1 record, but coached phenomenal tailback Lorenzo White to national fame as an All-America selection in 1985. White led the nation in rushing with 2066 yards on 386 carries. Quarterback Dave Yarema also shone, completing nearly 60 percent of his passes and leading the conference in passing in 1985 with 2581 yards.

Spartan fans hoped that Perles' strong defense could soon be matched to a capable offense, one worthy of Michigan State's dazzling performance in its first two decades in the Big Ten.

Above: *Tailback Lorenzo White (34) sparkled for the 1985 Spartans.*

Left: *Quarterback Brian Clark (14) calls a play versus the Buckeyes, 1978.*

Right: *Dave Yarema provided superior quarterbacking in 1985 and 1986. He led the conference in passing in 1986 with a phenomenal 2581 yards.*

# UNIVERSITY OF MINNESOTA

Founded: 1851

Location: Minneapolis

Total Enrollment: 44,950

Colors: Maroon and Gold

Nickname: Golden Gophers

As a charter member of the Western Intercollegiate Conference, which would become the Big Ten, the University of Minnesota has a gridiron history woven into the very fabric of the conference. From Bronko Nagurski to Coach Bernie Bierman, from the conference cellar to two consecutive Rose Bowls, the Golden Gophers and their fans have thrown themselves wholeheartedly into college football, savoring the rivalries, the trophies, the wins and sometimes even the well-played losses.

The origins of the Golden Gophers team nickname go back to 1857, when Minnesota was dubbed 'The Gopher State' after a newspaper cartoon appeared satirizing a bitterly opposed railroad loan bill pending in the state legislature. The cartoon depicted a 'Gopher Train' drawn by nine of the striped animals with human heads. The state has borne the 'Gopher' nickname ever since, and this was the early designation by which University of Minnesota football teams were always known. But it was not until the 1930s, when Bernie Bierman's crushing teams were being called 'the golden-shirted horde' because of their gold jerseys, that the nickname 'Golden Gophers' evolved.

Big Ten records show that Minnesota went 3-0-1 in 1900, and by 1903 the first of its players to be recognized as among the best in the nation, or 'All American,' caught national attention. He was tackle Fred Schact.

Also immortalized during the 1903 season was a somewhat homely looking piece of pottery, the water jug used on the sidelines by Fielding Yost's 'Point-A-Minute' Wolverines. After the Gophers, under the coaching of Dr Harry Williams, had tied Michigan, Yost hustled his dejected players out of town, leaving the jug behind. The Gopher's trainer sent a note to his counterpart at Michigan telling him if they wanted the jug back to 'come and get it.' Subsequent Michigan and Minnesota teams have been trying to 'get' the Little Brown Jug, the most famed football trophy for decades, ever since.

In 1904 both Michigan and Minnesota went undefeated, but unfortunately they never met each other to determine who was really Number 1. The Gophers amassed 618 points and gave up only 12 to their opponents during their perfect 11-0 season.

Meanwhile, Coach Williams, a member of the conference football rules committee, was among the very first to argue for the legalization of the forward pass. Two years later the technique was adopted.

In 1906 Minnesota shared Big Nine conference honors with Wisconsin, as both went undefeated. Perhaps even more notable was the fact that the Gophers' great end, Bobby Marshall, was the first black to play in the conference. Meanwhile, Michigan was protesting new conference rulings which prohibited playing more than five games in a season. Many conference teams played up to 12, often adding several games with prestigious Eastern schools to boost attendance. Michigan pulled out of the Big Nine in 1907 and ceased to play conference games until 1917.

Minnesota was a perennial conference power during this period. Tiny quarterback Johnny McGovern, only 5-feet 5-inches and weighing 155 pounds, made All-America in 1909. The pint-sized terror was speedy and a master tactician, although it certainly helped to take coaching from Dr Williams. Williams had come to Minneapolis in 1900 amid great fanfare to take the job of Minnesota's first full-time head football coach – but under one condition. The former Yale halfback and world record hurdler would coach only if he were allowed to continue his medical practice at the same time. He soon proved he could handle both tasks. By the middle of the 1905 season, the Gophers had already compiled a total 52-3-3 record under Williams.

In 1910 Williams came up with his greatest innovation, the 'Minnesota Shift.' In those days, backfield players remained motionless until the ball was snapped to one man who either ran it or passed it. It was fairly easy for smart defensive players to 'read' the offense and respond accordingly.

Under Williams' direction, however, Minnesota backs would, on a prearranged signal, leap over to other backfield patterns just

before the ball was snapped from center, much as they do today, leaving the defense confused. Within two seasons the Minnesota Shift had swept the nation and many football historians mark its development, along with that of the forward pass, as the beginning of football's modern era. The contributions of Williams to Minnesota football during his 21-year tenure are even more remarkable when one considers that he managed a thriving medical practice throughout his coaching career, and that he never had more than one varsity coaching assistant.

In 1910 the Gophers played only two conference games and won both, though Illinois was generally acclaimed champion that year. Tackle James Walker, however, was voted All-America that season. In the 1911 season the Gophers again went undefeated, but this time they were recognized as the Big Nine football champs. In fact, for the next six seasons the Gophers would rank no lower than third in the conference. They again took the crown in 1915.

The 1915 Gophers featured perhaps the finest passing combination in college football prior to World War I: the duo of halfback Arnold 'Pudge' Wyman and end Bert Baston. Wyman-to-Baston passes figured in several Minnesota victories that season, and Gopher fans had high hopes as their undefeated cham-

*Above: All-American fullback Herb Joesting, the 'Owatonna Thunderbolt' totaled 2018 yards rushing and averaged 4.53 yards per carry for Minnesota between 1925 and 1927.*

*Left: Bernie Bierman was Minnesota's team captain in 1915. He returned to his alma mater as football coach in 1932 and led the Golden Gophers to five undefeated seasons, seven Big Ten championships and five national championships in 18 years.*

pions entered a contest with similarly unbeaten Illinois to decide the conference title.

During practice the week prior, Minnesota's ace running back, Bernie Bierman, sprained an ankle. His absence blunted the ground attack which usually complemented the aerial game, and the Illini managed to eke out a 6-6 tie and a share of the title. Bert Baston's pass-catching heroics were enough to earn an All-America selection that year, and the talented end repeated the honor in 1916, a season in which the mighty Gophers fell victim to a stunning upset.

The 1916 Minnesota team was considered Williams' best ever and all but unbeatable. The Gophers had romped through their season with scores of 67-0 over Iowa, 81-0 over South Dakota, 54-0 over Wisconsin and 49-0 over the University of Chicago. Coach Bob Zuppke's Illinois team was considered a three-touchdown underdog, yet Williams had worked the Gophers ragged in practice all week before the match, perhaps remembering the tie of the year before.

Zuppke, who in time would coach Red Grange and be considered among the greatest coaches in college athletic history, felt that a light touch was needed and purposely gave a funny speech right before the game to loosen up the Illini players. He also outlined a brilliant game plan that called for a concentration of defense on three specific Gophers players, as well as passing on first down – unheard of at the time. The strategy worked, and the Illini pulled off one of the upsets of the century right in front of Walter Camp himself, who had attended the game to see for himself the wondrous Gophers. Embarrassed Minnesota finished in a tie for second in the conference.

Whether the Illini upset was a turning point or not, the next few seasons belonged to Ohio State and Illinois. Although Gopher football produced outstanding individual players such as All-Americans Shorty Long, George Hauser, Earl Martineau and Herb Joesting, the Gophers would not win another conference football title until 1934. In the late 1920s, however, just as things seemed darkest, along came a young giant by the name of Bronislaw Nagurski.

The boy from International Falls came to the Minnesota campus without fanfare. His high school team had never won a game. He'd been known as 'Bronko' ever since a grade school teacher tried, without success, to pronounce his Christian name. The story goes that when the young Nagurski reported for freshman football in the fall of 1926 Gopher coach Clarence Spears wandered over to meet him, offered his hand and said in a friendly way, 'My name's Spears – what's yours?' The lad replied, 'Nagurski – Bronko Nagurski.' Spears smirked and said, 'Bronko, eh? That's a strange name!' The freshman frowned darkly and muttered, 'Well, Clarence ain't so hot, either!'

Though it began on the wrong foot, a strange and wonderful relationship developed between the coach and the mild-mannered crusher with the high-pitched voice. In Nagurski's first scrimmage as a freshman, it became obvious that he could play both fullback and tackle with equal force, as the stunned varsity soon learned. Spears already had All-American Herb Joesting at fullback, so he began using Nagurski at end, tackle – anywhere he needed a 220-pound battering ram. Before he was through at Minnesota, 'The Bronk' had played every position but quarterback, halfback and center.

It is ironic that in Nagurski's three varsity years – the seasons 1927, 1928 and 1929 – he was never a part of a conference championship

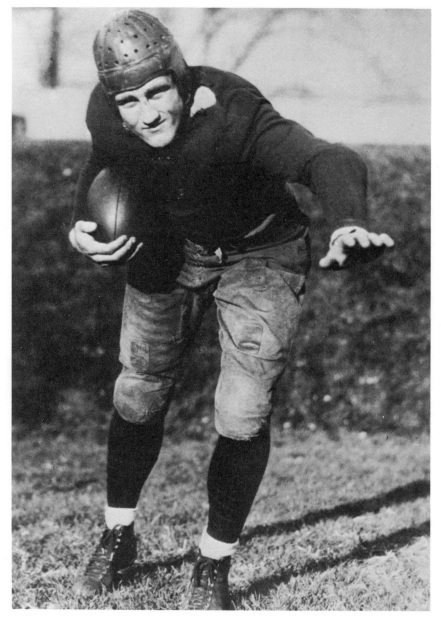

Below: *Huge both in stature and legend, Bronko Nagurski is probably Minnesota's best-known football hero. He played nearly every position with equal effectiveness, mauling the opposition from 1927 to 1929.*

team, even though the Gophers lost only four games, and never by more than two points. His legendary style of play, however, brought Minnesota fans some of their biggest thrills.

One came in a game against Northwestern when the Gophers had the ball on the Wildcats' 12-yard line. Nagurski received the handoff and hurtled forward into the Wildcat line, shucking aside defenders as he powered ahead over the goal line. His momentum carried him past the line, through the 10-yard end zone and into a pile of 100-pound bags of cement intended for a construction project. Legend has it that even the wall of cement bags went down under the Bronk's onslaught.

Bronko was injured for the only time in his college career in the 1928 game against tough Iowa. The young giant, who now played fullback, as well as sometimes helping out on defense, had taken a hard hit and could not bend over to receive the snap from center. So he simply went on to play tackle throughout the remainder of the game. It was later discovered that three ribs had been torn away from Nagurski's sternum. Yet Nagurski demanded a special back brace and came back four weeks later for the traditional finale against Wisconsin. He carried the ball five straight times for a grueling 18-yard drive and a score. Minnesota won the game 6-0 and knocked the Badgers out of title contention.

Despite his legendary strength and bruising determination, Bronko Nagurski was a gentle and mild-mannered man who rarely became angry even when repeatedly gang-tackled by the opposition. In vain, Spears attempted to rile up 'The Bronk,' thinking it might help him to play even better. It never worked, but then there wasn't much room for improvement in Nagurski's play anyway.

Once in 1927 the Gophers trailed Notre Dame – always tough at home in South Bend – 7-0 at halftime. Gale-force winds, sleet and rain had pounded the Gopher players and had caused the usually-steady quarterback, Fred Hovde, to fumble, setting up the Notre Dame touchdown. Spears knew something had to be done to turn the game around. As his players wearily trotted out for the second half, Spears grabbed Nagurski and began shaking him by the shoulders.

'Bronk,' he hissed. 'You should be able to beat that Notre Dame single-handed. I want you to go out there and tear 'em apart. You're going out there and kill 'em, kill 'em, KILL 'EM!'

The impassive giant stared at the frenzied Spears for a moment, then replied mildly 'You bet, Coach.' Then he loped back on to the field

and went on playing just as he had been before – which is to say, spectacularly. Late in the fourth quarter Nagurski, playing tackle, burst through the Irish line and hit the runner so hard he dropped the ball, which the Bronk recovered on the Irish 15. With only seconds left the Gophers were able to score and convert, ending the game in a tie. Not many teams had ever come from behind to deprive one of Knute Rockne's teams of victory, and this was the first time in 22 years that the Irish had not won on their home field. But then this was also the first time they had had a chance to see what Nagurski could do, even when he wasn't mad.

When the time came to compose the All-America teams for 1929 Bronko Nagurski made every list, either at tackle or at fullback. The *New York Sun*, apparently unable to decide between the two positions, simply picked only 10 players and selected Nagurski as its All-American at both positions. The Heisman Trophy had not yet been instituted, but Nagurski did not need any award to add to his fame. Grantland Rice, the most respected of American sportswriters, said of him, 'Nagurski may well have been the greatest football player of all time.'

Nagurski, of course, went on to sign with George Halas' Chicago Bears and became the scourge of professional football for the next eight seasons. Benny Friedman, of Michigan fame, who played against Nagurski both as a collegiate and as a pro, described him this way: 'He was the greatest fullback I ever played against, in college or the pro game. He bucked

*Above: Quarterback Fred Hovde benefited from the gargantuan blocking and solid running supplied by Bronko Nagurski.*

Above: *Clarence 'Biggie' Munn played guard for the Gophers and was All-American in 1931.*

Right: *Halfback Francis 'Pug' Lund captained the stupendous 1934 squad which Coach Bernie Bierman called his greatest team ever.*

Opposite top: *Minnesota's 1934 national football champions: (front row) Johnson, Tenner, Bengtson, B Bevan, Lund, Rennebohm, Occh, Widseth, Roning; (second row) Rork, Clarkson, Bruhn, D Smith, Kostka, Proffitt, Anderson; (third row) Seidel, Roscoe, Knudsen, Wilkinson, J Bevan, Freimuth, W Smith, Dallera, Antil, Potvin; (back row) Alfonse, Svendsen, Rennix, LeVoir, Beise, Coach Bernie Bierman, Athletic Director Frank McCormick, Student Manager Paul Bergren, Munson. Frank Larson is not shown.*

Opposite bottom: *Guard Bud Wilkinson was All-American in 1935. He went on to greater fame as coach at Oklahoma.*

the line harder than Ernie Nevers. He did everything better. I never saw a greater blocker or a more deadly, brutal tackler.'

Red Grange, Nagurski's teammate on the Bears after his own famed career at Illinois, said of him, 'When it comes to picking the greatest player ever, there is no contest: It's the Bronk.' Nagurski's jersey number, 72, was retired by the Gophers in 1979.

Dr Clarence Spears left Minnesota at the same time as Bronko Nagurski, after the 1929 season. The Gophers' coach for the next two seasons was Herbert Orrin 'Fritz' Crisler, who would go on to nationwide fame as coach of several championship Michigan Wolverine teams. Although in 1931 guard Clarence 'Biggie' Munn made All-American, Crisler's fine recruiting efforts were appreciated only after he had left to take a coaching job at Princeton. Many of the freshmen he recruited went on to stardom under his successor, Bernie Bierman.

Bernard W Bierman, who had captained the 1916 Gopher team, coached Minnesota football teams from 1932 to 1941 and again from 1945 to 1950. Bierman had enjoyed great success at Tulane, but when given a chance to coach at his alma mater, he didn't hesitate for a moment.

He was recognized as the greatest college football coach of his time, and the statistics suggest that he may have been: an overall record of 93-35-6, five undefeated seasons, five national championships, seven Big Ten titles (five outright and two ties), 12 All-America selections, and not one but two 21-game winning streaks.

Bierman's numerous innovations, which included the single-wing formation from an unbalanced line, were matched by his ability to instill perfect timing and flawless blocking. The coach would inspect his players' footsteps in the grass to see if they had followed the precise path he had prescribed. If not, they would receive a Bernie Bierman 'talking-to.' Bierman respected his players' ability to learn, and learn they did. 'Our kids were frequently referred to as "big dumb Swedes." ' he once remarked. 'I never saw one on my football teams.'

Bierman's Gophers enjoyed complete dominance of the Big Ten during the seasons from 1938 to 1940. Though Tom Harmon, Michigan's greatest star, was tearing up the rest of the conference, he never scored a single point on Minnesota, and Michigan lost to the Gophers all three years.

Minnesota fans had many stars to cheer during Bierman's 'Golden Decade' of 1932-1941. There were, for example, the irrepressible halfback Pug Lund, selected All-America in 1934, along with end Frank Larson and guard Bill Bevan. Bierman later called the 1934 team his greatest, and virtually every observer of the day agreed. As usual, Grantland Rice, writing from Minneapolis, had the last word on the 1934 Gophers:

*Football fans here are no longer discussing whether Minnesota's team is the best in the country. They are taking it for granted. What they want to know is: Shouldn't it be rated the greatest of all time? In this debate they speak in terms of a squad — not eleven men — as they point to at least thirty men, most of whom are big, fast and replete with skill . . .*

The year 1935 brought another undefeated season, another national title and more All-Americans: guard Bud Wilkinson, also a star hockey player for Minnesota who would go on to coaching greatness of his own at Oklahoma, and versatile tackle Dick Smith, who also played guard.

A stunning upset by Northwestern marred 1936 for the Gophers. The Wildcats, under Lynn 'Pappy' Waldorf, were on their way to their first undisputed conference championship. The Gophers finished third in the conference overall. But tackle Ed Widseth, the latest in Bierman's string of 'superlinemen,' earned a well-deserved All-America selection.

End Ray King and fullback Andy Uram were selected All-Americans — it seemed that the Gophers turned out at least one per season — in 1937, ending a year in which Minnesota again won every conference game, although the Gophers had lost two tough non-conference

Right: *Minnesota's greatest coach, Bernie Bierman.*

Opposite top: *Guard Tom Brown was All-American and conference MVP for the 1960 season. He also received the Outland Award as the nation's best interior lineman.*

games to Nebraska and perennial spoiler Notre Dame. Guard Francis Twedell, tackle Urban Odson, halfbacks George Franck and 1941 Heisman Trophy winner Bruce Smith, and two-timer (1940-41) Dick Wildung completed the string of All-America picks during Bernie Bierman's tenure. The Minnesota star-machine just kept churning out brilliant players. The handsome Smith, Minnesota's only Heisman winner, was to serve as a Navy fighter pilot and play professional football with the Green Bay Packers and Los Angeles Rams. His Minnesota number, 54, was retired in 1977, ten years after his early death from cancer.

In the early 1940s the Gophers were still a force to be reckoned with. But now the world was at war, and across the country team line-ups were disrupted and schedules switched as military service drew more and more playing stars away from their campuses. Bierman coached through the end of the 1941 season and then he, too, entered the service until 1945. George Hauser handled the coaching duties in his absence, a period in which many Big Ten players found themselves on rival teams during their military duty. Thus fullback Bill Daley and end Herb Hein, after playing the 1942 season at Minnesota, attained All-America stat-

ure at Michigan and Northwestern, respectively, in the 1943 season.

Bernie Bierman returned to the Minnesota campus from the Marine Corps in 1945 to find that college football had changed. Freshmen were rubbing elbows with 25-year-old service-men returning from duty. The players did not mesh, and Bierman had trouble trying to effect a transition from the single-wing to the T-for-mation, which had now become popular. Two players from seasons of the late 1940s, however, must be mentioned: They were giant tackle-guard Leo Nomellini, All-American in both 1948 and 1949, and center Clayton Ton-nemaker, who joined Nomellini on the 1949 All-America team.

When Gopher teams failed to regain their prewar dominance, the critics, quick to forget the good years, began to hound Bierman, and he resigned after the 1950 season. But his coaching philosophy sounds as fresh today as it did when he first came to Minneapolis in 1932. 'Only one thing is worse than going into a game convinced you can't win,' he said. 'That's going into a game convinced you can't lose. The best is to feel you can win but will have to put out everything you have to do it.'

Anxious as the critics had been to hound Bierman out of town, they liked his successor little better. Wes Fesler became coach of the 1951, 1952 and 1953 squads. The former Ohio State great called his 1951 team, which won only two games, 'the world's worst squad.'

Below: *Halfback Bruce Smith won the Heisman Trophy in 1941.*

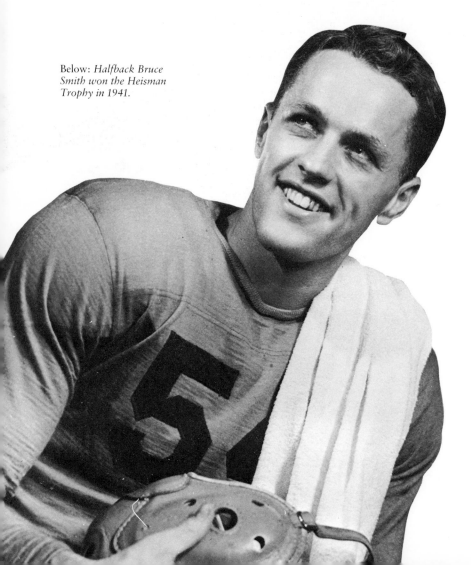

There was one bright spot, however, and it was bright indeed – the play of halfback Paul Giel.

In 1952 and 1953 Giel was just about the only thing going for Minnesota. He called the plays, passed, caught passes, ran with the football and kicked it, too. He even held the ball for PATs. In a 1953 game against Michigan, which the Gophers had not beaten in ten years, Giel handled the ball in 53 of 63 Minnesota plays, rushing for 112 yards, completing 13 of 18 passes – including his first 11 straight – for 169 yards, returned four punts for 49 yards and a kick-off for another 24 and made two interceptions. Minnesota stunned the Wolverines 22-0 on the strength of Giel's one-man show.

His efforts were certainly appreciated at awards time. Giel won All-America honors and conference MVP in both 1952 and 1953, and in 1953 he was a close runner-up to Notre Dame's Johnny Lattner for the Heisman Trophy. Giel was then also given the Walter Camp Award for Back of the Year, and was chosen UPI's Player of the Year. Yet his Gopher team had finished no better than fifth during his years there. Also a fine baseball player, Giel went on to play professional ball with several clubs before returning to Minnesota as athletic director in 1971.

Coach Murray Warmath took over the reins from Fesler in 1954 and guided the Gopher program until 1971. Although his overall record of 86-78-7 doesn't match that of Bierman, Warmath did lead the Gophers through two of their most exciting seasons: 1960 and 1961, in which Minnesota played in two consecutive Rose Bowls.

In the 1960 season, Iowa and Minnesota were deadlocked for the conference title, but the Gophers beat the Hawkeyes in a head-on clash, so it was off to Pasadena for Warmath's Gophers. Disappointment followed, as the Washington Huskies made the Gophers their 17-7 victims, managing to hold off the surging Minnesota offense, led by quarterback Sandy Stephens, in the second half. Still, the award picks were satisfying: Magnificent guard Tom Brown was chosen All-American and conference MVP, and became the Outland Award winner as best interior lineman. Coach Warmath was recognized for his strong efforts with Coach-of-the-Year honors.

The following season, 1961, Minnesota put together a 6-1-0 record, losing only to conference champ Ohio State. At first, it appeared that the Gophers had fallen short. But the Ohio State faculty, which in those days could refuse a Rose Bowl bid, did just that – and the Gophers, as runners-up, were California-bound again. This time they made a better showing.

Left: *Quarterback Sandy Stephens headed the strong offense of the 1960 Gophers. They made it to the Rose Bowl but lost to the Washington Huskies, 17-7.*

Above: *The Paul Bunyan Trophy passes to the winner of the Minnesota-Wisconsin game.*

Top: *Quarterback Philip Hagen (15) in action for the 1968 Gophers.*

Quarterback Stephens, seasoned after the previous year's loss and aided by breakaway halfback Bill Muncey, called for a number of daring fourth-down plays to take an early lead over opponent UCLA. The capper came late in the fourth quarter when Stephens spearheaded an 84-yard drive in 19 plays, scoring his second touchdown from the two-yard line. The Gophers trounced the Bruins, 21-3. Coach Warmath was carried off the field by his players, a broad smile on his face, and back in Minneapolis the home celebrations began. Stephens carried off the conference MVP and All-America honors that year as well.

To say that Minnesota's football fortunes tumbled after that New Year's Day would not be an exaggeration. The Gophers finished as conference runner-up in 1967, but in years following Michigan and Ohio State's dominance was only occasionally challenged. Only five All-Americans wore the Minnesota uniform in two decades. They were tackle Bobby Bell in 1961 and 1962, tackle Carl Eller in 1963, and ends Aaron Brown in 1965, Bob Stein in 1967

and Doug Kingsriter in 1971. Yet new coaching blood and increased emphasis on recruiting in the 1980s led Gopher fans to hope that new generations of Minnesota stars were on the horizon. And respectable (7-5 and 6-6), if not overwhelming, seasons in 1985 and 1986 did nothing to dampen that hope.

Minnesota has continued to enjoy its great rivalries. In addition to the Little Brown Jug contest with Michigan each season, Gopher teams vie for a hog and an axe. Floyd of Rosedale, once a real champion pig and the wager between the governors of Minnesota and Iowa on the 1935 game between the two schools, is now a bronze statue of the beloved animal, and the prized trophy of each year's contest. And what more appropriate trophy between the schools of the 'Great North,' Minnesota and Wisconsin, than Paul Bunyan's axe? The National 'W' Club of Wisconsin donated the colorful axe to the Gophers after their victory in 1948, and the prized implement has passed to the winner of the Minnesota – Wisconsin game ever since.

Above: *The 1968 Gophers in action.*

Left: *The Minnesota sideline cheers a touchdown versus Southern California, 1968.*

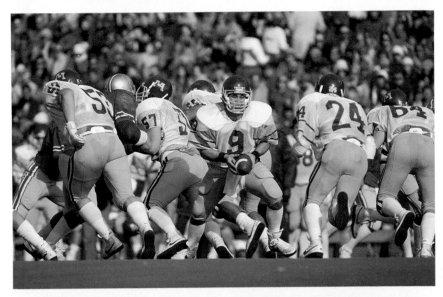

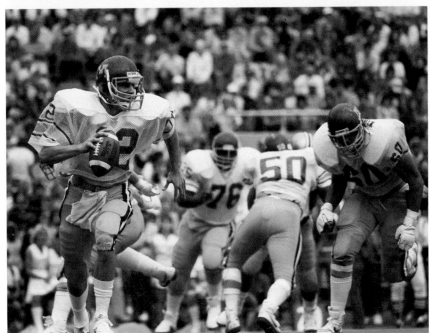

Left: *Andy Hare (12) makes a move against OSU, 1 October 1983.*

Center: *Quarterback Mike Hohensee (9) looks for a handoff versus OSU, 1982.*

Opposite: *Fullback James Carter (34) grabs a pass in a 1968 game against the Buckeyes.*

Above: *Quarterback Dungy (9) calls a play, November 1975.*

Top: *The 1975 Golden Gophers trot down the field at Columbus before they meet the Buckeyes. Shown are Luckemeyer (7), Midboe (78), Weber (28) and Avery (1).*

# NORTH-WESTERN UNIVERSITY

Founded: 1851

Location: Evanston, Illinois

Total Enrollment: 15,951

Colors: Purple and White

Nickname: Wildcats

Football had already been played at Northwestern University for 14 years when the Western Intercollegiate Conference, later to become the Big Ten conference, was formed in 1896. On 11 November 1882 an energetic band of Northwestern students played a 'football heat' against their neighbors further north on the Michigan shore at Lake Forest College. The scoring was as follows: Lake Forest won the contest with one goal, two touchdowns and two safeties, against nothing for NU – numerical scoring would not be introduced to football for another two years. In a return match in Evanston, Northwestern 'evened the series,' scoring a goal and a touchdown against two safeties for Lake Forest.

Northwestern's football history is as illustrious as it is long. Upsets, daring plays and contests played ankle-deep in mud have all contributed to Wildcat football lore. Well into their second century of competition, fans of the Purple and White are justifiably proud of the achievements of their athletes, as players and as scholars. Perhaps no other Big Ten institution has so well demonstrated the combination of athletic competition and scholarship in molding the character of its students.

The first year of football competition for the newly-formed WIC conference featured a pair of star Northwestern halfbacks who brought national attention to the Midwest. Jesse Van Doozer and Albert Potter led the Purple to a 46-6 victory over the University of Chicago Maroon, coached by the immortal Amos Alonzo Stagg. A *Chicago Tribune* sportswriter later described the surprised Maroons as falling 'like straw men before the driving wind.'

Northwestern had lost only one contest that 1896 season, when they met undefeated University of Wisconsin for the first league championship game. In the rain and mud, Van Doozer was able to slither through opposing tacklers for a touchdown late in the game. But as time was running out Wisconsin managed to down a bad Northwestern snap behind the goal line for a touchdown, a tie game and the first Western Conference title.

Still, Van Doozer and Potter were awarded All-Conference honors, and are remembered as the first in a long line of outstanding players to wear the 'N.'

Another well-remembered game in those early days of Northwestern football was a 2-0 victory over Notre Dame in 1901 – NU's first defeat of the scrappy Irish. It is recorded that Harry Allen tackled a Notre Dame player named Salmon in back of the goal as the Irishman attempted to punt a soggy football – scoring the only points of the contest.

One of the great players of that era was Northwestern quarterback Alton Johnson, who played for the Purple from 1898 to 1902. Johnson may have, quite by accident, invented the huddle about twenty years before it became popular. During a contest with the Maroon of Chicago in 1901 Johnson apparently suffered partial amnesia after a blow to the side of the head while running back a punt. Although he could think clearly, he was unable to remember signals or numbers and was forced to gather his teammates around him before each play to go over the pattern. Northwestern won the game 6-5.

Johnson became Northwestern's first All-American that year, although he himself seems to have been unclear about the honor. Several decades after he left Northwestern, he wrote to *Collier's* asking for official confirmation of the fact, explaining that he needed to convince a skeptical daughter.

Northwestern's first great coach was Walter McCornack, a former Dartmouth star who brought with him several training and practice procedures that were standard in the East, where football was better established. Such innovations as the tackling dummy and longer practice hours, including early morning signal drills, improved the Northwestern football effort considerably. In a one-year turnaround the Evanston team rose from last place to third in the conference. Over McCornack's three years, the Purple's record was 25-6-4.

Meanwhile, there was still a general uproar, even in the Western Conference – now called the Big Nine, thanks to the addition of Iowa and Indiana in 1899 – about the rough and sometimes violent nature of the young sport of college football. In 1906 Northwestern's officials voted to ban intercollegiate play. They were back in the race two years later, however, when a committee of trustees, responding to

Left: *Halfbacks Jesse Van Doozer and Albert Potter were the first Northwestern players to bring fame to the Purple.*

Page 128: *Quarterback Kevin Strasser in action for the 1978 Northwestern Wildcats.*

Below: *John 'Paddy' Driscoll was quarterback and captain of the 1916 team which lost only one game, to the OSU Buckeyes, and won the conference title.*

Above: *Super kicker Ralph 'Moon' Baker with Coach Glenn Thistlethwaite.*

Below: *Dyche Stadium home of the Northwestern Wildcats.*

pressure from student and alumni groups, decided that the reforms recently introduced to make the game safer and to regulate conduct and eligibility made the game acceptable.

Still, Northwestern remained near the bottom of the conference heap for the next seven years while the conference was being dominated by Chicago and Minnesota. Then, in 1915, along came pint-sized Paddy Driscoll.

Though small of stature – he never weighed more than 150 pounds in his career – John Leo Driscoll proved himself the equal of much larger men on the football field. After a grim 1915 season, during which the Purple failed to win a single conference game, Driscoll led the team to a 6-1 record for 1916. This remarkable 1916 team, captained by the compact quarterback and coached by Fred Murphy, reached its high point with a 10-0 win over powerful Chicago, when Driscoll scored a touchdown and dropkicked a 43-yard field goal. Northwestern's only loss that year was to Ohio State, when the Purple ran into a buzz saw in the form of Buckeye great Chic Harley, who led the team's fourth quarter scoring blitz to take the game 23-3 and win the conference title. .

Yet Northwestern had now proven it could play with the 'big boys,' and for Paddy Driscoll this was only the beginning of a lifelong love affair with the game of football. Driscoll dropped out of school in 1917 to join the Navy, and he played for the Navy Great Lakes team that went to the 1919 Rose Bowl. One of his teammates at Great Lakes was a young man who had played for Illinois, George Halas, the future great owner-coach of the Chicago

Bears. Driscoll went on to play professional football for three teams, including Halas' Bears, and his deadly dropkicking earned him several career NFL records which still stand.

The war years were sub-par for Northwestern and the rest of the Big Ten conference, as many of the organization's stars had gone into active military service. During seasons from 1918 through 1921, the Purple posted no better than a 2-3 conference record, and went winless in 1921. After that disastrous season university officials began the search for a coach to replace Elmer McDevitt, who had coached for two years. More than anything else, the Purple team needed discipline, and Northwestern found its disciplinarian in Coach Glenn Thistlethwaite.

Thistlethwaite came from nearby Oak Park, Illinois, High School. To some it seemed foolhardy to entrust a high school football coach with the task of turning around a floundering program, but officials liked what they saw in the new coach. A stern taskmaster, Thistlethwaite taught fundamental football and tolerated no nonsense. Soon the embarrassing losses were over, and by the 1924 season Thistlethwaite's style of football was firmly established at Northwestern and was starting to get good results. During that season, in the game against Chicago, the team earned a new nickname.

The Maroons of the University of Chicago, still coached by Stagg, were heavily favored going into the contest, but Northwestern managed to keep them off the scoreboard until the waning minutes of the game. Chicago's Bob Curley finally managed to drill a 28-yard dropkick through the uprights and end the game 3-0. Yet a *Chicago Tribune* sportswriter's post-game analysis gave credit to the scrappy Purple. 'Football players had not come down from Evanston,' wrote Wallace Abbey. 'Wildcats would be a name better suited to Thistlethwaite's boys.' Thus, as a souvenir of the game Northwestern's football team went home with the name 'Wildcats.' It was punchier than the 'Fighting Methodists' and certainly more descriptive than the 'Purple,' the two names by which the team had previously been known. Ever since, Northwestern athletic teams have been Wildcats, or sometimes just Cats.

Another highlight of that 1924 season was a contest against Knute Rockne's mighty Notre Dame team. The Irish were galloping across the Midwest on their way to a national championship, led by their legendary Four Horsemen,' Don Miller, Elmer Layden, Harry Stuhldreyer and Jim Crowley. Notre Dame would

Above: *Moon Baker played for Northwestern from 1924 to 1926, and was admitted to the NU Hall of Fame in 1984.*

Above: *Dick Hanley, the Wildcats' football coach from 1927 to 1933.*

win the Soldier Field game, but with considerably more trouble than expected, thanks to the heroics of a Wildcat named Ralph 'Moon' Baker.

Baker, a splendid kicker, nailed two drop-kicks during the first half to give Northwestern a 6-0 lead. Only when the Irish had scored and Baker had narrowly missed a 40-yard attempt did the tide turn toward Notre Dame, which then intercepted a desperation pass and ran it in for a touchdown to end the game 13-6. But the fearless play of Northwestern and Moon Baker had given the Notre Dame juggernaut a bad scare.

Thistlethwaite's Wildcats had already built a reputation as tough competitors and occasional spoilers when they entered their memorable 1925 game against Fielding Yost's Michigan Wolverines. More than 75,000 fans had purchased tickets for this Soldier Field contest, but it had rained so hard all morning the day of the game that postponement was seriously considered. As it was, only 40,000 were in the stands at the start of the game, staring down at the sea of mud and standing water that was supposed to be the field of play.

Early in the game Wolverine quarterback Benny Friedman fumbled the ball in the slop, and it was recovered on Michigan's five-yard line by Northwestern. A few minutes later big Wildcat fullback Leland 'Tiny' Lewis kicked a field goal to draw first blood for the Cats. Soon it became apparent that the contest was going to be against the elements, as neither side could put back-to-back first downs together. It was a

day for the punters until the fourth quarter, when Michigan drove to Northwestern's 10-yard line but failed to keep the ball. The Wildcats took over, deep in their own territory and with gale-force winds driving the rain into their faces.

Wildcat captain and center Tim Lowry knew that punting into the wind would lead to disaster. Huddling with quarterback Bill Christmann, he decided to take a safety and hope to hold on for the remaining few minutes. Tiny Lewis, standing on the goal line, took the snap from Lowry, backed up two or three steps, then downed the ball. After a desperate free kick, the Wildcats managed to hold off Michigan until the final gun. The improbable 3-2 score wrecked Michigan's perfect season, and although the Wolverines went on to win the conference title, the memory of that mud-soaked Soldier Field would haunt their dreams.

A long time had passed between All-American selections from Northwestern, but Tim Lowry was awarded the honor, virtually unanimously, as well as being selected conference MVP. Lowry's blond good looks and movie-star smile had endeared him to Wildcat fans, especially the females, and he was also a good enough student to graduate from Northwestern's law school, going on to practice law in Chicago for many years.

The 1926 season was even better for fans of Northwestern football. Thistlethwaite's Wildcat team was solid in all departments, with the amiable giant, Moon Baker, and crunching Tiny Lewis returning to lead the attack. Bob Johnson was a standout at tackle, and Waldo Fisher, who starred at end, would also win All-Conference honors in basketball. Sophomores too talented to be kept out of starting positions included Justin Dart at tackle, Luke Johnson at end and a sterling backfield runner named Walt Holmer.

Double shutout wins over Indiana and a shutout victory over Purdue were sandwiched around a 6-0 defeat at the hands of nemesis Notre Dame, which won with a fourth-quarter touchdown pass. The Wildcats knew they were in great shape as they headed into the final two games of the season against Chicago and Iowa.

It was also the dedication year for a new football stadium at Northwestern, christened Dyche Stadium in honor of William A Dyche, the school's longtime business manager and an avid football fan. Wildcat officials knew that scheduling arch-rival Chicago for the dedication game would boost attendance. Chicago Coach Stagg's worst fears about the improved

Wildcats were confirmed when the contest turned into a 38-7 rout for Northwestern. Wildcat Vic Gustafson began by running the opening kickoff back 88 yards for a touchdown. Quarterback and captain Moon Baker passed to Fisher and Gustafson for two more scores, and the Wildcats topped the humiliation in the third quarter with touchdown runs by Tiny Lewis and Gustafson. Amos Alonzo Stagg vowed never to schedule Northwestern again, and in fact the University of Chicago would drop intercollegiate football in 1939 and leave the conference altogether seven years later. But the 1926 Wildcats were a victory away from an undefeated conference season.

In ice and snow at Iowa City, Northwestern hung on with teeth gritted to pull out a 13-6 victory over a stubborn Iowa team. But pesky Michigan had managed to win a thrilling 17-16 victory over Ohio State and was undefeated also. Thus the two teams had to share the conference crown, since they had identical 7-1 overall records. When the season was over the unbeatable Moon Baker had won All-American honors, along with tackle Bob Johnson. But the Wildcats' post-season celebrations were suddenly cut short when Coach Thistlethwaite announced that he would not consider renewing his five-year contract and would instead become head football coach at rival Wisconsin.

Yet all was not lost, for Thistlethwaite's replacement as head coach was a man named Dick Hanley. By the end of 1931 he would produce two championship teams and eight All-Americans.

The 1930 Wildcat team is remembered as one of the finest in Big Ten history. It featured tackles Dallas Marvil and Jack Riley, the Big Ten's best guard in Wade 'Red' Woolworth and talented sophomore end Dick Fenol. In the famed backfield were quarterback Felix 'Lefty' Leach, captain Hank Bruder at halfback and two big newcomers – Pug Rentner and Reb Russell at halfback and fullback, respectively. Hank Bruder would gain fame as 'Hard Luck Hank,' due to the star halfback's uncanny injury jinx, which included broken legs, shoulder injuries, and even a bout with smallpox. These and other mishaps kept the triple-threat Bruder from ever playing a complete season with Northwestern.

Nevertheless, the 1930 Wildcats swept through their conference schedule on Rentner's passing and the smashing fullback play of Reb Russell. The final game was one of the most anticipated in history, as it matched the undefeated Wildcats with also unbeaten Notre Dame for the probable national champion-

ship. The Irish were loaded with All-American talent as well, including watch-charm guard Bert Metzger and quarterback Frank Carideo.

Fans in jam-packed Dyche Stadium bit their nails for 53 minutes as a scoreless deadlock unfolded. Then, with seven minutes to play, Irish halfback Marchy Schwartz galloped 27 yards for a touchdown. A few minutes later, Carideo intercepted a Wildcat pass that would turn into another Notre Dame score.

The exhausted Wildcats were unable to retaliate, and the game ended 14-0 – the only shutout of the Wildcats that season. Northwestern again shared the conference title with Michigan, with identical 5-0 conference records. Pass-catcher Frank Baker, Reb Russell and Wade Woolworth made All-Americans that year, and Notre Dame's Knute Rockne later called Russell 'the greatest plunging fullback I ever saw.' Northwestern's football fortunes were again looking up.

The 1931 season proved to be a wild one in the Big Ten, winding up in a bizarre three-way tie for the conference crown. One of the teams was Northwestern, which had stormed back with Pug Rentner, Jack Riley and Dal Marvil to pound its Big Ten opposition and fight the Irish to a scoreless standoff. After beating Iowa

*Above: Tackle Joshua 'Dallas' Marvil of the superb 1930 Wildcats, who were defeated only by the rampaging Irish of Notre Dame. Northwestern and Michigan shared the conference title that season, with matching 5-0 conference records.*

7-6 in the season finale, Northwestern was the undisputed champion – until it was announced that five post-season games would be played in the Big Ten with proceeds going to the poor of the Depression-ridden nation. The results were to count in the final conference standings.

Northwestern was paired with Purdue for a Soldier Field contest. The night before the game an elevator at the Chicago hotel where the Purple team was staying fell out of control with several Wildcat players inside. Although no one was seriously hurt, some were shaken up and the mishap was taken as a bad omen. The next afternoon, the whole team appeared sluggish as 50 scoreless minutes were ground out. Then, Fred Hecker of Purdue intercepted a pass and minutes later Boilermaker Jim Purvis turned it into the only touchdown of the game. Northwestern had fallen into a tie both with the tough Purdue team and with Michigan. One Wildcat fan said of the charity game, 'We gave more than our share – we gave up an undisputed title!'

Pug Rentner, Jack Riley and Dal Marvil earned All-America honors during that 1931 season when it seemed that Fate was a Purdue fan. And of those Wildcat greats of the 1930-31 seasons, several went on to further stardom. Jack Riley, also a wrestling champion at NU, won a 1932 Olympic silver medal in wrestling and later coached the sport back at Northwestern. Reb Russell enjoyed a career in movies, making 12 westerns with his friend Tom Mix. And Ernest 'Pug' Rentner went on to play professional football with the Boston Redskins and Chicago Bears.

Again, in 1936, Northwestern rose to the top of the conference heap – this time under Coach Lynn 'Pappy' Waldorf. Minnesota's Golden Gophers, coached by Bernie Bierman, had been the undisputed champions in 1934 and 1935 and were expected to keep rolling in

*Left: Ernest 'Pug' Rentner of the stellar 1930-31 Wildcats.*

*Below: Coach Lynn 'Pappy' Waldorf (left) with Alex Kaster in 1942. Waldorf took the job at Northwestern in 1936 and saw the Wildcats to the Big Ten championship that same year. He also was named Coach of the Year for his superb performance. In his 12 years at NU Waldorf produced 7 All-America players, one of whom was the dynamic Otto Graham.*

1936, but Waldorf's Wildcats were undefeated and had three conference victories going into the game with the Gophers.

The muddy field of a wet Homecoming afternoon didn't seem to bother the Northwestern team, and they held their own in a scoreless defensive battle until the third quarter. Then came the break. A flag was thrown against Minnesota for unnecessary roughness, and the penalty yards put the ball on the Gopher one-yard line. Wildcat fullback Steve Toth, with opposing hands trying in vain to grab him, slipped over the goal line for the game's only score. Minnesota's string of 28 games without defeat was broken, and two victories later Pappy Waldorf's Purple team had at last won an undisputed Big Ten title.

But the national championship again eluded the team as Notre Dame took its revenge for the previous season's defeat by beating the Wildcats 26-6. Still, captain and guard Steve Reid attained All-America that year.

Thereafter Northwestern football went into a kind of slump that lasted the better part of 12 years. But of course no slump of such duration could be without its bright spots. Northwestern's 1938 team, although posting only a 2-1-2 record, nevertheless produced All-American

tackle Bob Voigts, who was later to figure even more prominently in Wildcat grid history. And though Pappy Waldorf left Northwestern after the 1946 season, he did so without regrets. In his 12-year coaching tenure, Waldorf's team had finished in the lower half of the Big Ten only three times, and he had produced seven All-Americans. One of these was the great Otto Graham.

This triple-threat tailback, who actually believed basketball was his best sport and was eaded for a musical career, had to be talked into reporting for spring practice in 1941. Once he put on the cleats, the rest was Northwestern football history. A natural athlete, Graham dazzled fans and opponents alike throughout the 1941-43 seasons, his skills put to maximum use by the wily Waldorf. 'With Otto's sense of timing, his peripheral vision, and his natural gifts of size, strength and toughness, he was the ideal running-passing threat,' Waldorf later commented.

Although Graham labored on some mediocre Northwestern teams, he compiled some almost unbelievable career statistics. He completed 157 of 320 passes for 2181 yards and 15 touchdowns; gained 823 rushing yards and another 17 touchdowns on the ground; and tallied a grand total of 3004 yards in total offense and 115 points – half the points scored by the entire team during his three seasons. One of Northwestern's greatest stars, Graham earned All-America honors and the conference MVP award. He went on, of course, to an even more brilliant career, as pro football's premier quarterback from 1945 to 1955, with the Cleveland Browns under Coach Paul Brown.

But even with occasional outstanding players, Northwestern began finding it hard to compete. Superlative runners such as Don Heap and Bill DeCorrevont stood out in the late 1930s and early 1940s, but players of their caliber were few and far between. Northwestern was the only private school in the Big Ten and was being decisively out-recruited by neighbors Iowa, Michigan and Ohio State, who were picking the local high schools clean.

How, then, did Northwestern's Wildcats go to the Rose Bowl after the 1948 season? They did it with Coach Bob Voigts, the 1938 gridiron star who had returned and was in his second year at the helm. They did it, too, with Alex Sarkisian, captain and center, and a host of other smart, hungry players. The 1948 Wildcat team finished second in the Big Ten with a 5-1-0 record – second to the only team that had beaten it, Michigan. The Big Ten, having finally signed a Rose Bowl pact with the Pacific Coast Conference, had decreed that no

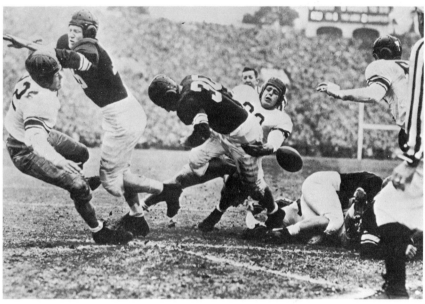

Big Ten team could go twice in a row. Rules were rules, and 1947 Rose Bowl winner Michigan would have to sit this one out, so Northwestern was in its first, and only, Rose Bowl.

The scrappy team, accompanied by a huge group of its fans, did its best to make the 92,000 Rose Bowl spectators forget that it was the second place Big Ten team. The Wildcats also tried to ignore the fact that the coach of their opponents, the California Golden Bears, was none other than Pappy Waldorf.

Midway in the first quarter Northwestern's Frank Aschenbrenner broke off right tackle for a 73-yard scoring run. The Golden Bears soon evened the score and kept it there until early in the second quarter, when Wildcat Art Murakowski crashed into the end zone from the two-yard line. He fumbled as he crossed the goal line, but officials ruled that he had had possession long enough for the score to count.

In the second half the Wildcat defense repelled drive after drive by the Bears, who had scored early to lead 14-13. Finally, Northwestern owned the football on their own 12-yard line with three minutes to go in the contest.

*Above: The 1948 Wildcats went to the Rose Bowl to meet the California Golden Bears when Michigan, the previous year's Big Ten entry at the Rose Bowl, had to stay home. Northwestern's first two scores came on a brilliant 73-yard run by Frank Aschenbrenner and a two-yard plunge by fullback Art Murakowski, the legality of which has never been satisfactorily ascertained. As this photo shows, the ball seems to be falling off his left hip while both of his feet are still on the field of play. The Wildcats won the Rose Bowl, 20-14.*

*Top: The great Otto Graham (48) twists and turns his way through the opposition. He became one of NU's all-time greats in the 1941-43 seasons.*

After a first down, Aschenbrenner, who seldom passed, electrified the crowd by tossing a spiral to Don Stonesifer on the Wildcats' 30-yard line.

With only seconds left for another play, right halfback Ed Tunnicliff took a direct snap from center and, aided by magnificent blocking, raced 45 yards for a touchdown. The Bears had time for a desperation pass after the kickoff, but the throw was intercepted. Northwestern had won the 1949 Rose Bowl 20-14. The goal posts were torn down as delirious Wildcat fans, who had followed their team by train, plane and automobile, began celebrating the biggest thrill in the history of Purple football. To cap the season, Art Murakowski and Alex Sarkisian wound up as All-America picks, with Murakowski adding conference MVP honors.

Bob Voigts went on to coach the Wildcats through the 1954 season, during which time Wildcat fans enjoyed the exploits of such players as Don Stonesifer and Joel Collier. Stonesifer, one of the heroes of the Rose Bowl victory, had his finest year in 1950, when he set Big Ten records with 28 receptions for 394 yards. Another record was established when he made 13 receptions in a 13-6 defeat of Minnesota. An All-American in 1950, Stonesifer went on to play professional ball with the Chicago Cardinals for several years, earning All-Pro honors. Wide receiver Joel Collier shone in 1952, earning All-Conference and All-America status and playing in two All-Star games his senior year. Collier turned down a pro offer from the New York Giants in order to continue his education. Western Illinois, the Buffalo Bills and the Denver Broncos have all benefited from his decision to enter coaching.

But otherwise, Northwestern was in the doldrums again. Voigts departed after the 1954 season, and Lou Saban's 1955 Wildcats finished dead last in the conference with an 0-6-1 record. It was time for a change, and Ara Parseghian, Northwestern's coach for the next eight years, was definitely a change.

The energetic, outspoken young Parseghian took the Wildcats, the Big Ten's doormats and by 1962 had them contending for the Big Ten crown. Along the way, Dyche Stadium crowds were treated to some fancy play, especially in 1958 by guard Andy Cverko, who was named an All-American that year, and halfback Ron Burton. That was Burton's junior year, but he managed to figure in just about every offensive category in the Big Ten, finishing second in scoring, first in pass receiving, fourth in rushing and third in punt returns.

Burton, who starred in some stunning upset victories over Michigan (55-24) and previ-

ously unbeaten Ohio State (21-0) in the 1958 season, went on to earn All-America honors in 1959 and play professional football for the Boston Patriots. He was joined on the All-America team in 1959 by Northwestern's fine center, Jim Andreotti.

Everything seemed to come together for Parseghian's Wildcats in 1962. After trailing Ohio State 14-12 at the half, the Purple put together a 42-yard fourth quarter scoring drive which put them ahead, 18-14, and they held off the Buckeyes to win by that score. More fourth-quarter fireworks were in store for Wildcat fans in the Indiana game, courtesy of quarterback Tom Myers. The plucky Myers completed four passes for 54 yards and a touchdown as time wound down, pulling out a 26-21 victory over the Hoosiers. The Wildcats had their sixth straight victory, and were briefly ranked first in the nation. But losses to Wisconsin and Michigan State ended the season with disappointment. Tom Myers was All-American, along with guard Jack Cverko.

Ara Parseghian left Northwestern after the 1963 season for the coveted Notre Dame head coaching job, where he proceeded to bring the Fighting Irish eight Top Ten rankings and two national championships in the next 11 years. His former assistant for eight years, Alex Agase, an All-American at both Illinois and

*Above: Coach Dennis Green, who joined the Wildcats in 1981.*

*Below: Frank Aschenbrenner (left) takes a handoff from Don Burson during practice.*

Purdue, was selected as Parseghian's replacement at NU.

In 1968, 'Little Big Man' Mike Adamle appeared on the Wildcat scene. At only 5-feet 9-inches and 190 pounds, Adamle had been recruited by only one Big Ten team – Northwestern. He soon avenged himself on the doubters by compiling some eye-opening statistics. By the end of his college career in 1970, Adamle held six new conference records, including rushing yardage in a game (316 against Wisconsin in 1969), season (1255 in 1970) and career (2105). Named an All-American as well as conference MVP in 1970, the stubby, powerful fullback went on to professional football with the Kansas City Chiefs, New York Jets and Chicago Bears. A leg injury brought his pro career to an early end, but Adamle, who had the looks of a matinee idol as well as a breezy wit, soon found a niche as a sportscaster.

Agase, named national 'Coach of the Year' in 1970 by the Football Writers of America, left Northwestern after the 1973 season to accept the head coaching duties at Purdue, where he had starred as a player. The 1970 and 1971 seasons had brought a rise in Wildcat fortunes, with defensive safety Eric Hutchinson thrilling crowds and the Purple finishing third and second in the conference, respectively – not bad considering Michigan and Ohio State's almost complete domination of the conference from 1968 to 1982.

Agase was succeeded by John Pont, who coached the Wildcats from 1973 to 1977 after a stint at Indiana. He compiled an unspectacular record of 10-31-0. Nevertheless, Mitch Anderson quarterbacked the team brilliantly from 1972 to 1974, leading the conference in passing yardage in 1974 with 1098.

Rick Venturi handled the coaching chores from 1978 to 1980, when the Wildcats lured coach Dennis Green away from Stanford, where he had served as their offensive coordinator. Green had also served a stint at Iowa as quarterback-receiver coach, and a year in professional football coaching under Bill Walsh. In his first season, 1981, Green emphasized football fundamentals and year-round athletic conditioning. He also stressed the oft-neglected local recruiting effort. Although Northwestern consistently found its layers on Academic All-Big Ten lists, and although scholarship would always be the first priority at NU, Green took aim for heightened recognition of Northwestern as an athletic institution. In 1986 Northwestern shared seventh place in the conference standings with Illinois, its best finish in three years, and fans could hope for better things to come.

Well into its second century of football competition, Northwestern has evolved several colorful football traditions, including the NU Marching Band and the 'Sweet Sioux' Tomahawk, the trophy which goes to the winner of the annual contest between the Wildcats and downstate conference rival Illinois. First established in 1945, the 'Sweet Sioux' trophy was a real cigar store wooden Indian statue. Posing a transportation problem as it was passed back and forth between Evanston and Champaign, it was eventually replaced by the Tomahawk. In either form it has been a symbol of a proud university.

Above: *Fullback Mike Adamle compiled an awesome record in his three seasons at NU, 1968-70.*

Top: *All-American quarterback Tom Myers in 1963.*

Top left: *NU's Mike Fieldler (57) fights off OSU's Tim Sawicki (68) in Columbus, 6 October 1979.*

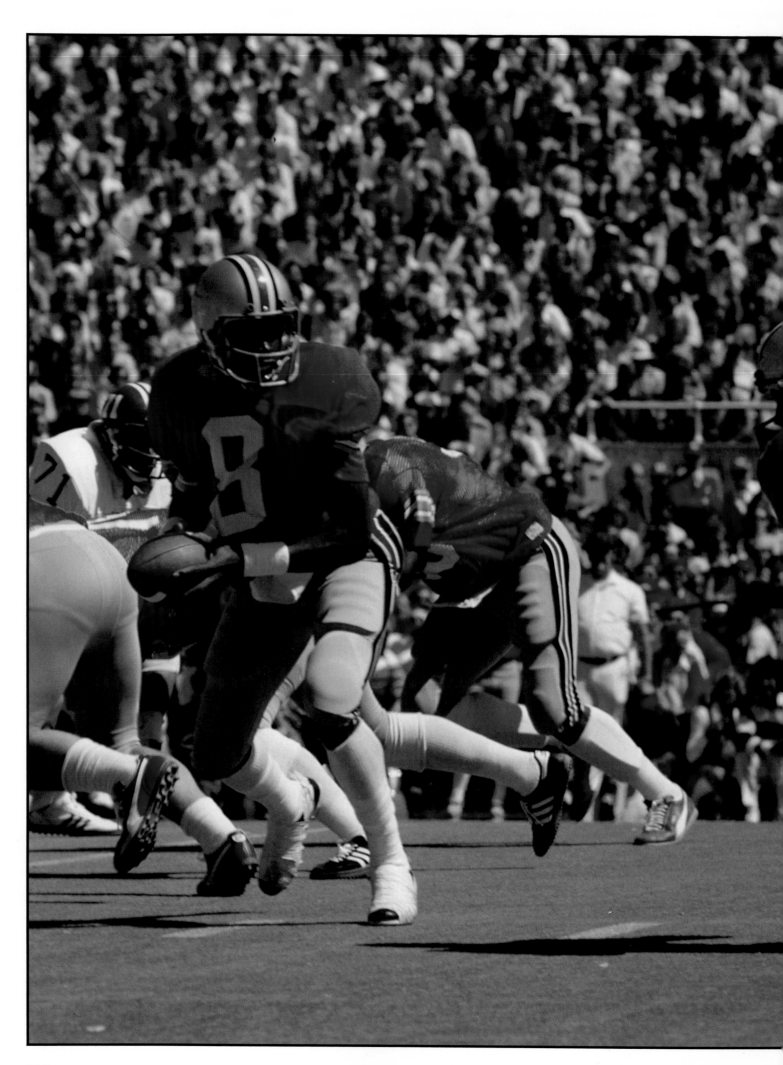

# OHIO STATE UNIVERSITY

Founded: 1870

Location: Columbus

Total Enrollment: 53,199

Colors: Scarlet and Grey

Nickname: Buckeyes

Ohio State's earliest gridiron contest was held on 3 May 1890 in the village of Delaware, Ohio, home of Ohio Wesleyan, a small Christian college. Play began at 9:30 AM so that the Ohio State team would have time to find their way back to Columbus, 17 miles to the south, before dark. Coached by Alexander S Lilley and Jack Ryder, the Buckeyes won their first contest 20-14, a fitting start for a school that would someday rank among the nation's driving forces in collegiate football.

The Buckeyes' early exploits in the game, however, were often uneven, if not disastrous. The small school, which had been founded as Ohio Agricultural and Mechanical College 17 years before its first football game, was first a member of the Ohio Athletic Conference. Opposition teams came mostly from church-affiliated schools scattered across the state, such as Ohio Wesleyan, Akron, Case, Denison, Kenyon, Oberlin, Otterbein and Wooster. Some opponents weren't even schools, but simply organizations that ran teams of OSU's caliber: Army bases, for example, whose squads included the Western Reserve, 17th Regiment and the Columbus Barracks, or the Dayton YMCA.

It wasn't until 1897 that tiny Ohio State took on a team from the Western Conference, later the Big Ten. The Buckeyes were immediately sacked by Michigan 34-0 but entered into a rivalry that today is the most publicized in all of college football. The loss wasn't a surprise to Ohio State fans, who watched their team fall scoreless to six other opponents that year and gain only one win and one tie.

Early Buckeye football fortunes were spotty, with victories almost equally matched by losses. Much of the inconsistency on the field owed to inconsistency in leadership. A revolving door ushered ten coaches in and out of Columbus before any continuity was established in 1913 with the hiring of John W Wilce.

The first three years of relative joy for Ohio State students and fans were brought by the teams of 1899-1901, under the tutelage of John B C Eckstorm. In the first year, the Buckeyes went undefeated, stalled only by a tie with Case. The 1900 team went 8-1-1, the one tie coming in a scoreless shownown with Michigan at Ann Arbor. Eckstorm finished his term with a 5-3-1 record in 1901.

Those happy years were darkened only by the loss of center John L Sigrist in the Western Reserve game of 1901. Sigrist was the first and only player in Ohio State history to sustain fatal injuries on the field.

In the following year, Perry T W Hale replaced Eckstorm, and coached his team to 14

wins and five losses over two years. Western Conference play was limited to the traditional Michigan game, and fledgling OSU could do nothing to stop Fielding Yost's 'Point-a-Minute' teams featuring the magnificent halfback Willie Heston. The Buckeyes were embarrassed first by an 86-0 route – which remains Ohio's worst loss ever – at Ann Arbor before 6000 spectators, 'the largest crowd that had assembled on the local gridiron this season,' according to the *Cleveland Plain Dealer*. The following season, the Wolverines rolled over OSU 36-0.

Coaching in 1904-05 was E R Sweetland, who posted successful 6-5 and 8-2-2 records. The Scarlet and Gray demonstrated, as usual, its dominance over Ohio Conference teams, with the continual exception of Case, but obviously had not yet mustered 'big league' stamina. OSU suffered shutouts at the hands of Illinois, Indiana, Michigan and the upstart Carlisle Indian School teams during Sweetland's two years, but it at least had the satisfaction of stomping Miami University of Oxford, Ohio 80-0.

Ohio State football enjoyed continued victories under the youthful direction of A E Herrnstein, a former Michigan football star, who coached during the following four years. Herrnstein's team lost only to Michigan in 1906, and even then held the Wolverines to just six points. The team gave up only 14 points that season. The next season was almost as exciting to OSU fans, with only two losses, one each to Michigan and Case. The Buckeyes slipped a notch in 1908 with a 6-4 season, but received a first-time invitation to play Vanderbilt. The afternoon the Buckeyes were to leave for Nashville was declared a holiday, and 1000 enthusiastic students escorted their team to Columbus' Union Station in a snake dance. OSU pulled out a 17-6 victory the next day.

Howard Harding Jones, the first Ohio coach to be named to the National Football Foundation Hall of Fame, took over coaching duties in 1910 and upheld Herrnstein's record with a 6-1-3 season, including a tie with Michigan. Jones brought OSU its first taste of Eastern-style coaching, and an emphasis on a strong defense, having served Syracuse and Yale. But he returned to Yale the following year, and later went on to coaching fame at Iowa and Southern California.

Replacing Jones the following year was Harry W Vaughn, who also came to Ohio State from Yale. He coached the Buckeyes for only one season, helping them achieve a 5-3-2 record. School spirit ran higher than ever in 1911, reaching a peak with the Syracuse and

Above: *Alexander Spinning Lilley, Ohio State's first football coach, in 1890.*

Page 138: *Quarterback Rod Gerald of the Ohio State Buckeyes in action versus the Michigan State Spartans in 1976.*

Michigan games. The athletic board, catching the general mood, budgeted for the first paid cheerleader to attend a road game.

John R Richards filled the coaching position in 1912 and led the school to a 6-3 record. The football roster indicated a shift away from Ohio Conference games, long sought by students and coaches, yet OSU fell to Michigan, Michigan State and Penn State. The Buckeyes did not play MSU's Spartans for another 39 years, and they may have wished the same of Penn State. Coach Richards had continually complained to officials about Penn's rough tackling throughout the 37-0 rout, and he finally pulled his men from the field with five minutes left to play. Officials duly noted Richards' complaint, but awarded the game as a forfeit to Penn, jotting a score of 1-0 in the books.

Yet by playing bigger, tougher out-of-state teams, Ohio State was increasingly able to test its mettle and was growing ever more restless with the Ohio Conference roster. And the student rolls were finally growing large enough – about 3500 in 1912 – to provide something of an athletics talent pool.

After years of serious consideration, the University finally applied for membership in the Big Nine under Richards' leadership. In some ways the decision had been agonizing; membership in the conference would mean an end to competition with the Wolverines, always the most popular rival on the athletic rosters, because Michigan had withdrawn in 1907 over a disagreement on policy.

But in spite of the Big Nine's new 'non-intercourse' rule – which prohibited play with any former conference team – Ohio State tend-ered an application, and was voted into the Western Inter-Collegiate Conference on 6 April 1912. Within a few years Michigan would be re-enrolled, making possible not only the continuation of a longstanding rivalry, but also the conference moniker, 'Big Ten.'

For those students and athletes who had for years dreamed of walking with the giants of the Western Conference, the arrival of Lynn Wilbur St John and John W Wilce in 1913 seemed the final step. Legend has it that upon Richards' resignation as coach and athletic director in early 1913, the faculty selected and appointed a successor, St John, without even asking him if he wanted the job.

'Saint,' as he was known to his students and athletes, had played halfback while a freshman at OSU in 1900, but had dropped out of school when his father died. He went on to coach boys' football at other schools, and was splitting his time between coaching at Ohio Wesleyan and studying at Starling-Ohio Medical College when he was informed of his surprise appointment to athletic director at OSU. St John decided medicine could wait.

One of St John's first moves was to hire a new football coach. He sniffed out leads from other Big Nine schools, and picked Wilce, a 25-year-old assistant coach at Wisconsin who had once starred as a player with the Badgers. Wilce stayed for 16 years, at last putting a stop to Ohio State's revolving door.

Wilce must have felt some hesitation about the task before him. In five years OSU had played 14 games against conference opponents and had failed to win even one. The 1913 roster, shortened from nine to seven games in

*Above left: Coach John W Wilce (center) with outstanding end Wes Fesler (left), who dazzled Buckeyes fans from 1928-30 and who was All-American for three successive years, and Dick Larkins (right), who later became OSU's athletic director.*

*Above: Coach Albert 'Hernie' Herrnstein in 1907.*

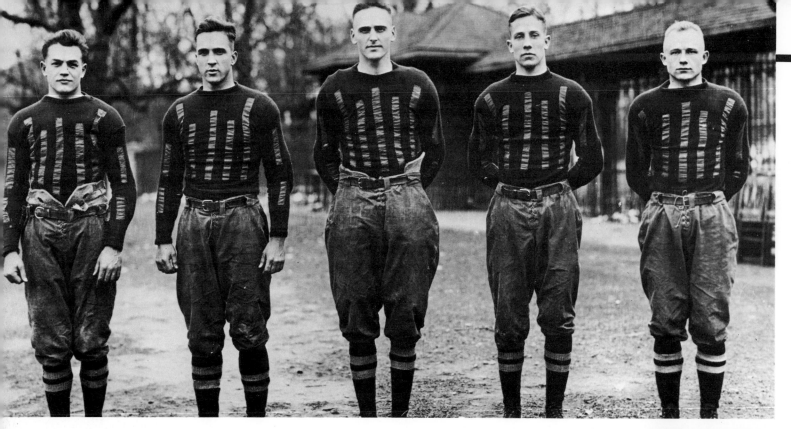

accordance with Big Nine rules, include three conference games with Indiana, Wisconsin and Northwestern. Wilce's players were beaten by the first two but polished off the Purple 58-0 at the end of a 4-2-1 season.

The Wisconsin match was OSU's first road game in conference play, and true to the Bucks' reputation for boisterous boosterism, 76 students went along to offer moral support. Four of them shipped themselves as baggage at a cost of 80 cents apiece.

Wilce's team fared a little better in conference play the next year, and added Illinois as an opponent. The Buckeyes fell to the Illini and to Wisconsin, but beat Indiana 13-3 and Northwestern 27-0 for a season record of 5-2. As if building toward the spectacular era just around the corner, OSU again went one better in 1915, chalking up a 5-1-1 season. This time the young Buckeyes, in spite of the loss of eight graduating gridmen in the spring, fell to Wisconsin, tied Illinois and beat Indiana and Northwestern. If students thought they had cause to celebrate, they also had reason to think twice. The program for the Illinois game carried the following message on the cover:

*Students: If you did not get to register in Columbus DON'T fail to go home and cast your vote to make OHIO DRY. You have a right to vote somewhere. To do it MARK your BALLOT like this Nov 2: YES – Prohibition of the sale and manufacture for sale of intoxicating liquor as a beverage.*

But the seasons of 1916 and 1917 would put any attempt at sobriety to the test. For across town, at Columbus East High School, varsity star Charles W 'Chic' Harley was preparing for a career that would put Ohio State on the nation's football map. The wiry 162-pound Harley had drawn bigger crowds to high school games than those at many OSU matches in his three years of play. His team won all but one game – his last – in those years, and the dark-eyed boy was the target of heavy recruiting efforts in the summer of 1915. But Harley wanted only to play for his hometown college, and he quickly distinguished himself in freshman scrimmage at OSU as a player of outstanding versatility.

Former Big Ten commissioner Kenneth 'Tug' Wilson later wrote of Harley's debut before Wilce, who was asked what Harley could do best.

*Wilce pondered a bit and said: 'Probably run.' Then, after a pause: 'No, he's possibly a better punter.' Another pause. 'Could be as a passer.' A final hesitation: 'Of course, you ought to see him drop kick!'*

Harley demonstrated his versatility in his first varsity games against Ohio Wesleyan and Oberlin with a dramatic flair that became his trademark. The Buckeyes easily beat Wesleyan 12-0, but Harley put on his first real show the next week for Oberlin. He dominated the field, adding two touchdowns to a winning score that is still the highest ever tallied by Ohio State: a whopping 128-point shutout.

Harley fared even better in the face of Big Nine competition. The sophomore's dazzling style prompted an unprecedented horde of

Above: *Halfback Gaylord 'Pete' Stinchcomb in 1920.*

Top: *The devastating 1917 OSU backfield: (l-r) Charles W 'Chic' Harley, Frank Willaman, Richard Boesel, Howard Yerges and Fred L Schweitzer.*

hopeful Ohioans to head for Illinois to see the Buckeyes meet Bob Zuppke's famous Illini. The fans' hopes slowly sank during the game, played in ankle-deep mud and with mounting Buckeye injuries.

Illinois' Macomber had kicked two impressive field goals during the game, but the Buckeyes were still scoreless in the fourth quarter as Harley passed the ball to advance OSU to the Illini 13-yard line. With a minute left Harley faked a pass and tore outside, zipped around the left end and between two tacklers to dive for a touchdown, tying the score 6-6. OSU took a time-out and Harley went to the sidelines to change his mud-filled shoes.

The crowd held its breath while Harley casually laced up his new shoes, patted them with satisfaction and trotted back to join his team at the line of scrimmage. A beat passed, and suddenly Harley had the snap from center. He took one step forward and neatly drop-kicked the extra point, driving fans to their feet. Harley had secured the Buckeye's first victory over Zuppke's mighty Illini, and the first UI defeat on home turf in four years.

The sports press sat up and took note of OSU's feat. Certainly writers didn't classify Wilce's scrappy eleven as a threat to Big Nine superpowers, but they did paint a picture of an up-and-coming team with great potential. That potential was to be fulfilled but two weeks later on Ohio State Homecoming Day.

Guest Wisconsin was leading 7-0 in the Homecoming Game's third quarter when Harley took the ball and spun a 33-yard pass to end Dwight Peabody, landing the ball on the Badger 25-yard line. Next Harley faked a punt and ran around the left end, cut back across tackle and dodged the halfback and safety for a touchdown. A perfect drop-kick by Harley tied the score at 7-7.

With just a few minutes left in the final quarter, Harley, playing defensive quarterback, nabbed a Wisconsin punt on his own 22-yard line. Led by a one-man interference, Chic slipped through the oncoming forward line, then brushed past virtually every Badger on the field in a spectacular 78-yard run for the goal. Harley's extra-point kick yielded a 13-7 lead.

Wisconsin made one more touchdown, but missed the extra point by flubbing an easy catch on the 'kickout.' (In early football, goals made in a corner were followed by an unimpeded kickout from the sideline to a spot closer to center, which had to be caught. Ohio State's yearbook, *The Makio*, teasingly commiserated with the Badger receiver: 'Try to catch a twisting football yourself with eleven opponents running toward you and yelling in true

Comanche style – at least that is the best alibi quarterback Taylor of the Badgers had.' The Buckeyes had come home to victory, the final score 14-13.

As if to prove that Ohio State was by no means a one-man team, the Buckeyes went on to plaster Indiana 46-7 the following week. Ironically, it was Indiana Coach Stiehm, and not the press, who was the first to admit that 'The team is the best I've seen and should win the conference championship.' The sort of hysteria that would, in later years, bring Columbus its identity as the football capital of the world began to spread, and a record crowd of 12,000 packed old Ohio Field for the 25 November contest with undefeated Northwestern.

For the first three quarters Ohio State rode 3-0 on the tails of Harley's 33-yard field goal. Early in the fourth, Northwestern star Paddy Driscoll tied the score with a 40-yard drop kick. Snatching the ball from Northwestern's kick at the Ohio 37-yard line, Harley took OSU fans' breath away with his famous dog-trot – a slow, almost hesitant little run he would make while sizing up his plan of attack for the onrushing forward line. As always, Harley finally switched gears and careered 67 yards for a goal, touched not once by the Northwestern eleven.

Following a fumble recovery from Northwestern a few minutes later, Harley tore around the Purple right end on a faked pass and ran 20 yards to bring the score to 16-3. Chic punted the second of two drop-kick extra points, and went on to hit MacDonald with a perfect 38-yard pass that set up OSU for one more touchdown and an extra point. At 23-3 the Purple were thoroughly beaten. The Buckeyes had pulled down their first championship.

Walter Camp selected OSU tackle Bob Karch and Harley for his All-America team and wrote of Chic, 'It doesn't seem possible he could have done everything credited to him but the fact is he did, and proved he is as great as any claim made for him.' And the *Chicago Tribune*'s Walter Eckersall noted, 'Chic Harley will be placed on my All-America team. He's one of the greatest players I've ever seen.'

All the nation's sports fans looked upon the upstart Buckeyes and wondered if they could possibly prove their worth in another season. Coach Wilce and his players snuffed out any doubts by reigning undefeated for a second straight season in 1917, beginning with four shutouts over Case, Ohio Wesleyan, Northwestern and Denison. Indiana posed more of a challenge, and though Wilce had thought of letting Harley have a rest, it became obvious in

Above: *Quarterback Harry 'Hage' Workman, one of the stars of the brilliant 1920 season.*

the first quarter that the Hoosiers were no easy prey. Wilce tossed in Harley late in the second quarter to break up a scoreless deadlock, and Chic did just that. His four long open-field runs of 25 to 50 yards resulted in Ohio State's only touchdowns, so that it seemed Chic himself handed Indiana its 26-3 defeat.

Harley let his teammates shine in the following games against Wisconsin and Illinois. Frustrated in running attempts by Badger ends, Harley instead made fruitful passes to Bolen and Courtney to set up two touchdowns, and kicked a 40-yard goal to clinch the 16-3 victory. In the championship game with tough Illinois the combination of Harley and Courtney managed the only touchdown scored against Zuppke's team that season. Two field goals by Harley brought the score to 13-0, and once again Ohio State took to the fore in the Big Nine. Both Harley and guard Charles Bolen were named to All-America teams.

Along with scores of other college students and athletes, Harley and the rest of the lettered squad joined the armed forces in 1918. In a season that is often regarded as unofficial, a makeshift team of freshman players went 3-3. The losses were all to conference teams, including the returning Wolverines, who had just rejoined the Big Ten.

If Michigan thought it could go back to kicking OSU around, there were surprises in store. Harley and his pals were back in 1919, and, joined by younger talent – Gaylord 'Pete' Stinchcomb and Iolas Huffman, among others – proceeded to set the Big Ten record straight with a 6-1 season.

Harley had reached the pinnacle of national fame upon his return from World War I, and he became the first collegiate football star whose public and private accomplishments were inflated to superstar proportions. Wrote Tug Wilson: 'In Chic Harley the press had its first post-war, all-purpose football hero. The headlines and pictures could have tripped a more sophisticated, more out-going boy, but fame never once threw the quiet, humble Harley for a loss.'

Yet if Harley is remembered by Ohio State fans for anything – and often, he is regarded as the man who invented OSU football as it is known today – it is for his part in bringing down arch-rival Michigan for the very first time. In 20 years of battle with Michigan, the Buckeyes had never won. In fact, they had gained only three touchdowns in the 15-game history. Harley would change all that.

Ohio State went to its conference opener at Ann Arbor with plenty of support, contributing to the 27,000-plus crowd at Ferry Field.

Ohio scored first, the conversion kicked by Harley, and the Wolverines answered with a field goal, putting OSU's lead at 7-3. The scoring stalled until the third quarter, when Harley took over an offensive drive that had landed the ball on the Michigan 40. On the snap Harley clamped the ball under his arm and ran for the right end, cut back sharply to avoid a menacing blocker and ran 40 yards through the remaining Wolverines for the winning touchdown. Michigan at last was beaten!

At day's end Harley had intercepted four of the Wolverines' 18 passes and averaged 42 yards on his 11 punts; one kick had flown 60 yards. The victory, so long in coming, had some Buckeyes weeping in the stands, and Wolverine Coach Fielding Yost made a rare appearance in the visitor's locker room to personally congratulate Harley.

Yet Chic would end his collegiate career with a heartbreaker. In the championship game with Illinois, Zuppke's formidable defense held Ohio State to just one touchdown, by Harley. Illinois gained a touchdown of its own, but missed the extra point, and OSU held a one-point lead until the final moments of the game.

The student editor of the OSU *Lantern* felt confident enough to order the presses to roll with a special issue, complete with banner headline claiming a Big Ten championship for Ohio State. Just after the game, the freshly printed papers would be run from the journalism plant to nearby Ohio Field for fans to take home, a souvenir of Harley's last game.

But the Illini offense had its own ideas for a headline and managed to intercept one of Harley's long passes. Zuppke's team launched an offensive that brought them to the Ohio 12 with just eight seconds left to play. Buckeye fans gasped as the Illini took to field-goal formation, and saw Bob Fletcher kick his first-ever field goal to clinch a 9-7 win. Ohio State had missed out on an unprecedented third straight championship by eight seconds.

The *Lantern* was not much of a seller that day, but no disappointment could darken the glowing record of Harley's career. In six years, he had lost only two games; in the last three, Ohio State's record was 21-1-1, thanks largely to his exploits. Harley had scored more than half his team's points in three years, had done almost all of its extra-point and goal kicking, all of its punting and most of the passing. The results: 23 touchdowns, 39 extra points and ten goals for a 201-point total. Harley was named All-American for a third time, one of the few players ever so honored.

Chic Harley lived to be 87 years old, long

Above: *All-American tackle Iolas Huffmann in 1921.*

Above: *Dick Larkins, OSU's athletic director of the 1940s.*

Above: *Versatile Buckeyes star Wes Fesler.*

Right: *The annual meeting of the American Football Coaches' Association at New York in 1928: (l-r, standing) Dr J W Wilce, Ohio State; Charlie Crowley, Columbia; Glenn Thistlethwaite, Northwestern; (l-r, seated) Hugo Bezdek, Penn State; Major Frank Cavanaugh, Fordham; Lou Young, University of Pennsylvania; Bill Roper, Princeton; and Fielding Yost, Michigan.*

enough to see his brand of playing matched by Howard 'Hopalong' Cassady and Archie Griffin, but never to be displaced as the man who put Ohio State on the football map.

With Harley gone in 1920, Pete Stinchcomb was able to shine even brighter than before. The senior halfback, a brilliant runner and receiver, was joined by Huffman, quarterback Harry Workman and fullback Frank Willaman in an unbeatable team. The season opened with the usual shutouts over Ohio Conference teams, and led to wins over every Big Ten opponent, including a 14-7 rout of Michigan and a narrow clip of first-time opponent Chicago.

One final score remained to be settled, that with Illinois, which had stolen the championship from OSU in the final seconds one year before. The weather was bitterly cold at Illinois on game day, and both teams, too frozen to mount an effective offense, were deadlocked down to the last minute of play. Finally, with a few seconds left on the clock, Buckeye Workman fired a pass to end Meyers at the Illinois 27-yard line, and somehow 'Truck' was able to motor through to the goal. Fans of Illinois, which would have been champion even with a tie because of its longer game roster, watched speechless as the Buckeyes skipped off the field with their third championship in six years.

The season was marred only by a final, postseason game. Ohio State was invited to play in the Rose Bowl – an honor, since only Michigan had played a Rose Bowl game, the series opener in 1902 with Stanford. The Wolverines had slaughtered Stanford 49-0, and the annual contest had been scrapped through 1916.

This time, though, it was the Big Ten that would sever ties with the West Coast. The University of California outplayed the Buckeyes at every turn, taking a decisive 28-0 win in their native 85° climate, and embarrassed the Midwestern conference into banning Rose Bowl play for the next quarter of a century. Nonetheless, Stinchcomb was unanimously voted All-American that year.

If nothing else, the Rose Bowl convinced OSU followers and the rest of the nation that Ohio State was a national football giant. Columbus had indeed become the capital of football, at least in the Midwest, and in 1920 a movement began to replace the wooden stands of Ohio Field with a modern concrete stadium. Construction of the 66,000-seat wonder commenced in 1921 with a budget of more than $1 million. Ohio Stadium would later be expanded to hold 80,000 as OSU set and maintained national records for college athletics attendance.

If old Ohio Field held any magic for OSU players, it was lost for the next several years. Wilce's 1921 team did manage a 5-2 record, the two including a surprise defeat at tiny Oberlin and a disappointing loss of the conference title to Illinois. With 3-4 in 1922, Wilce chalked up his first losing season and the team's first in 24 years, and fell to Michigan in the first loss of six straight to the Wolverines. Beyond the Michigan game, OSU lost to every other conference contender except Illinois. Iolas Huffman, at least, made All-America tackle.

The Galloping Ghost, Illinois' Red Grange, was to grab the attention – and many of the victories – in the conference for the next three years. OSU teams posted unspectacular seasons of 3-4-1, 2-3-3 and 4-3-1 but did manage

Above: *Center Gomer Jones, All-American in 1935.*

to hold Grange to just one touchdown in two games with him. The great end Harold 'Cookie' Cunningham, who excelled in baseball and basketball as well, helped prevent Grange from scoring in his career finale with Ohio State in 1925, but Illinois still won the game.

In 1926 the sun shone again on Columbus, if briefly. Wilce's eleven won its first six games, but the Buckeyes could not squelch Michigan's spectacular pass-play duo, Benny Friedman and Bennie Oosterbaan. After a traumatic 17-16 loss to the Wolverines, the Buckeyes managed to deck Illinois and cap a 7-1 season. The 190-pound guard Edwin Hess was selected an All-American for his second straight year, and honors also went to whirlwind halfback Martin Karow. Tackle Leo Raskowski was selected in 1927, but his brilliance could not keep OSU from slipping back to 4-4 and 5-2-1 seasons the next two years. Aggravated by the frustrating losing streak to Michigan, boosters grumbled that Coach Wilce should pack his bags.

Wilce wanted to return to his medical career anyway, and after 16 years as head of Buckeye football he tendered his resignation. Wilce's final team of 1928 pulled a 19-7 win over Michigan – perhaps too late – contributing to a 78-33-9 career, one that thrust Ohio State into the national sports picture.

Athletic director St John chose one of Wilce's own, assistant coach Sam Willaman, to head the football program in 1929. Yet Willaman would do little to satisfy the increasing demands of OSU partisans. Fans now wanted a man who, if not winning over the Wolverines, at least would appear to die trying, an image that quiet, unassuming Willaman could not deliver. What he delivered instead was a steady and successful, if unspectacular, coaching style that adhered to fundamentals. Willaman led the Buckeyes to a winning record for the next five seasons and developed at least one national star, the amazing Wesley Fesler, Phi Beta Kappa.

A sophomore player under Coach Wilce, Fesler had gained fame as an end in 1928, particularly in an upset of Princeton. He displayed amazing versatility, and, at 6-feet, 180 pounds, was a marvel of conditioning. In three years of Buckeye football he played defensive and offensive positions with equal ease, including stints as center, end, halfback and quarterback. Fesler was an outstanding varsity basketball center for three years as well, and in the spring starred as first baseman on the Ohio State sandlot. Considered by some to be the greatest all-around athlete in OSU history, Wes once helped the Bucks to a 11-6 baseball win over Illinois with hits for 16 total bases. He drove in all 11 runs with, consecutively, a double, a homer, another double and two grand slam homers.

His gridiron feats contributed to winning seasons of 4-3-1 and 5-2-1 in 1929 and 1930 and earned him his second and third of three consecutive All-America team selections – a rare honor. Joining Fesler on the team was his close friend Dick Larkins, who in the 1940s would become OSU's athletic director, and Stu Holcomb, who later served Purdue and Northwestern athletics.

Willaman fared even better in 1931 in spite of Fesler's absence, chalking up a 6-3 record and the most wins for OSU in a season in five years. The Buckeyes, benefiting from a repeat performance by Holcomb and the playing of halfback Lew Hinchman, guard Joe Gailus and end Sid Gilman, remained contenders for the Big Ten title right up to the last conference game, and pleased fans with a 20-7 rout of an enormously talented Michigan team.

In 1932 Willaman's eleven produced an All-American, Gailus, and managed a 4-1-3 record. The only loss – to Michigan – stuck out like a sore thumb. All eyes were on the coach to see what he could deliver in the 1933 season, as if a winning record were not enough. Willaman already had received a few outbound train schedules in the mail from ill-willed detractors.

'Sad Sam' and his team responded with a fantastic 7-1 season in 1933, holding five of eight teams scoreless, including Northwestern,

Indiana, Wisconsin and, by 75-0, Virginia. But the single loss, again, stuck in the Ohio public's craw: Michigan had delivered its second straight dump, 13-0, of the Buckeyes before an overflow crowd of 83,000. Willaman might as well have thrown in the towel right there.

He waited, though, until season's end, when he finally bowed to pressure and took the coaching spot at nearby Western Reserve, leaving behind a highly respectable 26-10-5 record and a .695 winning average. Taking over next year would be the type of personality OSU craved – Francis Schmidt.

Schmidt was everything Willaman was not. Egocentric, loud and sometimes profane, the former infantry captain was also a brilliant play strategist who had shown striking imagination in his coaching at Tulsa, Arkansas and Texas Christian University. At TCU, he had helped snare a conference title and tallied an impressive 46-6-5 record. Pop Warner's old double-wing formation still dominated the gridiron of the 1930s, but the new coach brought to OSU a sensational playbook and a habit of running up huge point leads that would earn him the nickname, 'Close-the-Gates-of-Mercy' Schmidt.

He was a pioneer of the multiple offense. His teams could scramble into any of half a dozen formations and run off literally hundreds of different plays. In what would later be called the 'I' formation, Schmidt would assemble behind the quarterback a lineup of three men, any of whom could carry the ball. Liberal use of passing, including rapid-fire combinations of laterals, forward passes and reverses, dazzled the competition. Ohio backs Stan Pincura, Dick Heekin, Damon 'Buzz' Wetzel, Jack Smith and pint-sized William 'Tippy' Dye were Schmidt's 'I' formation handymen, and

enjoyed the protection of a hard-blocking line: Gomer Jones, Merle Wendt, Charlie Hamrick, Inwood Smith and Regis Monahan.

The Buckeyes of 1934 matched Willaman's 7-1 record, but without the smarting loss to Michigan. In fact, the unusually weak Wolverine team was trampled, as were all comers but Illinois. The Illini's coach Zuppke had a few tricks up his own sleeve, and pulled the old flea flicker play – two laterals followed by a forward – to help down the Bucks 14-13, keeping them from sharing the conference title with Minnesota, a team considered by some to be the greatest ever in college football. Bernie Bierman's Golden Gophers, though not on OSU's normal play roster, remained a target in the Bucks' sights going into the fateful 1935 season.

Schmidt's already talented eleven now included stand-out sophomore back Joseph 'Jumping Joe' Williams. The Buckeyes sailed through their first five games unscathed, and with four touchdowns by Williams 'closed the gates of mercy' on Drake, 85-7. Ranked number one in the country, Ohio State and its fans eagerly welcomed undefeated Notre Dame for its sixth game of the season. It has since been voted, on more than one occasion, the greatest college ball game ever played.

Buckeye fans inundated Columbus prior to game day, creating an atmosphere of near-hysteria which eclipsed even that of the Michigan rivalry. A rash of street bonfires kept the city's fire department hopping, and the level of alcohol consumption soared to heights that challenged otherwise resourceful liquor suppliers. More than 81,000 people jammed into Ohio Stadium for the event, including sportswriters from every major wire service and columnists from the big Eastern papers. Even NBC Radio's Ted Husing was on hand to share with the rest of America what was billed as the unofficial national championship.

Coach Elmer Layden, who had played as one of Notre Dame's legendary Four Horsemen, watched his team go through a first half that seemed to spell certain defeat for the Irish. Time and again Notre Dame's strong backfield tried to move the ball against Ohio, but was firmly held back. One pass by Irish quarterback Mike Layden, younger brother of the coach, fell into the quick hands of Ohio fullback Frank Antenucci, who lateralled instantly to Franklin Boucher. The big halfback tore downfield 70 yards for a touchdown, and a kick by reserve back Dick Beltz set the score at 7-0.

Taking the ball early in the second quarter, the Buckeye line proceeded to punch huge

*Below: Notre Dame's Bill Shakespeare punts in the game versus OSU, 2 November 1935. The Irish upset the Buckeyes, 18-13.*

Above: Francis Layden, Notre Dame right halfback (in lower right of picture) heaves the pass that was turned into Ohio State's first touchdown of the November 1935 game. Frank Antenucci, Buckeye fullback, intercepted the pass and flipped a lateral to Frank Boucher, who raced 65 yards for the score.

holes in Notre Dame's forward defense. A Schmidt-inspired double-lateral play advanced the ball to the Irish three, and Jumping Joe Williams plowed through for another touchdown. Beltz missed the extra point, but OSU took a solid 13-0 lead to the locker room at halftime.

During the break, Grantland Rice told the press, 'This Ohio State team in the first half has shown me the greatest display of football I've ever witnessed!' Colleague Paul Gallico quipped, 'It'll take Congressional action to stop these guys.'

But Layden had other ideas, and sent in his entire second string line to serve with the starting backfield. Backs Layden, Jim Miller, Bill Shakespeare and Andy Pilney began chipping away at a tiring Buckeye defense. In the fourth quarter a pass by Pilney set the ball at the Ohio two, and seconds later Miller fell on the line for a touchdown.

Notre Dame missed the extra point and with 14 minutes to play still lagged behind Ohio, 13-6. Time seemed to be running too swiftly for the Irish. Miller fumbled on the next drive, and Notre Dame did not take regain possession until the four-minute mark. But brilliant passing by Pilney put the ball at the Ohio 33, then the 15, and finally into the hands of Layden who tore before a stunned crowd into the end zone for a touchdown.

Notre Dame's Willy Fromhart missed the extra point, and with OSU ahead 13-12, Buckeye fans still believed the game was over. Who would have guessed that Beltz would fumble the ball on the next play from scrimmage? Notre Dame had found one last chance, one last minute with the ball against OSU's reserve defense. The bigger, older linemen had been pulled by Schmidt in the fourth quarter, and rules prevented them from rejoining the game.

Pilney managed to run the ball to the Ohio 19 before being brought down for good – aides needed a stretcher to take him away. Replacement Shakespeare pitched the ball again, and this time Ohio's Beltz popped up for an interception – almost. Beltz lost his grip and the ball skittered away, the play incomplete. With just twenty seconds left, Shakespeare took the snap and desperately streaked between charging Ohio linemen, searching for a receiver. In the end zone he spotted Wayne Milner, and a split second later the big end was pulling in the ball for six points.

Horrified OSU fans didn't even notice Notre Dame's futile extra point attempt, or the last-ditch pass play by Ohio. As an overjoyed Irish team ran frenzied about the field, the Buckeyes stared in disbelief at the scoreboard: OSU had lost, 18-13. Perhaps only Schmidt believed it. As pandemonium ensued, he managed to run across the field to shake Layden's hand. A half an hour later many fans still sat dumbfounded in the stands.

It was the beginning of the end for Schmidt, who would never live down the defeat in spite of a 34-0 rout of Michigan, a 7-1 season finish and a share of the 1935 conference title beside the mighty Minnesota Gophers. OSU contributed the line trio of Wendt, Jones and Smith to All-American teams. Notre Dame subsequently lost to Northwestern, a team which Ohio, ironically enough, had earlier squashed by three touchdowns.

The Irish victory over Ohio State still rankled in the memories of OSU boosters in the following three seasons, during which the Buckeyes compiled records of 5-3, 6-2 and 4-3-1. Schmidt committed the cardinal sin of tilting ever more sharply to subjective judgement of coaching. He lost to Notre Dame again in 1936, 7-2; and his team was squeezed out of conference championship twice in his last five years (no matter that OSU snared it in 1939 with a 6-2 season). Worse, he continued to manage the football team as a dictator, alienating not only his own staff but also many players, university officials and alumni.

Schmidt's last two games with Michigan resulted in disaster, dealt by Wolverine star Tom Harmon, and a 1940 slate of 4-4 was the final straw. A sullen Schmidt resigned at season's end, his legacy a shining 39-16-1 record and a .705 winning average. The coach accepted a job at Idaho, where he served two years until his death.

Several players benefitted enough from Schmidt's drill-sergeant coaching to attain All-America honors in his last years. Among them were guard Gust Zarnas in 1937 and, two years later, triple-threat halfback Don Scott and end Esco Sarkkinen. Both were effective in defensive and offensive positions, Scott sharing the same brand of versatility that Iowa's star, Nile Kinnick, enjoyed. Like Kinnick, Scott was lost while serving as a flyer in World War II.

Replacing Coach Schmidt was one of his own assistants, Paul Brown. The methodical, no-nonsense young man of 32 was a proven winner at Massillon High School, which, under Brown's coaching, had not lost a game in six years. Brown placed renewed emphasis on the fundamentals, relying often on the double-wing but adding an occasional twist with the increasingly popular T formation.

Brown had to work with whatever talent was available in wartime, but he managed to produce good players and winning records in his three years at Columbus. He helped Jack Graf, who had been a mere substitute for two seasons, become Big Ten MVP material in 1941. Graf figured prominently in a zig-zag 20-20 tie with Michigan, a game that saw the teams trade off a total of six touchdowns and four extra points. Ohio State closed the season at 6-1-1.

The Buckeyes went a step further in 1942, thanks largely to the talents of quarterback George Lynn and halfbacks Leslie Horvath, Paul Sarringhaus and Tommy James, to take the conference title with a 9-1 record. The amazing end-tackle-guard trio of Bob Shaw, Charles Csuri and Lindell Houston was the first ever to be named All-America simultaneously. Only Boston College ranked above OSU nationally; Boston lost its last game of the season, and Ohio won over a tough Iowa service team that had lost only to Notre Dame. Within the odd parameters of wartime athletics the Buckeyes had nevertheless nabbed their first national title.

By 1943, however, all of the talent had been drafted. Brown fielded a team comprised of freshmen and 4-F draftees for a 3-6 season and then joined the military himself, going on to coach the team at Great Lakes Naval Training Center in Chicago. He appointed assistant coach Carroll Widdoes to fill his shoes in his absence, but when the war ended Brown chose to manage and coach Cleveland's professional ball team, leaving mild-mannered Widdoes in charge at OSU.

Widdoes certainly lucked out when Les Horvath returned from Army duty in 1944 on a deferment for dental studies. The mature Horvath became the captain and moral leader of a fuzzy-cheeked freshman team. Along with freshman backs Bob Brugge, Dick Flannagan and Ollie Cline, and another All-American line trio of Bill Willis, Warren Amling and Bill Hackette, Horvath helped chalk up a perfect 9-0 season. Particularly satisfying was the season-closer, a victory over Michigan at 18-14, in which Horvath scored all three Ohio touchdowns. Horvath led the league in passing and rushing and became OSU's first-ever Heisman Trophy winner, and the unassuming Widdoes was surprised to be named Coach of the Year by his fellow coaches.

Widdoes enjoyed another successful year in 1945, 7-2, as did Warren Amling, who repeated as All-American, and Ollie Cline, chosen conference MVP. But even with a winning percentage of .889 under his belt, Widdoes decided that the stress of Big Ten coaching did not suit his personality. He became the first head coach to ask for a demotion to his prior post as an assistant and to recommend that his job be given to an aide, Paul Bixler. Bixler managed only a 4-3-2 season before moving on to coach at Colgate, and new athletic director Dick Larkins looked no further than former teammate and star Wes Fesler for a replacement.

Fesler, who had coached at Princeton and Pittsburgh in the prior two seasons, made a slow start in 1947 with a youthful, inexperienced team. Yet Buckeye fans were caught up in the struggling spirit of the squad. Amazingly, Fesler was spared the usual loud criticism when he delivered a 2-6-1 season, which placed OSU in the basement of conference standings for the first time. The next year, Fesler lost a few more players to professional teams, as he had in 1947, but led his maturing team to a 6-3 record.

Everything finally clicked for the Buckeyes in 1949, with the combined skills of quarterback Pandel Savic, a Yugoslavian immigrant, sophomore Victor Janowicz and others. Fesler had assembled a team of comeback darlings who pulled out most of their wins from crises. 'We never really felt comfortable until we fell behind and had to rally,' Fesler later kidded.

And rally they did to achieve a 7-1-2 season, the Big Ten championship and a trip to the Rose Bowl. As in so many other wins that year, the Buckeyes pulled out a heart-stopping victory over California, breaking a tie in the final two minutes with a field goal by Jimmy Hague to win 17-14. Yet for the first time since 1919 OSU failed to put a player on the All-America teams.

The 1950 season proved even more nerve-wracking. The team, aided by versatile halfback Janowicz and sophomore quarterback Tony Curcillo, began the season with a 32-27

*Above: Quarterback Don Scott, 1938.*

Above: *Aerial view of the infamous 'Blizzard Bowl', Michigan vs Ohio State, 1950.*

Above: *Wes Fesler.*

loss in the final moments of a match with Southern Methodist. The Bucks then embarked on a six-win rampage that included a 83-21 trouncing of Iowa and put OSU first in national rankings. But an underdog Illini team upset the Bucks 14-7, throwing the conference into a three-way battle for the crown between OSU, Illinois and Michigan. The Bucks were raring to come back and beat rival Michigan the next weekend to secure the Rose Bowl bid, but their biggest challenge turned out to be an unexpected one: a severe snowstorm that started the Friday before the game.

By Saturday afternoon parts of Ohio had been covered with two feet of snow and chilled by near-zero temperatures. Just why athletic officials allowed a game to be played in arctic conditions no one knows today; probably the arrival of 50,000 stalwart fans had something to do with it. Scores of Cub Scout ushers were called in to help cut and rip up the frozen Ohio Stadium tarpaulin, and the infamous 'Blizzard Bowl' was under way.

What ensued would, had it not been for the discomfort of the players and any fans who remained sober, have to be termed less football than comedy. Passing the ball became a near impossibility, as did running for any distance or, for that matter, making any real contact on the line of scrimmage. All that was left was the punt, itself no mean feat, considering that new snow kept the field a white quagmire. Simply seeing through the snow to other players and yard markers was a challenge.

Michigan tailback Chuck Ortmann punted a record 24 times for a total of 723 yards, nearly matched by Janowicz's 672 yards from 21 kicks. Ortmann slipped six yards to record Michigan's longest run in a 27-yard rushing total. Ohio State managed to rush 25, no thanks to poor Janowicz who, in spite of slosh-ing 11 yards for the game's longest run, carried 19 times for a net *loss* of nine yards. Michigan completed none of nine pass attempts; OSU fared better with 13 of 18 completed.

Janowicz somehow kicked a field goal for three points, but two of his punts, both made dangerously close to the OSU goal, were blocked. The first rolled across the line for an automatic Wolverine safety; the other was smothered by Michigan's Tony Momsen in the end zone for a touchdown. An extra point gave the Wolverines a 9-3 lead that continued through the second half and put them on the road to the Tournament of Roses.

Buckeye fans had barely recovered from the worst snowstorm in Ohio history and the most bizarre game yet played in the Big Ten, when Wes Fesler turned in his resignation for 'health reasons.' Reportedly on the verge of a nervous breakdown, Fesler told a friend, 'I was in the training room during the football season more often than the players – getting treatment for my head and neck.' Soon enough Fesler had a change of heart for football and barely two months later accepted the head coaching spot at Minnesota.

The only good news concerned Janowicz, who had led the league in scoring and offensive yardage and earned a triple honor: the Heisman Trophy, All-America selection and the conference MVP award. Joining him on the All-America team were Buckeyes Bob Momsen at guard and center Bob McCullough.

During the winter eight hopefuls interviewed for Fesler's job, and there was talk of a return by Paul Brown, whose campus visit was cheered by a huge mob of OSU students. When the Board of Trustees finally made its choice on 18 February 1951 it could not have known that it was beginning a new era – colorful and controversial – in Ohio State football, one that would span almost three decades. The Buckeyes' new coach was Wayne Woodrow Hayes.

'Woody' Hayes came from the head coaching job at Miami University in Ohio, where he had established a 13-5 record over two years, 1949 and 1950. Previously, at alma mater Denison, Hayes had amassed 18 straight victories. Aside from his professional record, Hayes impressed athletic director Dick Larkins and the board with his war experience – he had commanded a PT boat and a destroyer escort in the Pacific – and with his sheer enthusiasm. He promised to 'kick, scratch and churn up as much hell as I have to,' and, oh, how he delivered in the years ahead.

OSU boosters, students and alums who hadn't even heard of Hayes could be impressed by one thing only: victory over the dreaded

gained recognition as an outstanding guard, and represented OSU on the All-America team.

Ohio State football was also blessed with a freshman halfback named Howard Cassady. The 5-foot 11-inch, 175-pounder scored three touchdowns in his thrilling debut, a rout of Indiana, and rushed 119 yards in an upset of heavily-favored Wisconsin.

Most important, the Buckeyes smashed visitor Michigan 27-7 and giddily carried Hayes from the field on their shoulders. Among them were backs Robert Watkins and David Leggett, who would soon be writing OSU history with the help of fullback Hubert Bobo, the first charger in a series that was Hayes' offensive trademark.

For Coach Hayes 1954 was the year of affirmation. He had once again narrowly escaped hostile booster sentiment, which after a 6-3 season in 1953 and a crushing defeat at Michigan was ready to boot him back to Denison. That animus only served to strengthen Woody's already ample resolve to win. His men matched that commitment in spirit and form, taking on all the characteristics of a classic Hayes team; outstanding line blocking; discipline and executional skills that kept fumbling and penalties to a minimum; and an emphasis on an efficient, clockwork running game that downplayed the forward pass.

Hayes' 'machine' began the season by rolling over Illinois 28-0, and systematically mashed each successive opponent, including Number 2-ranked Wisconsin. In that game, Hopalong Cassady drew national attention by leading a three-touchdown rampage, including an 88-yard dash on an interception, that brought trailing OSU to a 31-14 victory. Hayes later called Hoppie's run 'the most spectacular play in 20 years of football in our stadium.' Victories over Pittsburgh and Purdue led to a dramatic finale with Michigan which would catapult the winner to the Rose Bowl.

The game was a 7-7 stalemate by the third quarter, but tension mounted as Michigan successfully drove to the Ohio one-yard line for a first down. Little breath was drawn in the stadium as the two mighty lines crashed together again and again. The Buckeye defense, led by mastodonic Jim Parker, performed the impossible and held the Wolverines to as little as 12 inches of turf for four downs.

After the turnover OSU methodically pushed the ball all the way back in 12 plays to the Michigan end zone for a winning touchdown. Three consecutive sneaks by quarterback Leggett for a first down and a 52-yard run by Cassady contributed to the campaign. The

*Left: Rushing star Howard 'Hopalong' Cassady earned the Heisman Trophy in 1955.*

*Below: Halfback Victor Janowicz won the Heisman Trophy in 1950, as well as All-America honors and a selection as conference MVP.*

Wolverines of Ann Arbor. But in 1951 it was not to be. Hayes inaugurated his OSU career with a 4-3-2 season, including a 7-0 loss to Michigan. He also got off to a bad start with his players, who resented being called 'muscleheads' in his press interviews, twice-daily gut-busting practice sessions and even a ban on singing in the shower.

Hayes answered critics and those who would oust him with his trademark modesty. 'I probably muffed a lot of chances to be a nice guy, but . . . I despise losing,' he said. 'I despise it, and if I honestly didn't believe we could get on the victory wagon next year, I'd resign right now.' Enough people – the people with power in OSU athletics – were sufficiently impressed to lend their support.

Hayes repaid them in 1952 by temporarily easing up on his crew – less yelling, more humor and a season record of 6-3. He worked to develop young quarterback John Borton while shifting Curcillo to defense – a controversial move, considering Curcillo had set a new conference mark for yards gained (308) against Iowa in 1951. But the move paid off as Borton completed 115 of 196 passes in 1952 for a new record. Teammate Mike Takacs also

Buckeyes capped the day with another 12-play drive, this time for 62 yards, ending with a Cassady touchdown and a final score of 21-7. The OSU marching band, which Hayes unsuccessfully had asked to stay off the field at halftime so as not to mutilate the turf, struck up 'California Here I Come,' and the Bucks gave their grouchy coach an impromptu shower-room dunking.

The team was the first in the conference since Amos Stagg's 1913 Chicago Maroons to go undefeated to the league championship. The Buckeyes lived up to the honor by defeating Southern California 20-7, and Cassady was selected All-American by unanimous vote.

Hayes' challenge of living up to that stellar 1954 season was all the more difficult the next year because only four of his starting eleven returned. Fortunately, they included Cassady and Jim Parker, but a new quarterback was needed to replace Leggett and a fullback to replace Bobo, who had been dropped because of poor academic standing.

In putting Frank Elwood, a mediocre passer but a brilliant academic, in Leggett's spot, Coach Hayes cemented an offensive style that would stand for decades: 'Three yards and a cloud of dust.' Fans whined that it lacked the excitement of aerial play, but Woody didn't care. He once sniffed, 'There are three things that can happen on a forward pass, and two of them are bad.'

Boring or not, the ball-control strategy led the Buckeyes to another Big Ten championship in 1955, garnering the first back-to-back pair of titles since 1917. Because conference rules prevented two consecutive Rose Bowl appearances the Bucks could only take joy in preventing rival Michigan from participating. They did so, delivering a 17-0 shutout that was Hayes' first victory in Ann Arbor and his 13th straight win for Ohio State. As the Wolverines' hopes for California sank late in the game, Buckeye fans shouted, 'Unpack! Unpack! You guys aren't going anywhere!' The game could barely be finished; one fight after another broke out on the gridiron. Michigan sustained six penalties, OSU two, and both sustained double penalties that cancelled each other. Two Wolverines were even ejected from play.

The Bucks had passed a mere 13 yards average per game that season, yet they ran for 310, a near-record. National superstar Cassady had rushed for 711 yards during the season with a six-yard average carry, and he had made 11 touchdowns for 66 points scored. It was no surprise when the 'redheaded speedster,' as some writers called him, was awarded the Heisman Trophy, the same honor accorded to

earlier. Buckeye legends Chic Harley and Les Horvath.

Not long after season's end Hayes became embroiled in the first of many controversies during his tenure at OSU. A *Sports Illustrated* article quoted Hayes as saying he had, over several years, given small loans to financially needy players out of a nominal TV-appearance income. Though Hayes' assistance was no doubt well-intentioned, it was also forbidden by Big Ten rules, and Commissioner Tug Wilson slapped Ohio State with a one-year conference probation that would rule out a Rose Bowl bid for another year.

With Cassady's departure to play with the Detroit Lions, OSU football fortunes slipped somewhat in 1956, the Bucks achieving a 6-3 record. Parker enjoyed a fantastic farewell season, winning the Outland Award as the nation's best interior lineman and a spot on the All-America team.

But by 1957 Hayes was back on track and out of Big Ten probation. He seemed more of a curmudgeon to some, less accommodating to the press which had 'burned' him and more resistant than ever to critics of his bulldozer-style ground offense. Another bright but weak-passing quarterback, Frank Kremblas, was installed in the backfield, flanked by Don Clark and Dick LeBeau at halfback and by fullbacks Galen Cisco and Bob White.

The team stumbled in its first game with Texas Christian, losing 18-14, but recovered to mount a tremendous nine-game winning streak that carried OSU all the way to the national championship and a Rose Bowl victory over the Oregon Ducks. White became the star of the season with a now-legendary performance before the favored Hawkeyes of Iowa. In its last offensive drive of the game, with OSU behind 13-10, Kremblas used White like a pile driver. He gave White the ball repeatedly — seven out of eight times — and hammered inside, outside and over tackle for a total of 66 yards, ultimately dragging two Hawkeyes with him over the goal line for an OSU victory. It was the kind of classic Hayes strategy that won him his first Coach of the Year honors from his peers.

The next season, at 6-1-2, was less dramatic, but saw standout performances in a game with Number 1 Iowa that Hayes later termed 'the greatest offensive contest I've ever been in.' In a closely matched battle it was Clark and again White who made spectacular gains of 152 and 209 yards, respectively, this time devastating the Iowa defense not only with short-run rabbit-punches but also long gains. At season's end Buckeye end Jim Houston, tackle Jim

Above: *The great Wayne Woodrow 'Woody' Hayes treated Buckeyes fans to historic displays and 27 years of superb football from 1951 to 1978. His 'three yards and cloud of dust' philosophy helped him to amass a tremendous career total of 238-72-10, 14 Big Ten titles and a .759 winning percentage, one of the five highest in football history.*

Marshall and the indomitable White were named All-Americans, with White having rushed a total of 713 yards with, amazingly, *no* losses on his 178 carries.

Woody Hayes posted his first losing season – 3-5-1 – in 1959, his team lacking the talent of earlier squads, but came back with a 7-2 record in 1960 thanks to the strengths of quarterback Tom Matte and All-America fullback Bob Ferguson. Yet Hayes made more enemies than ever with the press, slugging a Los Angeles sportswriter in 1959 following a loss to USC's Trojans and barring writers from the locker room after enduring a humiliation from Michigan.

Prospects continued to brighten for the coach, who had recruited backs Paul Warfield and Matt Snell. The 1961 squad was one of Hayes' best and amassed a 8-0-1 championship record using a running attack that averaged 371 yards and 20 first downs per game. After the defeat of Michigan 50-20, a perfect capper would have been a Rose Bowl game. But the Big Ten had withdrawn from its pact with Pasadena, and the OSU faculty opted not to accept a match. Students at Columbus reacted with a near riot on campus and could be quieted only by the football players themselves in a plea for peace. Ferguson repeated on the Big Ten's All-America lineup.

In 1962 and 1963 the Buckeyes failed to provide the same sort of spectacle fans had come to rely on. But Hayes maintained support by successfully battling to reinstate Rose Bowl eligibility, chalking up winning seasons of 6-3 and 5-3-1 and beating Michigan for two more consecutive victories.

A third would have made 1964 near-perfect. Except for an upset by Penn State, the Buckeyes enjoyed a stellar year, thanks in part to quarterback Don Unverferth, one of the best passers in OSU history. The team went into the Michigan bout with seven wins and one loss: The victor would earn a trip to the Rose Bowl. But Bo Rein, sophomore halfback, fumbled a punt return late in the first half, his hands stiffened by subfreezing temperatures. The Wolverines recovered and in two plays converted Rein's slip into a winning touchdown. The Bucks settled for a 7-2 record and placed safety Arnie Chonko, linebacker Dwight "Ike" Kelly and tackle Jim Davidson on All-America teams.

Woody Hayes had to pull together an almost all-new team in 1965, although he benefited from Kelly's return. Yet the squad proved remarkably talented, falling only to North Carolina in the season opener, 14-3, and to an outstanding Michigan State team, 32-7.

Ohio State finished as runner-up in the Big Ten for a second straight year. Kelly repeated on the All-America team and was joined by tackle Doug Van Horn.

The Buckeyes of 1966 were leaner still on talent, and Hayes produced his second losing record with 4-5, though at least Ray Pryor, who played center, made All-America. Hayes embarked on a recruiting drive in the early months of 1967 and pulled together a scrappy bunch of freshmen that would become his greatest squad ever. Coaches at rival schools could hardly believe the collection of talent Hayes, who had recently been criticized for a weak recruiting program, had somehow pulled together. After fielding a you-ain't-seen-nothin'-yet team in 1967 for a 6-3 season, Hayes put 13 of the recruits, now sophomores, into starting positions on the varsity to see what they could do.

What they did was to win 27 of their 29 games during their years at Ohio State. Hayes' 'Super Team' had arrived.

Among the Supermen were quarterbacks Ron Maciejowski and the amazing Rex Kern, whose 'magic ballhandling' would mark him as the nation's top collegiate quarterback for the next three years. Flanking them in the backfield were halfbacks Leo Hayden, Larry Zelina and John Brockington, and the great Jim Otis at fullback. Defense starred the

*Above: Star of the 1957 season, fullback Bob White smashed his way through the opposition to gain the Big Ten championship and a Rose Bowl victory for the Buckeyes.*

famous trio of backs Tim Anderson, Mike Sensibaugh and John Tatum. All were welded, physically and emotionally, into a virtually faultless football machine.

As freshmen they had terrorized their elders, the varsity team, in every practice scrimmage, and as starting sophomores they laid waste to the entire Big Ten roster. The Buckeyes went undefeated throughout the entire 1968 season, even bombing Michigan 50-14, for the conference title and a berth in the Rose Bowl. The

undefeated team rolled into Pasadena and used a crushing defense to hold Southern California's own 'Super Back,' O J Simpson, to 137 yards on 18 carries in the first half, and just 34 yards on 10 second-half carries.

With little dramatic offensive play OSU downed the Trojans 27-16, emerging triumphant in its first Rose Bowl in 11 years and taking the national title. O J is said to have dashed to the OSU dressing room after the game to shout, 'You're the best team I ever played against!' At the season's close, senior offensive tackles David Foley and Rufus Mayes were accorded All-America honors.

Throughout the following season the nation fully believed that Ohio State, the greatest college ball team of the modern era, simply could not be beaten. The Bucks made winning routine, picking off contestants almost effortlessly, and in some cases by huge margins: Illinois fell 41-0 and Texas Christian was swamped 62-0. Fans paid more attention to the fact that Hayes, who always was seen wearing a short-sleeve shirt regardless of sideline temperatures, finally donned a fuzzy red coat during the Purdue game, perhaps confusing and distracting the opponent into a 42-13 defeat.

After plastering Wisconsin 62-7 for its 21st consecutive win, OSU seemed destined to go undefeated for a second straight season. But fate finally interceded, and at the worst possible place, Ann Arbor, Michigan, with a loss to a fiesty pack of Wolverines. OSU managed to keep above water for the first half but for

*Left: Mike Sensibaugh (3) punts, 1968.*

*Below: Game action, 1968: fullback Jim Otis (35) crashes through with help from the offensive line.*

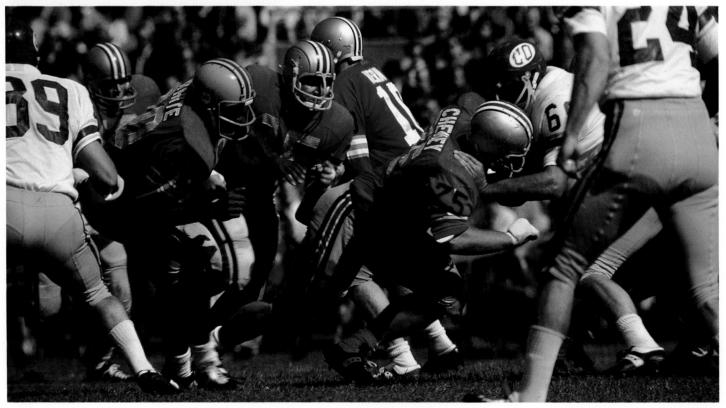

*Above: Quarterback Rex Kern (10), an integral part of Woody Hayes' 'Super Team' which wreaked havoc during the 1968-70 seasons. In 1968 and again in 1970 the Buckeyes went undefeated for the season, and in 1968 returned from Pasadena with a Rose Bowl victory to their credit.*

dence as they journeyed to California, and the players, subjected to Woody's usual harsh drilling the moment they arrived, finally rebelled and demanded a more relaxed practice schedule. Only after they threatened to quit the game did an infuriated Hayes relent. Whether mixed emotions contributed to OSU's downfall is not certain, but the unstoppable 1970 Buckeyes were finally stopped by Stanford, 27-17, in their farewell performance on New Year's Day 1971.

The year ended with a bumper crop of All-America selections. Stillwagon and Tatum were chosen once more, joined by Sensibaugh, Anderson, end Jan White and Brockington, who streaked for 1142 yards and 17 TDs. From that stable of talent, 17 seniors were graduated in the spring, leaving Hayes with a nearly blank slate. Only center Tom DeLeone remained. the usual solid defense combined with a ho-hum offense to produce a 6-4 season, and DeLeone made All-America. Most memorable was a nationally-televised temper tantrum by Hayes who, upset by an official's call during an ill-fated game at Ann Arbor, tore linemarkers off the sidelines and snapped them over his knee. 'They can call me anything,' Hayes once said, 'just so they don't call me a "nice old man." '

The Big Ten's new freshmen eligibility rule brought Hayes fresh talent in 1972, including the incredible Archie Griffin, a high school gridiron star from football's own home town, Columbus. This 185-pound tornado gave OSU boosters a sample of things to come in his starter against North Carolina: The tailback ran for 239 yards in seven carries. The only blemish on OSU's conference record that year was an upset by Michigan State, but it didn't keep the Buckeyes from Rose Bowl play. After assaulting a nosy newspaper photographer just before kickoff, Hayes was dealt his second loss in five trips to Pasadena. Southern California handily dispatched the Bucks 42-17, the biggest margin ever scored against a Hayes-coached OSU team. But defensive leaders Randy Gradishar and John Hicks shone in All-America lineups. Sharing the limelight was fullback Harold Henson, who led the nation in scoring with 120 points and 20 TDs.

Sophomore Griffin arrived at full-blown superstar status the following season by running for 1577 yards, carrying 30 times for 246 yards in the Michigan game alone. Hayes again proved one could win football through defense, and his mammoth line in 1973 held all Big Ten comers to a paltry 43 point total. The Bucks easily rolled over Minnesota 57-7; Iowa, 55-13; Northwestern, by the biggest

some reason took its offense to the air in the second. Hayes shuddered as he watched half a dozen of Kern's passes being intercepted and Michigan topple OSU 24-12. But the conference co-champions were richly praised at season's end, with All-America teams scooping up Kern, who had contributed 1585 offensive yards; Otis, with 1027 yards and 15 touchdowns; and Stillwagon, Tatum and senior tackle Ted Provost.

The Bucks and their rambunctious coach were all but tasting revenge on Michigan by the end of the 1970 season, one which again saw an unbeaten Buckeye team dominate the national football scene. Michigan, too, had gone undefeated and 'clash of the titans' would have been a fair moniker for the bout. This time OSU played a straight ball-control offense. Combining it with the usual monolithic defense force, the Bucks carried the day with a 20-9 slap to Michigan and prepared to repeat history in sunny Pasadena.

The Big Ten champs exuded unusual confi-

Above: *Astounding tailback Archie Griffin (45) shows the Hoosiers how the game is played at Ohio Stadium, 1975. Hayes' greatest star, Griffin became the only collegiate athlete ever to win the Heisman Trophy twice, and was selected to All-America teams three times in his dazzling career with the Buckeyes.*

OSU victory margin ever at 60-0; Michigan State, 35-0; and Illinois, 30-0. The Michigan game once again represented the conference title and a Rose Bowl berth, and an all-time record 105,223 football fans invaded Ann Arbor for the event.

Each team fought gallantly, and each won a half of the game, figuratively and literally, resulting in a 10-10 tie. The conference had to vote which of the undefeated teams would represent at the Rose Bowl; OSU, considered the more likely to win for the Big Ten at Pasadena, was given the nod, much to the outrage of Wolverine coach Bo Schembechler. The Buckeyes lived up to the honor and trampled USC 42-21. Snaring All-America honors for a second time were Hicks and Gradishar, joined by first-timers Griffin and defensive end Van DeCree.

The 1974 season seemed a carbon-copy of the year prior, with Hayes' machine shaking the Midwest for another ten wins. The only bitter medicine was dispensed by Michigan State, in a narrow 16-13 defeat. But the Bucks overcame the Wolverines 12-10, setting the two teams in yet another tie for the conference title and the Rose Bowl honors. And once again, the conference voted to send Hayes' tribe against USC. Hayes accepted with grace and seemed determined to revamp his poor image among the West Coast press by playing

the role of a good-natured gentleman during his visit to Pasadena. Players were asked to practice just once a day, not the usual twice, and even were allowed to spend their breakfast money on pizza.

But image wasn't enough, and the Bucks took a heartbreak loss to the Trojans by a score of 18-17. Nothing could tarnish the brilliant season of Archie Griffin, however, who became the fourth man in Ohio State football history, and one of the few underclassmen ever, to win the coveted Heisman Trophy. The tailback, who had rushed for a phenomenal 1695 yards and 12 touchdowns, also repeated All-America standing, as did DeCree. A wave of newcomers piled onto the same team for an unheard-of OSU contribution of seven men: stunning tackles Kurt Schumacher and Pete Cusick, center Steve Meyers, back Neal Colzie and punt kicker Tom Skladany. 'I'd love to win the national championship,' the modest Griffin said, 'and if trading this award for a win over Michigan State would mean being Number 1 . . . yes, I'd trade it.'

The 1975 season brought OSU a retaliatory 21-0 victory over MSU in the Buckeye's season opener. Hayes went on to lead his team to eleven straight regular-season victories, including a decisive win over Michigan 21-14. Behind a marauding defense led by safety Tim Fox, Hayes' sixth undefeated team led the

Above: *Fullback Pete Johnson (33) rolls in for a touchdown in 1976.*

Above left: *Coach Earle Bruce in a characteristic pose, 1979. Though neither as cranky nor quite as successful as his predecessor Woody Hayes, he continues to produce winning teams at Ohio State.*

nation in scoring with 374 points, an average of 34 per game. Junior fullback Pete Johnson topped the count with no less than 26 TDs for 156 points.

Griffin slashed and darted for 1450 yards and became the only athlete in collegiate history to win the Heisman a second time. Again he would have preferred a national title, but that remained elusive: UCLA toppled Number 1-ranked OSU in its fourth straight Rose Bowl appearance, the Bucks dazed by the shining pass plays of Bruin quarterback John Sciarra. Hayes had blown his eighth, and final Rose Bowl bid. But the Big Ten leaders were showered again with All-America choices, including repeats for Skladany and Griffin (Archie's third) and first-time picks of Fox and Ted Smith.

Hayes slipped a bit in his next two seasons at OSU, producing a 9-2-1 record in 1976 that included a 27-10 rout of former assistant coach Bill Mallory's Colorado Buffs at the Orange Bowl. The slate was 9-3-0 in 1977, with Hayes posting a co-championship with Michigan for two straight, but OSU ended the year with an embarrassing 35-6 blow by Bear Bryant's Alabama team. Both years were marked by painful losses to the Wolverines, 22-0 and 14-6, that did little to bolster Buckeye fans' spirits or improve Hayes' irascible nature, even though All-America honors were given to Skladany

for a rare third-year selection, and to Bob Brudzinski, Tom Cousineau and, both years, Chris Ward.

Things came to a head in 1978 when Hayes' Buckeyes dropped one more notch for a 7-4-1 season and another humiliation at the hands of Michigan, 14-3. At the previous Michigan game, a frustrated Hayes had punched out an ABC-TV cameraman on the sidelines. This year, at the Gator Bowl, Woody's temper finally became his undoing. With two minutes left in a game with Clemson, the Bucks trailing 17-15, Charlie Bauman intercepted an OSU pass and hurtled across the sidelines near Hayes. The great coach angrily shook the Clemson linebacker by his face guard, and a Buckeye who tried to intervene got punched in the face. Just hours later Hayes' three-decade career at OSU was history.

The 1978 season was the first in seven years in which the Buckeyes failed to conquer or share in the conference championship. Ken Fritz made All-American, and Cousineau was selected a second time, but sadness prevailed as OSU boosters adjusted to the idea of a new coach, Earle Bruce, knowing that an era had ended. Hayes, putting aside his infamous role of loudmouth, insisted that he had gotten what he had coming. 'Let's let it go at that,' he told the press quietly.

At 65 Hayes faded into retirement in

Above: *Running back Keith Byars (41) flies over his teammates toward a touchdown in this 1984 game against Michigan State. He led the nation in 1984 with 1655 yards rushing.*

Top right: *Wearing his trademark sneer and shirtsleeves, Woody Hayes surveys his team's performance during his last season as coach, 1978.*

Above right: *Quarterback Jim Karsatos (16) wheels and looks for his man, 1985. Coach Bruce made use of Karsatos' passing skills to achieve a total of 2311 yards passing in 1985, 25 yards more than rushing for the season.*

Columbus, resting comfortably on laurels of a 238-72-10 career, 14 Big Ten Titles and an enviable .759 winning percentage, one of the five highest in football history. He was the only man elected Coach of the Year three times by his peers. Woody spent his last years as an ardent supporter of OSU football and occasional advisor to Bruce. He died quietly in his sleep early in 1987.

Earle Bruce, his predecessor's assistant and the keeper of the Hayes style, didn't miss a beat in rallying the Buckeyes back to glory. In 1979, OSU regained the conference title, stomping undefeated through the regular season to meet USC at the Rose Bowl. Quarterback Art Schlichter contributed 2246 yards to the offensive, helping to tally 374 points for the season. But another narrow defeat was handed out by a clever Trojan team, and the Buckeyes struggled unsuccessfully to revisit Pasadena for the

next several years.

Beginning in 1980 Bruce began to compile the kind of record – successful, but to Columbus football fanatics boring – that would give him the nickname, 'Ol' Nine-and-Three Earle.' In fact, Earle's record was exactly 9-3-0 for six straight seasons; it qualified the Buckeyes for a co-championship with Iowa in 1981, but never for the Rose Bowl.

A coach in any other town would be glad to win nine games a year, and to produce the players and numbers Bruce did. Schlichter continued to rack up offense yardage, reaching a peak of 2392 in 1981, with Tim Spencer rushing for 1371 of it. In 1982, back Marcus Marek starred on defense and took All-America honors. And a new star was born in 1983 with the addition of running back Keith Byars who went on to make All-America teams and led the nation in 1984 with 1655 yards.

In his endless quest for the title Bruce in 1985 mounted an effective passing attack, radical for OSU, using the talents of junior quarterback Jim Karsatos, who made 2311 yards to help OSU average 25 more yards passing than rushing for the season. Bruce had every reason to be pleased. Although persisting in his '9-3 complex,' by season's end he had helped Ohio State to become one of the winningest teams in football history: 598-236-48 over 96 years, for a whopping .705 percentage!

In 1986 he broke out of the 9-3 rut with a 10-3 season and contributed wide receiver Cris Carter and linebacker Chris Spielman to All-America. Woody Hayes would have been happy to hear about this well-deserved success. 'Without winners,' he said, 'there wouldn't be any civilization.'

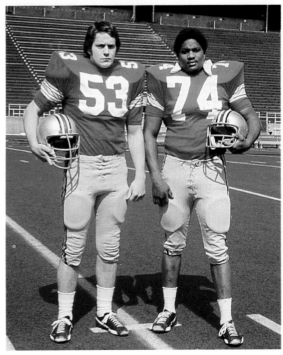

Above: *Quarterback Art Schlichter in 1979.*

Left: *Star defensemen Randy Gradishar (53) and John Hicks (74) in 1973.*

Top: *Wide receiver Cris Carter (2) reels one in vs Texas A & M, 1987.*

# PURDUE UNIVERSITY

Founded: 1869

Location: West Lafayette, Indiana

Total Enrollment: 31,987

Colors: Old Gold and Black

Nickname: Boilermakers

Page 160: *Purdue quarterback Scott Campbell (10) in 1981.*

Right: *Blond powerhouse Elmer 'Ollie' Oliphant arrived at Purdue in 1910 and went on to become one of the finest all-around athletes ever to come out of the Big Ten. A hefty and speedy runner, it normally took several tacklers to bring him down; his punting and dropkicking saved the day for the Boilermakers on several memorable occasions.*

Why are they called the Boilermakers?

The first thing anybody wants to know about Purdue football is how the team got its odd nickname, perhaps the most esoteric in all of college sports. The answer is simple, but it's *not* that the team enjoys a shot of whiskey with every glass of beer. Rather, it has to do with the fact that at the time Purdue University was founded, its home of West Lafayette, Indiana was known mostly for its foundries and for the workmen who toiled to produce many of the nation's steam-generating boilers.

Thus the sons of those industrialist forefathers proudly bore the 'Boilermaker' name when Purdue played its first football game in 1887, a somewhat humbling loss to Butler College 48-6. They had a little more to be proud about two years later when Purdue scored its first victory, 34-10, over DePauw, and in 1892, when the team went undefeated against eight contenders by outscoring them 320-24. In 1893 the Boilermakers had grown strong enough to vengefully stomp Butler 96-0, still the record high score for Purdue, and the following year they lost only to Minnesota for a 9-1 season. During that early golden period Purdue chalked up its longest winning streak ever. The school won 16 straight games between 1891 and 1893 before finally being toppled by Michigan.

Only ten years into its football career, Purdue had already established itself as a serious contender in the collegiate arena. In years ahead Purdue would continue to snare a respectable, if unspectacular, share of victories in the Big Ten, whose competition would give the Boilermakers considerably more trouble.

Interestingly, it was Purdue University President James H Smart who played a key role in the formation of the league. Smart was prominent among those who wished to free amateur football of violence and vestiges of professionalism. In the interest of establishing reforms, on 11 January 1895 Smart invited the presidents of other Midwestern universities – Chicago, Illinois, Lake Forest, Minnesota, Northwestern and Wisconsin – to Chicago's Palmer House hotel to meet and bring some semblance of order to the fledgling sport. By the following year a new conference, the precursor of the Big Ten, had been born, governed by specific guidelines on ethics, rules and arbitration that would eventually become the foundation for most amateur athletic organizations and their codes.

Smart's leadership may have been inspired, but Purdue football coaching itself seemed to lack direction. From the sport's inception at Purdue, coaches came and went every two or three years until 1922, after which terms of six or more years became common. Yet the coaches' departures could not be blamed entirely on losing streaks, for the Boilermakers had their share of winning seasons.

The team went 7-2-1 in 1902, for instance, losing only to the all-powerful Chicago Maroons and Illinois. The following year was one of tragedy for Purdue because a special train carrying the team to a meet with Indiana was wrecked, and about 20 team members were injured or killed. Amazingly, the team got back

Right: *Whirlwind halfback Ralph 'Pest' Welch ran, passed, kicked and played defense superbly for the Boilermakers from 1927 to 1929. He is best-remembered for his singlehanded rout of the Michigan Wolverines in 1929: He led the fourth-quarter 24-point drive that handed Purdue its first defeat of Michigan since 1892.*

on its feet in 1904 to produce a 9-3 record, and the following year shut out six opponents, losing only once, to unbeaten national champion Chicago.

A number of talented athletes contributed to Purdue's early success, but the school's first 'star' was featured on the marginally successful teams of 1911 to 1913. The legendary Elmer 'Ollie' Oliphant had versatility almost matching that of athletics phenomenon Jim Thorpe. A stocky blond youth who had spent many summers of his life in the coal mines of southern Indiana, Oliphant collected conference onors as a halfback and also shone in basketball. In baseball, as well, he was an impressive catcher, outfielder and batter, and his track skills earned him a world record for low hurdles on turf.

Oliphant enjoyed four more years of athletic stardom at West Point, where he won All-America honors. As a punter, he was favorably compared to Thorpe and Charley Brickley of Harvard; as a ball carrier, he was a terror. 'Nobody has ever seen a more devastating stiff-arm in the history of football,' one columnist wrote. Would-be tacklers who managed to latch on to Oliphant were frequently dragged in groups for five or ten yards. Even his own team preferred to avoid contact with this dynamo. One teammate at Army said the greatest fear among his fellow linemen was old Ollie, 'with those churning legs of his, running up our backs if we don't charge fast enough.'

All-America honors were accorded mostly to championship teams in those days, and Oliphant missed out because of Purdue's mediocre records: 3-4, 4-2-1 and 4-1-2. Many of the wins could be attributed to his kicking alone, including one in a famous match with Illinois in which Oliphant broke his ankle but continued to play, even whacking out a field goal. In a blitz of Rose Polytechnic in 1912 he scored five touchdowns and made 13 of 13 conversion attempts. At Wisconsin in 1913 Ollie plunged past four tacklers, ran 32 yards for the goal line and slipped by two more tackles to tie a powerful Badger team 7-7. After that Badger fans would 'wake up screaming, nightmared by a herd of pink Oliphants,' chortled sportswriter Harry Grayson.

Oliphant collected nine letters at Purdue in a variety of sports, and went even further as an Army Cadet, adding no less than 15 more letters in football, basketball, baseball, swimming and track. He captained several different squads, including the hockey team. He broke Army's record for the 220-yard hurdles, and though he weighed only 178 pounds, he won the West Point heavyweight boxing champi-

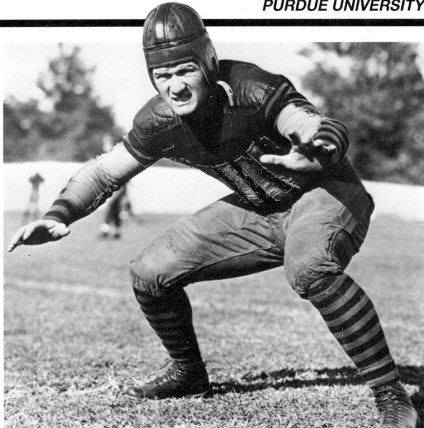

onship. All this while he diligently worked at two or more jobs at a time to keep himself in school.

After Oliphant left Purdue the Boilermakers fell back into a slump, but in 1922 they landed their first long-term coach, James Phelan. His term lasted from 1922 to 1929 and brought Purdue its first, long-awaited taste of national football glory. The bright young coach had an eye for talent, and in halfback Ralph Welch he developed Purdue's first All-America selection – a unanimous selection at that. Purdue was the last of the Big Ten members to contribute an All-American, but 'Pest' Welch seemed to make up for the school's tardiness.

Phelan produced excellent teams in 1924 and 1927 and in those years earned 5-2 and 6-2 records, marred only by close losses to Big Ten superteams Chicago, Ohio State and Wisconsin. Welch, though only a sophomore, contributed much to the 1927 record. Phelan first played the rangy triple-threat player from Whitesboro, Texas, as his secret weapon against top-rated Harvard. The Pest earned his nickname, zinging past the Crimson line for two touchdowns and passing 40 yards to Leon Hutton for a third. The Boilermakers stole a 19-0 upset and went on to win all but two contests for the season.

In the next two years Welch was the core of a hard-hitting eleven that helped the Gold and Black skyrocket in the Big Ten standings. Welch combined with tackle Elmer 'Red' Sleight and quarterback Glen Harmeson in the 1929 season to write a chapter in Purdue football history. Phelan's squad began the con-

Above: *Tackle Elmer 'Red' Sleight joined with quarterback Glen Harmeson and halfback Pest Welch in 1929 to produce the first ever undefeated Boilermaker team.*

ference season with a thrilling match against Michigan's favored Wolverines, unbeaten by Purdue since 1892. Michigan dominated the first three quarters of play, piling up a strong 16-6 lead that had fans from Ann Arbor reaching for their hats. But they stuck to their seats to watch a fourth-quarter Purdue comeback that is fondly remembered as the Pest's greatest moment. Welch pulled out all the stops, tearing off runs against the Wolverines for two touchdowns and spearheading a 24-point effort that settled the final score at 30-16. Welch's drive set the stage for Purdue's first undefeated season and Big Ten crown. Sleight joined Welch in accepting consensus All-America honors. Harmeson also garnered his own share of attention as a three-sport star, collecting nine letters in football, basketball and baseball between 1927 and 1930.

Phelan left a 35-22-5, .614 Purdue career coach at the University of Washington, assisted for 12 years by his star, Welch. The Pest replaced his mentor as head coach there for six more years, before finally retiring from the gridiron for good and opening an insurance business.

Replacing Phelan at Purdue in 1930 was his assistant, Noble Kizer, the youngest coach in the Big Ten and the only one in the nation under the age of 30. Boyish Kizer had come to the Purdue coaching staff in the late 1920s, fresh from a career as one of the famed 'watch-charm' guards for the legendary Four Horsemen of Notre Dame. The 160-pound Kizer, a

football and track prodigy from the farmland of Plymouth, Indiana, had also become the star and captain of the first Notre Dame basketball team to gain any national attention.

Over the next seven years Kizer brought the Gold and Black to new heights, including one unbeaten team and a Big Ten title. His first team of 1931 finished second in the conference and shared the title with Northwestern and Michigan, shutting out six and losing only to Wisconsin 21-14. The following year was just as impressive, with all opponents falling except a vengeful Northwestern, which having been denied an undisputed title the year before by the Boilermakers, held Kizer's men to a 7-7 tie. Purdue once again took a share of the Big Ten title beside undefeated Michigan, although the championship is not acknowledged in some circles today, for by modern rules the tie game would have reduced Purdue's standing.

Kizer's top men included Paul Moss, a do-everything end, and bruising fullback Roy Horstman. Moss made All-America in 1931, along with Charles Miller, a strong center. Moss' spectacular pass catching helped him repeat in 1932, joined by Horstman.

Kizer, a brilliant tactician, was rewarded with the Purdue athletic directorship post in 1933 and was selected by a national poll to coach the first collegiate All-Star team in 1934, a team that battled the fearsome Chicago Bear pros to a scoreless tie. By 1933 he had produced Purdue's longest string of wins, 20,

which was finally broken by Joe Laws and his band of Hawkeyes in a 14-6 Iowa game. Kizer's star that year was one of the game's last true triple-threats, Duane Purvis, a tailback who ran, passed and kicked with equal ease. The imaginative back, whose brother Jim had played at Purdue in the same position three years prior, took All-America honors in both 1933 and 1934. Purvis also distinguished himself in track as a javelin thrower and won a national championship.

Purvis is particularly remembered for a wild pass play that he devised in secret with Jim Carter before a game with Minnesota. The two conspired to run to opposite sidelines after one man had received the opening kickoff. Whoever had caught the ball would wait for the impending Gophers to surround him and would then lob the ball straight across the field to his partner, who presumably would streak downfield for a heroic touchdown.

'I carried out my part of the bargain,' Purvis later recalled to *Sports Illustrated*'s Mervin Hyman. 'I caught the kickoff and just as I was about to be tackled, I turned to throw a pass to Carter across the field.' Even though a big Gopher was looming right in front of Carter, it was too late to hold back on the pass, and Purvis let it go. 'By the grace of a kind providence, Carter caught it, even though he was downed in his tracks.'

Back at the bench, Kizer was less than thrilled with his duo's little surprise. 'Where the hell did you dig up that one?' he snapped.

'Why, we saw it work in high school and figured . . .' they began.

'This is not high school!' the coach thundered. 'Remember that!'

Kizer's last surprise gift to Purdue was the amazing Cecil Isbell, a halfback with terrific running and passing skills which somehow went unhindered by a very odd handicap: Isbell dislocated his left shoulder in his premier game, against Northwestern, and for the next three years had to play with a chain device rigged to his arm to prevent him from raising it above shoulder level. Isbell became a top performer in spite of the rig and later was drafted by the Green Bay Packers, with whom he played before returning to coach at Purdue from 1944 to 1946.

Coach Kizer left Purdue in 1936 following an illness; sadly, he died three years later at age 40, a victim of kidney disease. His legacy was a great one: the most successful coaching record ever at Purdue, 42-13-3 for a .764 winning percentage.

Had Kizer lived, Purdue football over the next several years might have had an entirely different history. A series of three coaches spanning the next ten years failed to produce teams with consistent winning spans, even though individual teams stood out. Coach Mal Edwards' 1938 squad, for example, lost only to Minnesota, thanks in part to halfback Isbell. Edwards also helped swift end Dave Rankin to the fore, and he made All-America teams in both 1939 and 1940.

The memory of Rankin continues to haunt certain Michigan State boosters, who recall when he broke his nose during a match with MSU but refused to quit, banging away at the Spartans until head linesman Mike Layden intervened. His white official's pants were dotted with Rankin's blood. 'Look at my pants,' he hollered to Rankin. 'Why don't you get the hell out of the game?'

Another share of the Big Ten title was claimed by Coach Elmer Burnham's 1943 team. Starring Alex Agase, 'the wandering guard,' and fullback Tony Butkovich, the Boilermakers ran roughshod over their entire conference lineup, outscoring foes 214-55 for a 9-0 season and matching Michigan's record. Purdue chalked up its second undefeated season in conference history, the other having been earned way back in 1929.

Agase earned his nickname as the only man ever to make All-America at two schools, having been designated the year prior when he was at Illinois. He was one of many Big Ten players shuffled to a different school for military training during the War, a phenomenon that made war-era college football a roulette-like game. Agase returned to Illinois in 1946 to be selected yet again.

Butkovich made his own name in 1943 with both All-America selection and a new Big Ten scoring record: 13 touchdowns for the season, a feat he accomplished in just four games,

Above: *Center Charles Miller, All-American in 1931, lent his considerable talents to Noble Kizer's first team.*

Opposite top: *Coach Noble Kizer works with his players, 1932.*

Opposite: *End Paul Moss' flying receptions earned him All-America selections in 1931 and 1932.*

helped by crafty halfback Boris 'Babe' Diman-cheff and guards Agase and Dick Barwegan. Butkovich was summoned for military duty before the season was over and was later killed in combat.

Dimancheff made All-America teams in 1944, and the following year tackle Tom Hughes was chosen, having contributed his skills to seven consecutive wins for a 7-3 season. Also grabbing the attention of fans was Bob DeMoss, a tall, angular freshman who was allowed to play varsity because of special wartime rules and who was the primary force behind an upset of Ohio State. In that game DeMoss completed his first six passes, totalled 138 yards on nine out of 11 attempts and contributed two touchdowns to a score of 35-13. DeMoss totalled 2790 yards on 192 passes over the next few years, setting a Big Ten record. After one year of pro ball he returned to Purdue as an assistant coach and would help to develop even greater passers.

First among them was the compact Dale Samuels, who completed for 3154 yards from 1950 to 1952, and Len Dawson, who comprised virtually the entire Purdue offense from 1954 to 1956. He gained 3325 yards and 29 touchdowns on 243 completions, throwing the ball 425 times. Dawson, who later achieved professional stardom with the Kansas City Chiefs, led the conference throughout his career in passing and total offense, the only Big Ten player to do so over three consecutive years.

The quiet, softspoken Dawson was dubbed 'The Golden Boy' by the press, and the director of Purdue's All-American Marching Band decided to add a counterpart during half-time parades. Thus began the dynasty of the Golden Girl, the baton-twirling, blonde princesses who have since entertained hundreds of audiences. As the unofficial queen of baton girls nationwide, each successive Golden Girl has demonstrated the same sort of precision attributed to Dawson himself. Assistant coach DeMoss, for his part, continued to produce a dynasty of ball-twirling star quarterbacks, especially during the 1960s.

Purdue's talent in the 1950s was by no means limited to passers. Leo Sugar, one of the most versatile wingmen the Big Ten had seen in a long time, pulled All-America honors in 1951. In the next year Stu Holcomb, whose coaching term lasted from 1947 to 1955, led a hard-hitting squad of Boilermakers to tie Michigan State for the conference title. The backfield, led by Samuels, was given ample opportunity by the front line, which included Bernie Flowers, an outstanding end, and

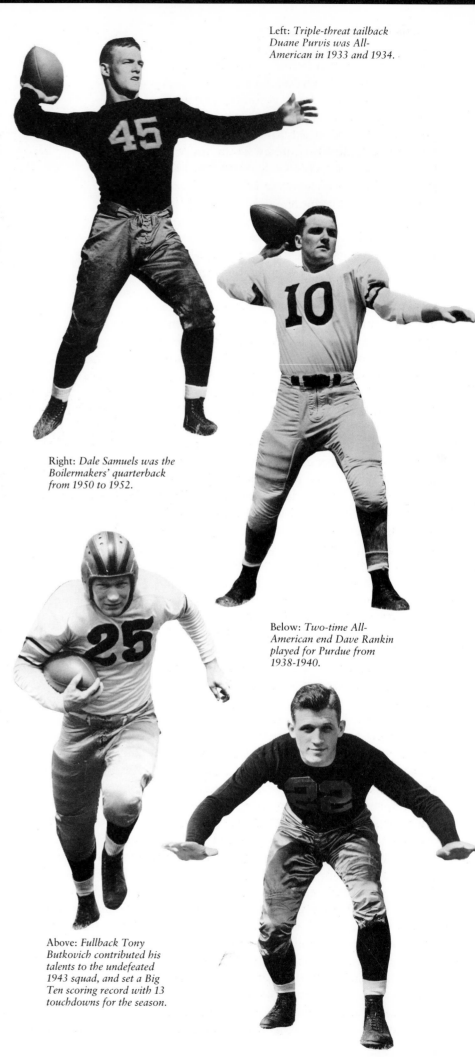

Left: *Triple-threat tailback Duane Purvis was All-American in 1933 and 1934.*

Right: *Dale Samuels was the Boilermakers' quarterback from 1950 to 1952.*

Below: *Two-time All-American end Dave Rankin played for Purdue from 1938-1940.*

Above: *Fullback Tony Butkovich contributed his talents to the undefeated 1943 squad, and set a Big Ten scoring record with 13 touchdowns for the season.*

guards John Houston and freshman Tom Bettis. Flowers took All-America honors in 1952, and Bettis continued to shine through 1954 when he, too, was selected.

The following year, 1953, quarterback Dawson made headlines again with an eye-popping 95-yard touchdown pass to Erich Barnes in a game with Northwestern. But with the exception of tackle Gene Selawski's election to All-America teams in 1958, the decade closed with little other limelight for the Boilermakers.

In 1955, however, there came portent of good things to come when Jack Mollenkopf replaced Coach Holcomb, beginning a 15-year stint that would be the longest – and the one with the most victories – in Purdue gridiron annals. Mollenkopf began assembling standout teams as early as his third year, 1958, when the Boilermakers went for 6-1-2, the sole loss being to Wisconsin 31-6.

Yet Purdue had to go on plodding through several unspectacular seasons while Mollenkopf tried again and again to find some 'magical' combination of talent. He was not entirely unsuccessful: Three more All-Americans were groomed within five years, including tackles Jerry Beabout and Donald Brumm in 1960 and 1962, respectively, and brilliant end Harold Wells in 1964. But for 10 whole years the ultimate magic eluded him.

In 1965 Mollenkopf finally brought the necessary elements together. Among them was quarterback Bob Griese, who after two mediocre seasons had developed into a fine passer, owing largely to Bob DeMoss' coaching. A brace of outstanding tackles, Jerry Shay and Karl Singer, headed a strong line and helped set the stage for Griese's aerial pyrotechnics.

The junior quarterback's 'coming out' game, played against Numbrt 1-ranked Notre Dame in 1965, is remembered as one of his greatest. Mollenkopf allowed Griese ample opportunity for pass plays, and Bob responded by completing 19 of 22 throws against the rival Irish, helping Purdue to a 25-21 victory. Griese was lauded for his ability to pass and run with equal effectiveness, since players' roles had grown increasingly specialized over the years. In fact, as one of the most versatile quarterbacks to come along in decades, Griese represented the advent of a new breed of running quarterback that would dominate the 1960s.

The Boilermakers finished with a 7-2-1 season, one of their best in 10 years, losing only to Illinois and to unbeaten national champion Michigan State by a mere 14-10. Griese passed for a total of 1719 yards and 11 touchdowns;

on the receiving end, Bob Hadrick caught 47 passes for 562 yards. Griese earned the first of two consecutive All-America selections, joined by teammates Shay and Singer.

Griese was truly primed for 1966, when he helped to boost Purdue to second place in the Big Ten. The quarterback completed 130 of 215 throws, gaining 1749 yards and 12 touchdowns. End Jim Beirne, one of the nation's leading receivers, caught 64 passes for 768 yards and eight touchdowns. Only national co-champions Michigan State and Notre Dame managed to beat the Boilermakers. Because the Spartans had played in the Rose Bowl the year prior, MSU was ineligible to play a second straight match and the honor went to Purdue. Mollenkopf's eleven was no disappointment. The Boilermakers upset a favored Southern California team 14-13 in their first-ever bowl game.

John Charles, a togch defensive back, was named Rose Bowl MVP and an All-American, along with Griese and Beirne. Yet Griese faced a major letdown at the selection of the Heisman Trophy winner. A favored candidate, Bob had been tipped to wait for a call on election day, and the eager quarterback did just that. The phone never rang; he was edged out by Florida quarterback Steve Spurrier. But, of course, thrills as great lay ahead for Griese

*Above: Quarterback Bob Griese began his highly successful football career at Purdue, where he led the Boilermakers to a 7-2-1 season in 1965 and its first-ever Rose Bowl victory in 1966. He went on to record-breaking fame with the Miami Dolphins, and took them to a Super Bowl championship in 1974.*

Above: *Coach Jack Mollenkopf took over the reins from Stu Holcomb in 1955, and in the next 15 years compiled one of the winningest records in Purdue football history.*

Top right: *Brilliant quarterback Mike Phipps (15) makes a handoff in 1968.*

Center right: *Master receiver and defense man Leroy Keyes (23) carries the ball against OSU, 1967. In his three years with the Boilermakers Keyes broke most of Ollie Oliphant's and Pest Welch's records and set a new career scoring record of 222 as well as a single season record of 114.*

Far right: *Otis Armstrong (24) shakes off the Michigan masses, 1971. His agility and speed helped him break records set by the great Leroy Keyes only a couple of years earlier.*

when he left Purdue for the pros. He would later lead his Miami Dolphins to a 1973 Super Bowl championship and surpass a variety of professional passing and other offensive records.

Passing coach DeMoss lost little time developing an heir to Griese's throne, and in 1967 sophomore Mike Phipps made his debut. Essentially a single-skill back, Phipps astonished Purdue audiences by rapidly chewing through Griese's collegiate passing records, and he soon became one of the first of his generation's high-yardage super-quarterbacks.

Phipps paired with national receiving phenomenon Leroy Keyes to form an efficient, fast-paced winning machine. Keyes, to some the greatest Boilermaker of all time, startled a nation that had grown unused to players able to play both defensive and offensive positions. Mollenkopf took advantage and allowed Keyes some impressive displays of versatility. As a rusher he was a wild, careering open-field runner who could find openings just about anywhere and, once on his way, could baffle would-be tacklers by constantly changing his pace. On the other hand, he was a quick-witted defense man who once, against Notre Dame, nabbed a Irish fumble in mid-air and ran the ball 95 yards for a touchdown.

Keyes blistered Iowa in 1967 with a four-touchdown performance, two on handoffs and two on pass receptions, and he scored three TDs each against Illinois and Minnesota, helping create Purdue victory margins of about 30 points. The Boilermakers finished the season

with 291 points and an 8-2 record, including a 41-6 plastering of mighty Ohio State, and shared the Big Ten title with Indiana and Minnesota. Phipps had passed for 1800 yards and 11 TDs; Keyes rushed 986 for 114 points and secured a unanimous choice as an All-American.

Keyes outdid himself in his senior year, 1968, rushing for 1003 yards in another 8-2, 291-point Boilermaker season. Keyes repeated as a consensus All-American, this time joined by guard Chuck Kyle, whose defense leadership helped limit defeats to those by unbeaten national champ OSU and a vengeful Minnesota. Before leaving, Keyes had broken most of Ollie Oliphant's and Pest Welch's records and had set new ones for scoring – 222 for a career, and 114 in a single season. His team lost only six games in three years, ample proof of his vast talents.

Even without Keyes, Purdue managed to chalk up its third straight 8-2 season in 1969, scoring 354 points, and Phipps' dazzling showmanship finally put him on the All-America team. He passed for a new record of 2527 yards total offense, good for 23 touchdowns. Phipps was helped by end Ashley Bell, who pulled in 49 passes for 669 yards and 11 TDs, and back Tim Foley, who starred on defense with five interceptions. Foley and tackle Bill Yanchar joined Phipps as All-Americans.

That 1969 team, Coach Mollenkopf's last, fell only to Michigan and Ohio State, teams that have since so completely dominated the Big Ten that some have called the conference 'the Big Two and the Little Eight.' But Purdue has never stopped producing players and seasons of distinction. The most famous man to grace West Lafayette's Ross-Ade Stadium in the modern Purdue era was probably runner Otis Armstrong, a boy from the Chicago ghetto who made audiences almost forget his team's 13-18 record during his three years at Purdue.

Under coach Bob DeMoss, who replaced Mollenkopf in 1970, Armstrong smashed through scrimmage to break many school records, including some set by Keyes, and he set a new conference record for rushing at 3515 yards – no easy feat, considering that Wisconsin's Alan Ameche had set the prior mark during a career of four years, not three.

Purdue fans vividly remember a 42-7 rout of Indiana in 1972 when Armstrong, in his final college performance, tore up a muddy field to gain 276 yards and three touchdowns on 32 carries. Moaned Indiana coach John Pont, 'We've looked at him for three years, and I can

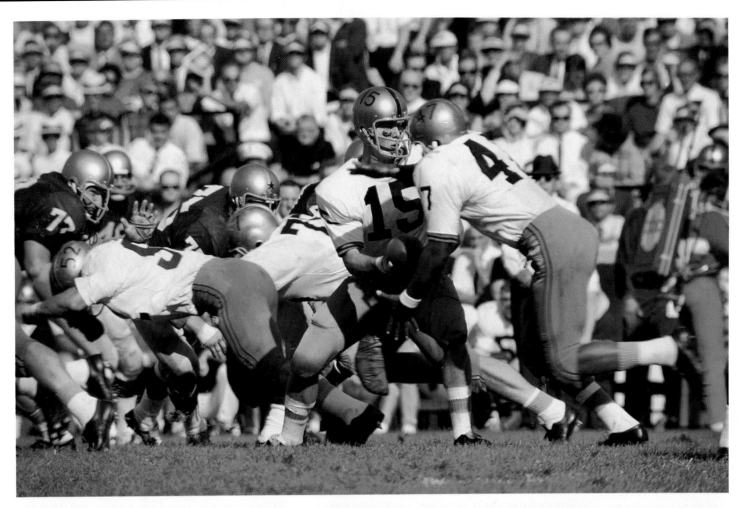

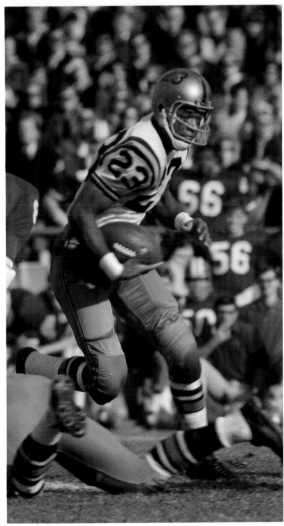

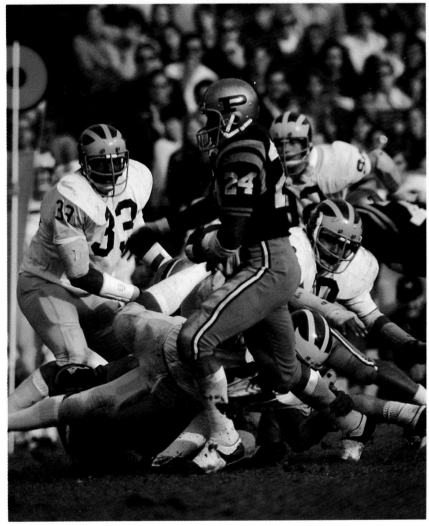

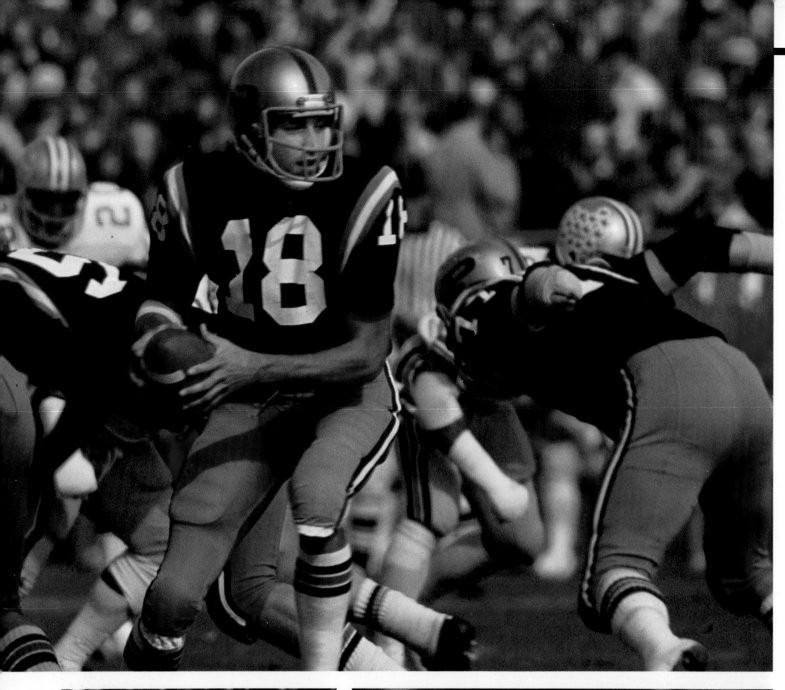

Above: *Sideline
entertainment provided by
the Silver Twins, 1980.*

Right: *Leroy Keyes (23)
catches his breath on the
bench.*

tell you, that's enough. He's the greatest, period.' Armstrong was easily elected to All-America teams that year, along with the big tackle Dave Butz. Later selections included Larry Barton and Ken Novak in 1974 and 1975, respectively.

Coach DeMoss moved on at the same time as Armstrong, and after an unsuccessful three-year term for former college football star Alex Agase, Jim Young stepped in to bring Purdue a new measure of excitement. Under Young the Boilermakers produced an 8-2-1 season in 1978, losing only to Notre Dame and Michigan, thanks in part to runner John Macon, who tallied 913 yards, in part to quarterback Mark Herrmann, who passed for 1904 yards and 14 touchdowns, and in part to Scott Sovereen, who kicked 15 field goals. The Boilermakers tromped on Georgia Tech in the Peach Bowl 41-21.

Young coached a 9-2 team in 1979, again starring Herrmann, who passed for 2377 yards and 16 TDs. Purdue scored double figures against all comers and beat Tennessee 27-22 in the Bluebonnet Bowl. The following year, Herrmann shared the limelight with end Dave Young in helping the Boilermakers to an 8-3 season. Herrmann sailed the ball for 3212 yards and 23 touchdowns, and Young caught 70 passes for 959 yards and nine TDs. At season's end, the team edged Missouri in the Liberty Bowl 28-25, and both Purdue stars were named All-Americans.

Coach Young left in 1981 with a 38-19-1 record, including three bowl championships, and an admirable winning percentage of .666. Taking over coaching duties was Leon Burtnett, who compiled a lackluster 18-26-1 record in his first four years. Yet as usual, there was no weakness in passing. In 1984 quarterback Jim Everett led the Big Ten by passing for 3003 yards, completing 58 percent of his 389 throws to a variety of good receivers, including the 1000-yard rusher Steve Griffin.

The arrival of Jeff George as quarterback in 1986 was cause for speculation that the Gold and Black might yet return to its former glory, for George had thrown for an unbelievable 8121 yards and 94 TDs at Indianapolis' Warren Central High School. Though his first season ended in a disappointing 3-8, he still has time to make the future of Boilermaker football something to remember.

Left: *Quarterback Jim Everett (14) led the conference in passing with 3003 yards in 1984.*

Top: *Rodney Carter (24) packs the pigskin for a short gain versus OSU, 1985.*

Opposite top: *Quarterback Mark Vitali (18) in action against OSU in 1975.*

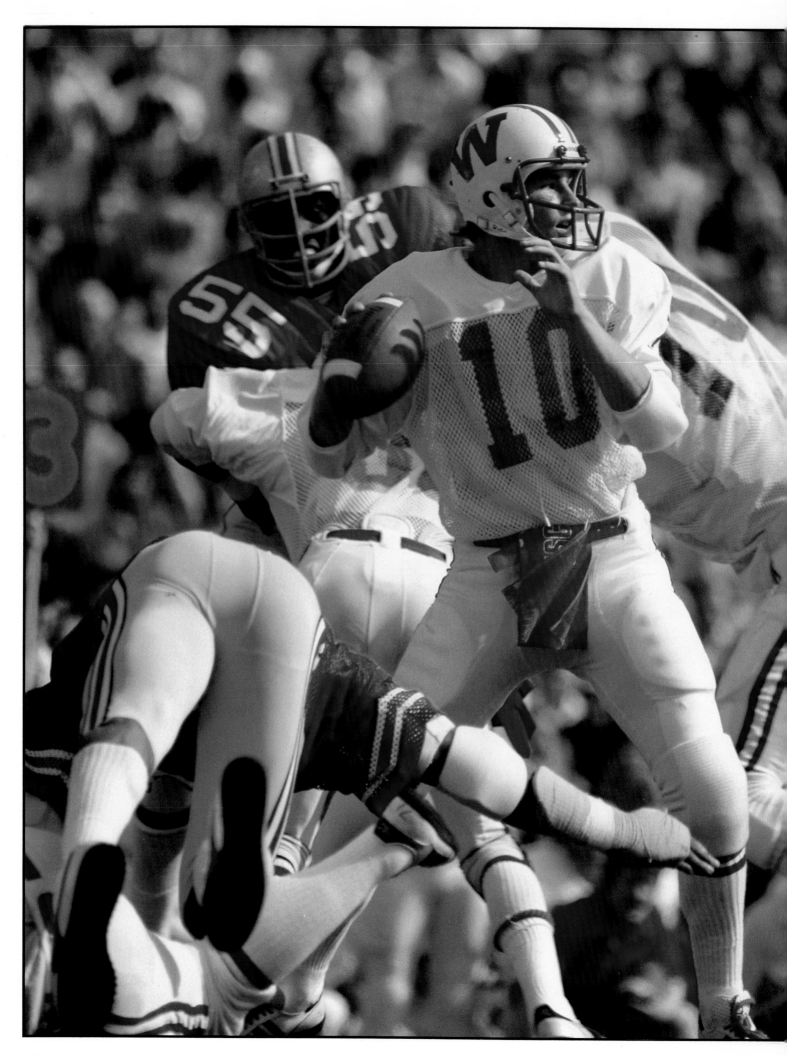

# UNIVERSITY
## OF
# WISCONSIN

Founded: 1848

Location: Madison

Total Enrollment: 45,050

Colors: Cardinal and White

Nickname: Badgers

The University of Wisconsin, a charter member of the Western Intercollegiate Conference when it was formed in 1896, had an authentic star in Pat O'Dea and was tearing up the turf before most of its conference rivals had even learned to play the 'new' game of football.

The fresh-faced, young Patrick John O'Dea had come to the Madison campus, where his older brother was crew coach, from Melbourne, Australia. The lad had played Australian football, which was a modified form of English rugby – with all scoring coming on drop -or placekicks. An outstanding kicker in Australia, O'Dea became an absolute sensation in America. Although weighing only about 170 pounds, he had tremendous leg strength and could be counted on to score from anywhere within the 50-yard line. Coach Phil King made the best use of his talents.

At the turn of the century field goals could be attempted on a free kick if a team signaled for a fair catch on a punt instead of running it back. The kicker could try for a five-point kick from wherever the catch was fielded. With O'Dea in his arsenal, King's team rarely returned a punt short of midfield, and scored often on O'Dea's 'magic toe.'

O'Dea's greatest afternoon came in a game against Minnesota in 1899. Midway through the second half in a hard-fought, scoreless game, Minnesota punted from deep in their own territory. O'Dea fielded the punt, and- ,hotly pursued by Gopher players, headed for the left sidelines and got off a dropkick without even coming to a full stop. The ball flew more than 60 yards and split the Minnesota crossbar as the longest dropkick in the history of American football. O'Dea had kicked it right-footed while running to his left!

Statistics were not kept in those days, but O'Dea may well have been the greatest kicker in athletic history. Unaccountably, he was left off the All-America team by Walter Camp and Caspar Whitney, who picked the collegiate honor teams for many years.

Although Wisconsin, like virtually everyone else, fell each season to Fielding Yost's 'Point-a-Minute' Michigan Wolverines in the early years of the century, Badger football made steady progress until 1906. In that year, new 'Big Nine' rules came out limiting the number of games in a season to five, and the Wisconsin faculty, disgusted with the violence of the game, also voted to ban Wisconsin's so-called 'big games' with traditional Badger rivals Chicago, Minnesota and Michigan.

Under the new rules Wisconsin excelled on the field, going undefeated in games against Lawrence, North Dakota, Iowa, Illinois and Purdue to share the conference title with Minnesota. But the lost revenue of the 'big games' made the season a disaster from a financial standpoint. By the 1908 season both Minnesota and Chicago were back on the Badgers' football schedule. Michigan had dropped out of the conference, not to return until 1917.

In 1912 the Badgers, under Coach Bill Juneau, clinched their first clear conference title with an undefeated season. The Wisconsin team was one of the most honored in history,

*Right: The undefeated Badgers team of 1912: (top row) Breckenridge, T Powell, Assistant Coach E Driver, All-American R Butler, Moffitt; (third row) Manager Brindley, W Powell, Keeler, Bright, Tanberg, Van Riper, Samp, Stenauer; (second row) Coach Bill Juneau, Lange, Gillette, Captain Hoefel, Bellows, Alexander, Wilce; (bottom row) Berger, Tormly, Ofatte, Gelin.*

*Above: Wisconsin's Camp Randall Stadium in 1910. The first football game played there was between the Badgers and the Minnesota Golden Gophers in 1917 on Homecoming Day.*

with nine players named to the *Chicago Tribune* all-conference team and with tackle Robert P 'Butts' Butler becoming the first Badger All-American. At the end of the season efforts were made to arrange a game between the Badger eleven and mighty Harvard for an unofficial 'national championship' game, but the Wisconsin faculty, perhaps still not entirely convinced of the benefits of a football program, nixed the contest.

Although the Badgers finished near the bottom of the conference heap the following season, guard Ray 'Tubby' Keeler made All-American. He was followed by guard Arlie Mucks in 1914, and Howard Buck in 1915. Center Charles Carpenter was so honored in 1919. But the war years played havoc with football personnel, since many Big Ten stars were called into military service. Despite this, attendance at games rose steadily.

In the late teens and early 1920s many of the Big Ten schools joined the trend toward building concrete stadiums for their football heroes. Wisconsin had a real stadium by 1913, but in 1915, during the climactic Wisconsin-Minnesota game, a large section of the wooden stands gave way and 20 people were hurt. In 1917 construction of a concrete stadium was begun with a $15,000 grant from the state legislature. Finding a name for it was no problem. The University's memorial athletic field had always been called Camp Randall, since a great military camp, named for a Civil War-era governor, had once stood on the site. The first football game played in Camp Randall Stadium was the 1917 Homecoming bout between the Badgers and Minnesota. At that time the

stadium held only 10,000, but seats were progressively added, with major enlargements being made in 1951 and 1958 and the enormous 13,000-seat upper deck being added in 1966. Capacity is now a whopping 77,280, making Camp Russell Stadium the seventh-largest college-owned stadium in the United States, surpassed only by stadiums at Michigan, Stanford, Ohio State, Tennessee, Penn State and Georgia. In 1926 the first electronic scoreboard was installed at Camp Randall and was first used in Wisconsin's game against Iowa – another illustration of how Wisconsin has in many ways been a Big Ten trendsetter in facilities and new technology.

Under Coach J R Richards Wisconsin was runner-up to Ohio State in 1920 with a 4-1-0 record, and it contributed end Frank Weston and tackle Ralph Scott to the All-America team. In fact, the only team to beat the Badgers that year was the rampaging Buckeyes, led by the brilliant running and pass-receiving of halfback Gaylord 'Pete' Stinchcomb. Ohio State went undefeated that season, only to be shellacked by the California Bears 28-0 in the Rose Bowl.

After the outstanding 1920 Badger team, however, Wisconsin fans suffered a long, dry spell. Wisconsin placed no better than third in the conference until 1928, when it again became runner-up to Illinois. Years had passed between All-Americans, too, with end Marty Below the lone All-American to be picked (1923) for the remainder of the decade.

Yet the 1923 season will always be remembered by Badger fans for another reason: the violently disputed call that cost Wisconsin a victory over mighty Michigan and that nearly touched off a riot at Camp Randall Stadium. The Badgers had plodded through a mediocre season, but one that could have been salvaged by a win over the mighty Wolverines. And Wisconsin had that victory in sight as they took a 3-0 lead on a field goal. The Badgers then played the defensive game of their lives to preserve the advantage. They had just punted, and Michigan safety Tod Rockwell had run the ball back about 20 yards before being brought down by a pair of Badger tacklers at midfield. The 20,000 or so Badger fans had breathed a sigh of relief, but what happened next caught them completely by surprise.

Rockwell strolled casually away from the pileup on the ground, still clinging to the ball — and suddenly began to run toward the goal line. As the stunned Wisconsin players watched, Rockwell crossed the goal line and field judge Colonel Mumma awarded him a touchdown!

Referee Walter Eckersall, a highly respected sportswriter and former University of Chicago star quarterback, had not blown his whistle to stop play after the Michigan runner had been brought down. Mumma ruled that the forward progress of the ball had therefore not been stopped, even though Badger tacklers had plainly stopped Rockwell. So Michigan was awarded both the touchdown and the game with a final score of 6-3.

Pandemonium broke out at Camp Randall. Coach Jack Ryan, the Wisconsin bench and 20,000 frenzied Badger fans pleaded, screamed, ranted and threatened, but to no avail. Walter Eckersall stood with his arms folded, refusing to reverse his decision. Michigan had preserved a tie for the conference crown and left the field hastily, no doubt glad to get out of town alive.

The Badger players took matters into their own hands and turned what could have been an actual riot into a moral victory. They surrounded Eckersall as he left the field, protecting him from their own fans. When the assembled crowd saw what the team was doing they dispersed, muttering to themselves but no longer in the mood for a lynching. The next day, a local sportswriter called the game 'the biggest robbery ever pulled off in Madison, Wisconsin.'

By 1930 Badger football had reached a low ebb. Dead last in the Big Ten ranking in 1927 and 1929, the fans had seen four head coaches come and go in ten years, with the latest, Glenn Thistlethwaite, departing in 1931 after only five years. Dr Clarence Spears, after a career at Minnesota coaching the likes of Bronko

Nagurski, followed Thistlethwaite but did little better.

In 1936 Wisconsin administrators decided it was time for a complete housecleaning. Under Spears the Badgers had not improved, and the coach had failed to win the support of the athletic director, Dr Walter Meanwell. Tensions between the two flared into public controversy during the 1935 season, when the exchange of accusations included everything from giving whiskey to players during halftime to promising football players coaching jobs in return for petition signatures calling for Spears' resignation. Exasperated, the Board of Regents dismissed both Spears and Meanwell, and the administration chose a single man to fill both jobs. The man was Harry Stuhldreher.

The name, of course, was well known to football fans all over the country, for he had been one of the legendary 'Four Horsemen' — the Notre Dame Irish backfield that had terrorized opponents in the early 1920s. After his career as Notre Dame's quarterback, Stuhldreher had played a year of professional football with the short-lived American Football League. From there he had gone on to coach for 12 years at Villanova.

Now, Stuhldreher was Wisconsin's coach and its director of athletics. He would stay until 1948, stopping the revolving door of coaches and overseeing improvements to the Badger football program that would bear fruit only in the 1950s and 1960s.

In 1938 Stuhldreher coached his first All-American: Howard Weiss, a line-smashing fullback. It had been, again, a lean period for Badger All-Americans, with tackle Milo Lubratovich the previous selection in 1930. But Weiss added conference MVP honors, and Badger fans felt that Wisconsin's football program was back on track.

Stuhldreher's 1941 and 1942 teams at last produced a few moments of glory as well as the heroes to go along with them. Fullback Marlin 'Pat' Harder and the versatile end Dave Schreiner, who could catch passes and block with equal ease, gave the Badger offense some punch in 1941. Unfortunately the opposition could quickly tie the score on Wisconsin's listless defense. A sample of scores for the season: a 27-25 win over Indiana, a 27-20 loss to Syracuse and a loss to the Ohio State Buckeyes in a scoring frenzy, 46-34. Still, the Badgers finished with a conference record of 3-3, and Dave Schreiner was selected an All-American.

In 1942, the last normal Big Ten season before the wartime emergency regulations interrupted scheduling and personnel, the Wisconsin Badgers piled up a gaudy five victories

and a 7-7 tie against Notre Dame. On Halloween they met unbeaten Ohio State at Camp Randall Stadium for Homecoming. The Buckeyes were favored by 10 points, but Wisconsin had some weapons: a canny quarterback, Jack Wing, who led a competent backfield including Pat Harder and a wild halfback named Elroy Hirsch, whose running style had already earned him the nickname 'Crazy Legs.' Up front was captain Dave Schreiner, who oversaw Paul Hirsbrunner at tackle, Fred Negus at center and talented guards Ken Currier and Evan Vogds.

The Buckeyes took to the field minus several players, victims to a mysterious illness that was attributed to tainted food or water, and that Badger fans dismissed as premature trick-or-treating. But the 'treats' definitely belonged to Wisconsin that day. The team struck early for a 10-point lead in the first half. Ohio State crawled from its sickbed for a third-quarter touchdown, but Wisconsin soon matched it and wrapped up a 17-7 win for its returning alumni and fans.

The resulting celebration was premature. Although Wisconsin laid claim to being the nation's best team by virtue of the Halloween win over the Buckeyes, the crunching hits had taken their toll — or perhaps the team had 'caught something' from Ohio State. The very next weekend a four-loss Iowa team handed Wisconsin a 6-0 heartbreaker at Iowa City. Wisconsin finished as conference runner-up to the Buckeyes, a bridesmaid yet again! Yet Badger fans could take consolation from the selection of both Harder and Schreiner as All-Americans.

'Crazy Legs' Hirsch went on to greater glory at Michigan the following year, where he had been assigned to a naval training program, and later in the National Football League with the Los Angeles Rams. In June 1945 Dave

*Above: Former pilot of the famed Four Horsemen of Notre Dame Harry Stuhldreher later became football coach for the Badgers. Here he is seen with his 1941 signal calling squad: (l-r) Coach Stuhldreher, Jack Wink, Paul Bronson, Ashley Anderson, Tom Farris and Bob Diercks.*

*Top left: Fullback Howard Weiss (70) was All-American and conference MVP in 1938.*

*Bottom left: Walter MacGuire, right halfback for the Wisconsin eleven under coach Glenn Thistlethwaite.*

Left: *Halfback Elroy 'Crazy Legs' Hirsch tore up the turf for the Badgers in 1942.*

Below: *Fullback Marlin 'Pat' Harder of the 1941-42 Badgers.*

Schreiner was killed in action with the Marine Corps on Okinawa. All of Wisconsin mourned his loss, and the Badger football team honored him by retiring his number, 80 – one of only two retired Badger numbers.

The 1943 and 1944 Badger football seasons were disappointments by comparison with 1942, but at least the Wisconsin faithful could boast of halfback Earl 'Jug' Girard, the whirling dervish who could run, pass and kick and was voted to the 1944 All-America team for those talents.

The 1944 season also brought unexpected tragedy to Wisconsin football. On 11 November, in the game against Iowa, Badger quarterback Allan Shafer was fatally injured in the second half of play. He died shortly after his team had defeated the Hawkeyes 26-7. A sorrowful University of Wisconsin, already mourning the deaths of so many promising young men overseas, paused to contemplate a young man's death on the gridiron. Shafer's Number 83 was retired in tribute.

The next few years were uneventful for Badger football. Wisconsin's best finish in the rest of the decade was a runner-up position to powerhouse Michigan in 1947. Coach Stuhldreher stepped down from his coaching position in 1948 to devote his full energies to the athletic director position. He was replaced by Ivan 'Ivy' Williamson.

The 1948 season prompted two comments in the Milwaukee newspapers which illustrate just how depressing the years of mediocrity had become. On Father's Day, the last game of the season, the Badgers lost to Minnesota, and a sympathetic Paul Gustafson of the *Milwaukee Sentinel* wrote: 'A bunch of conscientious boys, representing Wisconsin, set out to do a man's job at Camp Randall before their dads Saturday, and took a 16-0 bullying from the mighty Minnesota Gophers.' Oliver Kuechle of the *Milwaukee Journal* wrote of the same game: 'Wisconsin's dreary football season, which began with a licking, dragged through a succession of lickings, also ended here Saturday with a licking.' The school and the whole state needed a boost.

In Coach Williamson's first season, 1949, Wisconsin posted a 3-2-1 record, and the team was not eliminated from conference title contention until the last game. But it was perhaps the Homecoming rally of that year that fans remember most. It was at the rally that the first Bucky Badger mascot appeared. Bucky couldn't win the games, but he cheered things up nevertheless.

The devotion of the people of Wisconsin to the badger, both the animal and the athletic

Above: *Students Bill Sackse, Bill Segal and Connie Conrad with the first Bucky the Badger head, in 1949.*

symbol, is unequaled in the Big Ten. Nowhere else is the name of the football team so bound up in the history and psyche of the state. Before Wisconsin attained statehood, when it was still Indian country, the area that is now southwestern Wisconsin attracted large numbers of settlers. They came not only to farm, but to prospect for lead, which was in demand in the early 1800s for gunshot. Southwestern Wisconsin was full of lead – big chunks of it littered the ground – and by 1820 the Lead Rush was on. Many year-round prospectors sought shelter in the excavations they had made looking for lead ore, and naturally the miners were compared to badgers, which were then more plentiful. Eventually, the badger nickname was applied to the settlers of the new state, and it appeared on the Wisconsin arms beginning in 1851. More than 100 years later, in 1957, the badger was voted the state animal. Long before that it had become the symbol of Wisconsin football.

Live badgers, kept in cages or on a leash, had often been brought to football games as mascots, though the older animals sometimes displayed the feisty instincts of their wild natures, biting the luckless male cheerleaders whose task it was to lead them around. A humanized drawing of a badger first appeared on decals and in campus publications in 1940. Originally drawn by Art Evans, the popular figure sported the striped sweater, large letter 'W' and fighting stance that are still famous today.

In 1949, the Homecoming Pep committee organized a 'name the mascot' contest and also produced a costume badger head so that a 'live' badger mascot could provide some

Homecoming spirit. The mascot was christened Buckingham U Badger, and student tryouts for the honor of being Bucky draw many candidates. Today Bucky Badgers are pictured on milk cartons and Wisconsin state highway maps, and there are even Bucky Badger stuffed animals available at student stores, banks and other businesses.

In the 1950 season the Badgers finished third in the Big Ten, next to Michigan and Ohio State, with a 5-2-0 record, and halfback star Ed Withers made the All-America team. John Coatta, the Badger quarterback, set a conference pass completion record with 52 catches out of 81 attempts, a .642 average. Things were definitely looking up.

More success came in 1951. Wisconsin again finished third, with a 5-1-1 record, to Illinois and Purdue. Ends Hal Faverty and Pat O'Donahue were named All-Americans, and Coatta again led the conference in passing. Even a freshman got into the act by leading the conference in rushing with 774 yards. His name was Alan Ameche, and he had only just begun.

Big for his age, Ameche joined the Badgers during the Korean War when freshmen were allowed to play varsity. He crashed against opposing lines with such strength that he was soon dubbed 'The Horse' by delirious Badger fans. Ameche had plenty of help on the 1952 Badger team. Halfbacks Gerry Witt, Harland Carl, Bill Hutchinson and Archie Burks won praise, and sophomore quarterback Jim Haluska turned in a .587 pass completion mark that year. End Don Voss, also a sophomore, tackle Dave Suminsky, and guards Bob Kennedy, George O'Brien, Clarence Stensby and George Steinmetz completed the Badger picture – and it was a pretty one.

Upset by nemesis Ohio State early in the year, the Badgers won the rest of their conference contests and went into the Minnesota game needing at least a tie to clinch a share of the title. The ball changed hands five times in the last two minutes of the game, while Bucky Badger and the fans at Camp Randall screamed their support. The team posted a 21-21 finish. It had been 40 years since Wisconsin last earned the conference crown. Purdue shared the title with the Badgers – but not the Rose Bowl bid. Wisconsin had a better overall record and was Pasadena-bound.

Even a 7-0 loss to tough USC could not dim the fans' hopes for a new Badger football era, and they cheered the selection of Voss and Suminski as All-Americans. Ameche led the Big Ten in rushing again and was selected an All-American in both 1953 and 1954.

In 1954 Wisconsin put together a 5-2-0 season, finishing second to a great Woody Hayes Ohio State team. The 1954 season was also Alan Ameche's finest. Ivy Williamson had taken some of the pressure off of Ameche's running game in his junior and senior years by instituting more passing plays. Ameche was asked to also play defense because of the return to one-platoon football, and in addition to his rushing brilliance he became a feared linebacker on defense. His career at Wisconsin ended with 3212 yards rushing, the 1954 conference MVP award, the Heisman Trophy and a host of Wisconsin offensive records that would stand for 20 years. Ameche subsequently spent a brilliant pro career with the Baltimore Colts and was a perennial All-Pro selection at fullback. Yet he never forgot the University of Wisconsin. In the early 1980s he presented Wisconsin Athletic Director Elroy Hirsch with his Heisman Trophy, now on permanent display in the Wisconsin football office.

Coach Williamson left Wisconsin after the 1955 season, yielding to Milt Bruhn. In 1958, under Bruhn, Wisconsin again ran solidly in the hunt, finishing second to Iowa with a 5-1-1 record. In 1959 Wisconsin took advantage of a slack year elsewhere in the conference. Tackle Dan Lanphear, quarterback Dale Hackbart, end Henry Derleth and guard Jerry Stalcup led a standout Wisconsin team, which finished the Big Ten season with a 5-2-0 mark. Hackbart led the conference in rushing with 686 yards,

319 of them rushing and the other 367 passing. Dan Lanphear was the Badger's All-American that year. But again, the Big Ten titlist Badgers came up short in the Rose Bowl, losing 44-8 to awesome Washington.

In 1960 the Badgers placed far down in the conference pack, but by 1962 they were on top of the heap again. The 1962 Badger team enjoyed the return of end Pat Richter, All-American on the previous year's 4-3 team, and a host of other fine players — among them tackle Roger Pillath; speedy halfback Lou Holland (who would be the leading conference scorer) and at quarterback a third-stringer from the year before, Ron VanderKelen. VanderKelen was perhaps the best hunch Coach Bruhn ever played, and he went on to thrill Badger fans with his scrambling and passing.

An attempt to spell his name correctly was about all the competition could muster against the scrappy VanderKelen. He became the conference offensive leader with 228 yards rushing and an astounding 1009 passing, a combined record of 1237 yards. Lou Holland scored 11 touchdowns, and Pat Richter again

shone as the leading Big Ten pass receiver, with 33 receptions for 440 yards. With statistics like those, it was no wonder the Badgers recorded such pastings as a 42-14 win over Iowa, 34-12 over Michigan, 35-6 over Illinois and, to top it off, a 17-8 win over Notre Dame. Their only defeat came in the Columbus snakepit as Ohio State hexed them again with a 14-7 loss.

The Rose Bowl of 1963 is still often mentioned as one of the most exciting on record. The Badgers went into the third quarter trailing USC 35-14, then came back on Vander-Kelen's passing wizardry to score three touchdowns and a safety. But Wisconsin lost to the clock; the Trojans desperately hung on to the ball in the final minute to pull out a squeaker, 42-37. VanderKelen had completed 33 of 48 passes for 419 yards and two touchdowns — but time ran out just seconds too soon for the unlucky Badgers. At season's end, Pat Richter was again voted to the All-America team, and VanderKelen won well-deserved conference MVP honors.

After Milt Bruhn's departure Wisconsin's coaching duties passed to former quarterback star John Coatta, who returned to coach from 1967 to 1969; to John Jardine, who took over from 1970 to 1977; and to Dave McClain, who began his Wisconsin coaching career in 1978.

*Above: Quarterback Ron VanderKelen (5) drops back to make a pass versus OSU, 1962. The Badgers went to the Rose Bowl on the strength of VanderKelen's passing, but lost to a powerful USC squad, 42-37.*

*Left: Quarterback Mike Howard (7) in action, 1985.*

*Opposite top: John Coatta was Wisconsin's quarterback in the early 1950s. He became the Badgers' coach in 1967, and left in 1969.*

*Opposite bottom: Fullback Alan Ameche, 'The Horse', ran like the wind to lead the Badgers to the Big Ten championship in 1952. He won the Heisman Trophy in 1954, and has become a legend in Wisconsin football history.*

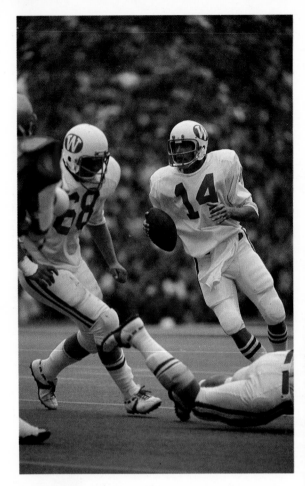

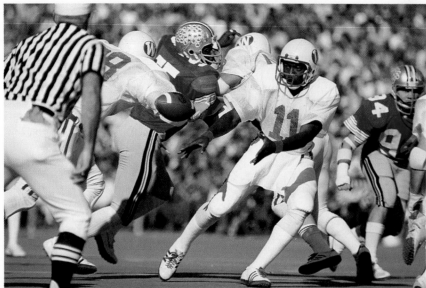

Above: *Quarterback Gregg Bohlig (14) in action, 1974.*

Top right: *Quarterback Charles Green (11) in action, 1975.*

Right: *Quarterback Randy Wright (12) looks for an opening while Chris Osswald (78) defends versus OSU, 1983.*

Below right: *Quarterback Bud Keyes (12) in action, 1985.*

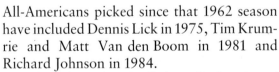

All-Americans picked since that 1962 season have included Dennis Lick in 1975, Tim Krumrie and Matt Van den Boom in 1981 and Richard Johnson in 1984.

Badger fans also thrilled to the heroics of Rufus 'Road Runner' Ferguson, who broke Alan Ameche's single-season rushing record in 1971, and Billy Marek. Marek compiled career totals of 3709 yards rushing and 46 touchdowns by his senior year of 1975, but had the misfortune of playing in the shadow of Ohio State star Archie Griffin.

The Wisconsin Badgers are still looking for respect, and under Dave McClain they made appearances in several post-season bowl games in the early 1980s. At present they may well be down on the conference list, but they do not doubt that someday soon they will be back in the Rose Bowl.

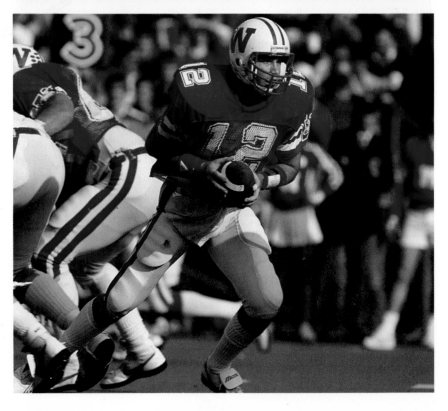

# Big Ten Conference Champions

| Year | School | Year | School | Year | School | Year | School |
|------|--------|------|--------|------|--------|------|--------|
| 1896 | Wisconsin | 1918 | Illinois | 1939 | Ohio State | 1965 | Michigan State |
| 1897 | Wisconsin | | Michigan | 1940 | Minnesota | 1966 | Michigan State |
| 1898 | Michigan | | Purdue | 1941 | Minnesota | 1967 | Indiana |
| 1899 | Chicago | 1919 | Illinois | 1942 | Ohio State | | Minnesota |
| 1900 | Iowa | 1920 | Ohio State | 1943 | Michigan | 1968 | Ohio State |
| | Minnesota | 1921 | Iowa | | Purdue | 1969 | Michigan |
| 1901 | Michigan | 1922 | Iowa | 1944 | Ohio State | | Ohio State |
| | Wisconsin | | Michigan | 1945 | Indiana | 1970 | Ohio State |
| 1902 | Michigan | 1923 | Illinois | 1946 | Illinois | 1971 | Michigan |
| 1903 | Michigan | | Michigan | 1947 | Michigan | 1972 | Michigan |
| | Minnesota | 1924 | Chicago | 1948 | Michigan | | Ohio State |
| | Northwestern | 1925 | Michigan | 1949 | Michigan | 1973 | Ohio State |
| 1904 | Michigan | 1926 | Michigan | | Ohio State | | Michigan |
| | Minnesota | | Northwestern | 1950 | Michigan | 1974 | Ohio State |
| 1905 | Chicago | 1927 | Illinois | 1951 | Illinois | | Michigan |
| 1906 | Michigan | 1928 | Illinois | 1952 | Purdue | 1975 | Ohio State |
| | Minnesota | 1929 | Purdue | | Wisconsin | 1976 | Michigan |
| | Wisconsin | 1930 | Michigan | 1953 | Illinois | | Ohio State |
| 1907 | Chicago | | Northwestern | | Michigan State | 1977 | Michigan |
| 1908 | Chicago | 1931 | Michigan | 1954 | Ohio State | | Ohio State |
| 1909 | Minnesota | | Northwestern | 1955 | Ohio State | 1978 | Michigan |
| 1910 | Illinois | | Purdue | 1956 | Iowa | | Michigan State |
| | Minnesota | 1932 | Michigan | 1957 | Ohio State | 1979 | Ohio State |
| 1911 | Minnesota | 1933 | Michigan | 1958 | Iowa | 1980 | Michigan |
| 1912 | Wisconsin | 1934 | Minnesota | 1959 | Wisconsin | 1981 | Iowa |
| 1913 | Chicago | 1935 | Minnesota | 1960 | Iowa | | Ohio State |
| 1914 | Illinois | | Ohio State | | Minnesota | 1982 | Michigan |
| 1915 | Illinois | 1936 | Northwestern | 1961 | Ohio State | 1983 | Illinois |
| | Minnesota | 1937 | Minnesota | 1962 | Wisconsin | 1984 | Ohio State |
| 1916 | Ohio State | 1938 | Minnesota | 1963 | Illinois | 1985 | Iowa |
| 1917 | Ohio State | | Purdue | 1964 | Michigan | 1986 | Michigan/OSU |

# Heisman Memorial Trophy Winners

Awarded annually to the nation's outstanding college football player. Presented by the Downtown Athletic Club of New York City, as selected by a poll of sports journalists.

| | |
|---|---|
| 1935 | Jay Berwanger, Chicago, HB |
| 1939 | Nile Kinnick, Iowa, HB |
| 1940 | Tom Harmon, Michigan, HB |
| 1941 | Bruce Smith, Minnesota, HB |
| 1944 | Leslie Horvath, Ohio State, QB |
| 1950 | Vic Janowicz, Ohio State, HB |
| 1954 | Alan Ameche, Wisconsin, FB |
| 1955 | Howard Cassady, Ohio State, HB |
| 1974 | Archie Griffin, Ohio State, RB |
| 1975 | Archie Griffin, Ohio State, RB |

# Outland Award Winners

Awarded annually to the outstanding interior lineman. Selected by the Football Writers Association of America.

| | |
|---|---|
| 1949 | Ed Bagdon, Michigan State, G |
| 1955 | Calvin Jones, Iowa, G |
| 1956 | Jim Parker, Ohio State, G |
| 1957 | Alex Karras, Iowa, T |
| 1960 | Tom Brown, Minnesota, G |
| 1962 | Bobby Bell, Minnesota, T |
| 1970 | Jim Stillwagon, Ohio State, LB |
| 1973 | John Hicks, Ohio State, G |

# Longest Winning Streaks
### (of more than 25 wins)

| Wins | Team | Years | Ended By | Score |
|------|------|-------|----------|-------|
| 29 | Michigan | 1901-03 | Minnesota | 6-6 |
| 28 | Michigan State | 1950-53 | Purdue | 6-0 |
| 26 | Michigan | 1903-05 | Chicago | 2-0 |
| 25 | Michigan | 1946-49 | Army | 21-7 |

# College Football Coach of the Year Winners

Selected annually by the American Football Coaches Association and the Football Writers Association of America.

| | |
|---|---|
| 1935 Lynn Waldorf, Northwestern | 1957 Woody Hayes, Ohio State |
| 1939 Eddie Anderson, Iowa | 1960 Murray Warmath, Minnesota |
| 1943 Amoz Alonzo Stagg, Pacific (formerly of Chicago) | 1965 Duffy Daugherty, Michigan State |
| 1944 Carroll Widdoes, Ohio State | 1967 John Pont, Indiana |
| 1945 Bo McMillan, Indiana | 1968 Woody Hayes, Ohio State |
| 1947 Fritz Crisler, Michigan | 1969 Bo Schembechler, Michigan |
| 1948 Bennie Oosterbaan, Michigan | 1970 Alex Agase, Northwestern |
| 1952 Biggie Munn, Michigan State | 1975 Woody Hayes, Ohio State |
| 1955 Duffy Daugherty, Michigan State | 1979 Earle Bruce, Ohio State |

# ALL-TIME BIG TEN FOOTBALL RECORDS

(All Games – Does not include 1986-87 Postseason Bowl Games)

## RUSHING (Season)

| | | Year | Yards | Atts |
|---|---|---|---|---|
| 1 | Lorenzo White, MSU | 1985 | 2066 | 419 |
| 2 | Keith Byars, OSU | 1984 | 1764 | 336 |
| 3 | Archie Griffin, OSU | 1974 | 1695 | 256 |
| 4 | Archie Griffin, OSU | 1973 | 1577 | 247 |
| 5 | Tim Spencer, OSU | 1982 | 1538 | 273 |
| 6 | Eric Allen, MSU | 1971 | 1494 | 259 |
| 7 | Rob Lytle, MICH | 1976 | 1469 | 221 |
| 8 | Butch Woolfolk, MICH | 1981 | 1459 | 253 |
| 9 | Archie Griffin, OSU | 1975 | 1450 | 262 |
| 10 | Ron Johnson, MICH | 1968 | 1391 | 255 |
| 11 | Gordon Bell, MICH | 1975 | 1388 | 273 |
| 12 | Lawrence Ricks, MICH | 1982 | 1388 | 266 |

## RUSHING (Career)

| | | Years | Yards | Atts |
|---|---|---|---|---|
| 1 | Archie Griffin, OSU | 1972-75 | 5589 | 924 |
| 2 | Butch Woolfolk, MICH | 1978-81 | 3861 | 718 |
| 3 | Billy Marek, WIS | 1972-75 | 3709 | 719 |
| 4 | Tim Spencer, OSU | 1979-82 | 3553 | 644 |
| 5 | Alan Ameche, WIS | 1951-54 | 3345 | 701 |
| 6 | Rob Lytle, MICH | 1973-76 | 3317 | 557 |
| 7 | Otis Armstrong, PUR | 1970-72 | 3315 | 670 |
| | Lorenzo White, MSU | 1984- | 3315 | 725 |
| 9 | Mike Harkrader, IND | 1976-80 | 3257 | 718 |
| 10 | Keith Byars, OSU | 1982-85 | 3200 | 619 |
| 11 | Marion Barber, MINN | 1977-80 | 3187 | 656 |
| 12 | Bill Taylor, MICH | 1969-71 | 3072 | 587 |
| 13 | Larry Emery, WIS | 1983-86 | 2979 | 582 |

## PASSING (Season)

| | | Year | Yards | Comp | Att | TD |
|---|---|---|---|---|---|---|
| 1 | Tony Eason, ILL | 1982 | 3671 | 313 | 505 | 18 |
| 2 | Jim Everett, PUR | 1985 | 3651 | 285 | 450 | 23 |
| 3 | Tony Eason, ILL | 1981 | 3360 | 284 | 406 | 20 |
| 4 | Jack Trudeau, ILL | 1985 | 3339 | 322 | 501 | 18 |
| 5 | Chuck Long, IOWA | 1985 | 3297 | 260 | 388 | 27 |
| 6 | Jim Everett, PUR | 1984 | 3256 | 249 | 431 | 18 |
| 7 | Mark Herrmann, PUR | 1980 | 3212 | 242 | 368 | 23 |
| 8 | Dave Wilson, ILL | 1980 | 3154 | 245 | 463 | 19 |
| 9 | Chuck Long, IOWA | 1984 | 2871 | 216 | 322 | 22 |
| 10 | Sandy Schwab, NU | 1982 | 2735 | 234 | 416 | 14 |
| 11 | Jack Trudeau, ILL | 1984 | 2724 | 247 | 378 | 18 |
| 12 | Scott Campbell, PUR | 1981 | 2686 | 185 | 321 | 16 |
| 13 | Scott Campbell, PUR | 1982 | 2626 | 218 | 399 | 14 |
| 14 | Jack Trudeau, ILL | 1983 | 2624 | 226 | 363 | 19 |
| 15 | Chuck Long, IOWA | 1983 | 2601 | 157 | 265 | 14 |

## PASSING (Career)

| | | Years | Yards | Comp | Atts | TD |
|---|---|---|---|---|---|---|
| 1 | Chuck Long, IOWA | 1981-85 | 10461 | 782 | 1203 | 74 |
| 2 | Mark Herrmann, PUR | 1977-80 | 9946 | 772 | 1309 | 71 |
| 3 | Jack Trudeau, ILL | 1981,83-85 | 8723 | 797 | 1248 | 55 |
| 4 | Scott Campbell, PUR | 1980-83 | 7636 | 609 | 1060 | 45 |
| 5 | Art Schlichter, OSU | 1978-81 | 7547 | 497 | 951 | 50 |
| 6 | Jim Everett, PUR | 1981-85 | 7411 | 572 | 965 | 43 |
| 7 | Tony Eason | 1981-82 | 7031 | 561 | 911 | 38 |
| 8 | Steve Bradley, IND | 1983-85 | 6579 | 532 | 1033 | 35 |
| 9 | Dave Yarema, MSU | 1982-86 | 5809 | 464 | 767 | 43 |
| 10 | Ed Smith, MSU | 1976-78 | 5706 | 418 | 789 | 43 |
| 11 | Sandy Schwab, NU | 1982-85 | 5679 | 533 | 973 | 23 |
| 12 | Mike Tomczak, OSU | 1981-84 | 5569 | 476 | 675 | 32 |
| 13 | Mike Phipps, PUR | 1967-69 | 5423 | 375 | 733 | 37 |
| 14 | Jim Harbaugh, MICH | 1983-86 | 5277 | 374 | 597 | 31 |
| 15 | Randy Wright, WIS | 1981-83 | 5003 | 377 | 714 | 38 |

## TOTAL OFFENSE (Season)

| | | Year | Yards |
|---|---|---|---|
| 1 | Tony Eason, ILL | 1982 | 3672 |
| 2 | Jim Everett, PUR | 1985 | 3589 |
| 3 | Tony Eason, ILL | 1981 | 3331 |
| 4 | Jack Trudeau, ILL | 1985 | 3321 |
| 5 | Jim Everett, PUR | 1984 | 3207 |
| 6 | Chuck Long, IOWA | 1985 | 3172 |
| 7 | Mark Herrmann, PUR | 1980 | 3026 |
| 8 | Dave Wilson, ILL | 1980 | 2960 |
| 9 | Scott Campbell, PUR | 1981 | 2809 |
| 10 | Jack Trudeau, ILL | 1984 | 2797 |
| 11 | Mike Phipps, PUR | 1969 | 2745 |
| 12 | Chuck Long, IOWA | 1984 | 2717 |
| 13 | Jim Harbaugh, MICH | 1986 | 2685 |
| 14 | Steve Bradley, IND | 1984 | 2561 |
| 15 | Sandy Schwab, NU | 1982 | 2555 |

## TOTAL OFFENSE (Career)

| | | Years | Yards |
|---|---|---|---|
| 1 | Chuck Long, IOWA | 1981-85 | 10254 |
| 2 | Mark Herrmann, PUR | 1977-80 | 9134 |
| 3 | Art Schlichter, OSU | 1978-81 | 8850 |
| 4 | Jack Trudeau, ILL | 1981,83-85 | 8640 |
| 5 | Scott Campbell, PUR | 1980-83 | 7526 |
| 6 | Jim Everett, PUR | 1981-85 | 7284 |
| 7 | Tony Eason, ILL | 1981-82 | 7002 |
| 8 | Steve Bradley, IND | 1983-85 | 6835 |
| 9 | Steve Smith, MICH | 1980-83 | 6554 |
| 10 | Rick Leach, MICH | 1975-78 | 6460 |

| 11 | Mike Phipps, PUR | 1967-69 | 5883 |
|----|------------------|---------|------|
| 12 | Archie Griffin, OSU | 1972-75 | 5589 |
| 13 | Mike Tomczak, OSU | 1981-84 | 5568 |
| 14 | Ed Smith, MSU | 1976-78 | 5556 |
| 15 | Jim Harbaugh, MICH | 1983-86 | 5484 |

## RECEIVING (Season)

| | | Years | No | Yards |
|----|------------------|-------|-----|-------|
| 1 | David Williams, ILL | 1984 | 101 | 1278 |
| 2 | Rodney Carter, PUR | 1985 | 98 | 1099 |
| 3 | David Williams, ILL | 1985 | 92 | 1156 |
| 4 | Ricky Edwards, NU | 1983 | 83 | 570 |
| 5 | Mike Martin, ILL | 1982 | 77 | 1068 |
| 6 | Jack Clancy, MICH | 1966 | 76 | 1079 |
| 7 | Dave Young, PUR | 1980 | 70 | 959 |
| 8 | David Williams, ILL | 1983 | 69 | 958 |
| 9 | Bart Burrell, PUR | 1980 | 66 | 1001 |
| | Cris Carter, OSU | 1986 | 66 | 1066 |
| 11 | Steve Griffin, PUR | 1984 | 64 | 1060 |
| | Keith Chappelle, IOWA | 1980 | 64 | 1037 |
| | Jim Beirne, PUR | 1966 | 64 | 768 |
| | Tim Brewster, ILL | 1983 | 64 | 688 |
| 15 | Steve Bryant, PUR | 1981 | 61 | 971 |

## RECEIVING (Career)

| | | Year | No | Yards |
|----|------------------|-------|-----|-------|
| 1 | David Williams, ILL | 1983-85 | 262 | 3392 |
| 2 | Rodney, Carter, PUR | 1982-85 | 181 | 1814 |
| 3 | Dave Young, PUR | 1977-80 | 180 | 2316 |
| 4 | Cris Carter, OSU | 1984- | 164 | 2664 |
| 5 | Anthony Carter, MICH | 1979-82 | 161 | 3076 |
| 6 | John Wright, ILL | 1965-67 | 159 | 2284 |
| 7 | Gary Williams, OSU | 1979-82 | 154 | 2792 |
| 8 | Steve Griffin, PUR | 1982-85 | 146 | 2234 |
| | Ronnie Harmon, IOWA | 1982-85 | 146 | 2045 |
| 10 | Mike Martin, ILL | 1979-82 | 143 | 2304 |
| 11 | Bart Burrell, PUR | 1977-80 | 140 | 2126 |
| | Ricky Edwards, NU | 1980-83 | 140 | 1056 |
| 13 | Jim Beirne, PUR | 1965-67 | 138 | 1795 |
| 14 | Jack Clancy, MICH | 1963,5,6 | 132 | 1919 |
| 15 | Al Toon, WIS | 1981-84 | 131 | 2103 |

## PUNTING (Season) (40 or more)

| | | Year | No | Avg |
|----|------------------|-------|-----|-----|
| 1 | Reggie Roby, IOWA | 1981 | 48 | 49.8 |
| 2 | Reggie Roby, IOWA | 1982 | 56 | 47.2 |
| 3 | Tom Tupa, OSU | 1984 | 45 | 47.1 |
| 4 | Ray Stachowicz, MSU | 1980 | 71 | 46.2 |
| | Adam Kelly, MINN | 1984 | 59 | 46.2 |
| 6 | John Kidd, NU | 1982 | 52 | 45.6 |
| 7 | Ralf Mojsiejenko, MSU | 1984 | 76 | 44.7 |
| | Greg Montgomery, MSU | 1985 | 76 | 44.7 |
| 9 | Ralf Mojsiejenko, MSU | 1982 | 77 | 44.6 |
| 10 | Ray Stachowicz, MSU | 1979 | 62 | 44.3 |
| 11 | Ralf Mojsiejenko, MSU | 1983 | 74 | 43.9 |
| | Chuck Razmic, IND | 1984 | 57 | 43.9 |
| 13 | Tom Orosz, OSU | 1978 | 47 | 43.7 |
| 14 | Tom Tupa, OSU | 1986 | 50 | 43.6 |
| 15 | Don Bracken, MICH | 1981 | 50 | 43.3 |

## PUNTING (Career) (100 or more)

| | | Years | No | Avg |
|----|------------------|-------|-----|-----|
| 1 | Reggie Roby, IOWA | 1979-82 | 180 | 45.5 |
| 2 | Greg Montgomery, MSU | 1985- | 114 | 45.3 |
| 3 | Tom Tupa, OSU | 1984- | 145 | 44.1 |

| 4 | Ralf Mojsiejenko, MSU | 1981-84 | 279 | 43.6 |
|----|------------------|---------|------|------|
| 5 | Ray Stachowicz, MSU | 1977-80 | 230 | 43.3 |
| 6 | Adam Kelly, MINN | 1983-85 | 136 | 43.2 |
| 7 | Tom Skladany, OSU | 1973-76 | 160 | 42.7 |
| 8 | Monte Robbins, MICH | 1984- | 143 | 42.6 |
| 9 | John Kidd, NU | 1980-83 | 261 | 41.8 |
| | Tom Orosz, OSU | 1977-80 | 162 | 41.8 |
| 11 | Scott Cepicky, WIS | 1984- | 192 | 41.5 |
| 12 | Jim Bakken, WIS | 1959-61 | 111 | 40.4 |
| 13 | Dick Milaeger, WIS | 1975-77 | 121 | 40.3 |
| 14 | Don Bracken, MICH | 1980-83 | 203 | 40.2 |
| 15 | Chuck Razmic, IND | 1981-84 | 242 | 39.9 |

## SCORING (Season)

| | | Year | TD | XP | FG | Pts |
|----|------------------|------|-----|-----|-----|-----|
| 1 | Pete Johnson, OSU | 1975 | 26 | — | — | 156 |
| 2 | Keith Byars, OSU | 1984 | 24 | — | — | 144 |
| 3 | Keith Byars, OSU | 1983 | 22 | — | — | 132 |
| 4 | Harold Henson, OSU | 1972 | 20 | — | — | 120 |
| 5 | Tom Harmon, MICH | 1940 | 16 | 18 | 1 | 117 |
| 6 | Ron Johnson, MICH | 1968 | 19 | 1† | — | 116 |
| 7 | Leroy Keyes, PUR | 1967 | 19 | — | — | 114 |
| | Billy Marek, WIS | 1974 | 19 | — | — | 114 |
| | Pete Johnson, OSU | 1976 | 19 | — | — | 114 |
| 10 | Eric Allen, MSU | 1971 | 18 | 1† | — | 110 |
| 11 | Stan Brown, PUR | 1969 | 18 | — | — | 108 |
| 12 | Rob Houghtlin, IOWA | 1985 | — | 48 | 19 | 105 |
| 13 | Mike Bass, ILL | 1982 | — | 32 | 24 | 104 |
| 14 | Chris White, ILL | 1984 | — | 31 | 24 | 103 |
| 15 | Tom Harmon, MICH | 1939 | 14 | 15 | 1 | 102 |
| | John Brockington, OSU | 1970 | 17 | — | — | 102 |
| | Jim Otis, OSU | 1968 | 17 | — | — | 102 |
| | Lorenzo White, MSU | 1985 | 17 | — | — | 102 |

† Two-point conversion

## SCORING (Career)

| | | Year | TD | XP | FG | Pts |
|----|------------------|---------|-----|-----|-----|-----|
| 1 | Pete Johnson, OSU | 1973-76 | 58 | — | — | 348 |
| 2 | Keith Byars, OSU | 1983-85 | 50 | — | — | 300 |
| 3 | Vlade Janakievski, OSU | 1977-80 | — | 172 | 41 | 295 |
| 4 | Rich Spangler, OSU | 1982-85 | — | 177 | 39 | 294 |
| 5 | Billy Marek, WIS | 1972-75 | 46 | 1 | — | 278 |
| 6 | Tom Nichol, IOWA | 1981-84 | — | 142 | 45 | 277 |
| 7 | Chris White, ILL | 1983-85 | — | 103 | 53 | 262 |
| 8 | Morten Andersen, MSU | 1978-81 | — | 120 | 45 | 261 |
| 9 | Anthony Carter, MICH | 1979-82 | 40 | 2† | — | 244 |
| 10 | Tom Harmon, MICH | 1938-40 | 33 | 33 | 2 | 237 |
| 11 | Hans Neilsen, MSU | 1974-77 | — | 98 | 44 | 230 |
| 12 | Howard Cassady, OSU | 1952-55 | 37 | — | — | 222 |
| | Leroy Keyes, PUR | 1966-68 | 37 | — | — | 222 |
| 14 | Paul Rogind, MINN | 1976-79 | — | 85 | 44 | 217 |
| 15 | Harold Henson, OSU | 1972-74 | 36 | — | — | 216 |
| | Jim Gallery, MINN | 1980-83 | — | 96 | 40 | 216 |

## FIELD GOALS (Season)

| | | Year | No |
|----|------------------|------|-----|
| 1 | Chris White, ILL | 1984 | 24 |
| | Mike Bass, ILL | 1982 | 24 |
| 3 | Todd Gregoire, WIS | 1984 | 20 |
| 4 | Rob Houghtlin, IOWA | 1985 | 19 |
| | John Duvic, NU | 1986 | 19 |
| 6 | Paul Rogind, MINN | 1977 | 18 |
| | Vlade Janakievski, OSU | 1979 | 18 |
| 8 | Hans Nielsen, MSU | 1977 | 17 |
| 9 | Rick Anderson, PUR | 1980 | 16 |
| | Tom Nichol, IOWA | 1984 | 16 |
| | Todd Gregoire, WIS | 1985 | 16 |
| | Mike Gillette, MICH | 1985 | 16 |

## FIELD GOALS (Career)

| | | Years | No |
|---|---|---|---|
| 1 | Chris White, ILL | 1983-85 | 53 |
| 2 | Todd Gregoire, WIS | 1984- | 49 |
| 3 | John Duvic, NU | 1983-86 | 46 |
| 4 | Tom Nichol, IOWA | 1981-84 | 45 |
| | Morten Andersen, MSU | 1978-81 | 45 |
| 6 | Hans Nielsen, MSU | 1974-77 | 44 |
| | Paul Rogind, MINN | 1976-79 | 44 |
| 8 | Vlade Janakievski, OSU | 1977-80 | 41 |
| | Mike Bass, ILL | 1980-82 | 41 |
| 10 | Jim Gallery, MINN | 1980-83 | 40 |
| 11 | Rich Spangler, OSU | 1982-85 | 39 |
| 12 | Dan Beaver, ILL | 1973-76 | 38 |
| 13 | Ralf Mojsiejenko, MSU | 1981-84 | 35 |
| 14 | Pat O'Dea, WIS | 1897-99 | 32 |
| | Rob Houghtlin, IOWA | 1985-86 | 32 |

## EXTRA POINTS (Season)

| | | Year | No |
|---|---|---|---|
| 1 | Dana Coin, MICH | 1971 | 55 |
| | Bob Wood, MICH | 1976 | 55 |
| 3 | Rich Spangler, OSU | 1983 | 53 |
| 4 | Morten Andersen, MSU | 1978 | 52 |
| | Tom Klaban, OSU | 1974 | 52 |
| | Jim Brieske, MICH | 1947 | 52 |
| 7 | Rob Houghtlin, IOWA | 1985 | 48 |
| 8 | Gregg Willner, MICH | 1978 | 47 |
| 9 | Tom Klaban, OSU | 1975 | 46 |
| 10 | Blair Conway, OSU | 1973 | 45 |
| | Rich Spangler, OSU | 1984 | 45 |
| | Vlade Janakievski, OSU | 1980 | 45 |
| | Kevin Rohde, WIS | 1983 | 45 |
| 14 | Vlade Janakievski, OSU | 1977 | 44 |
| | Jeff Jones, PUR | 1969 | 44 |
| | Tom Nichol, IOWA | 1983 | 44 |

## EXTRA POINTS (Career)

| | | Years | No |
|---|---|---|---|
| 1 | Rich Spangler, OSU | 1982-85 | 177 |
| 2 | Vlade Janakievski, OSU | 1977-80 | 172 |
| 3 | Tom Nichol, IOWA | 1981-84 | 142 |
| 4 | Morten Andersen, MSU | 1978-81 | 126 |
| 5 | Ali Haji-Shiekh, MICH | 1979-82 | 117 |
| 6 | Mike Lantry, MICH | 1972-74 | 113 |
| 7 | Chris White, ILL | 1983-85 | 103 |
| 8 | Tom Klaban, OSU | 1972-75 | 100 |
| 9 | Hans Nielsen, MSU | 1974-77 | 98 |
| 10 | Jim Gallery, MINN | 1980-83 | 96 |
| 11 | Gregg Willner, MICH | 1976-78 | 94 |
| | George Smith, MSU | 1947-49 | 94 |
| 13 | Mike Bass, ILL | 1980-82 | 89 |
| 14 | Bob Wood, MICH | 1975-76 | 87 |
| 15 | Paul Rogind, MINN | 1976-79 | 85 |
| | Rob Houghtlin, IOWA | 1985-86 | 85 |

## KICKING POINTS (Season)

| | | Year | No |
|---|---|---|---|
| 1 | Rob Houghtlin, IOWA | 1985 | 105 |
| 2 | Mike Bass, ILL | 1982 | 104 |
| 3 | Chris White, ILL | 1984 | 103 |
| 4 | Vlade Janakievski, OSU | 1979 | 97 |
| | Rob Houghtlin, IOWA | 1985 | 97 |
| 6 | Vlade Janakievski, OSU | 1980 | 90 |
| 7 | Tom Nichol, IOWA | 1984 | 89 |
| 8 | Rich Spangler, OSU | 1984 | 87 |

| | | | |
|---|---|---|---|
| 9 | Rick Anderson, PUR | 1980 | 86 |
| | Tom Nichol, IOWA | 1983 | 86 |
| 11 | Todd Gregoire, WIS | 1984 | 83 |
| 12 | Bob Atha, OSU | 1981 | 82 |
| 13 | Chris White, ILL | 1983 | 81 |
| 14 | Tom Klaban, OSU | 1974 | 79 |
| | Dana Coin, MICH | 1971 | 79 |
| | Mike Gillette, MICH | 1985 | 79 |

## KICKING POINTS (Career)

| | | Years | No |
|---|---|---|---|
| 1 | Vlade Janakievski, OSU | 1977-80 | 295 |
| 2 | Rich Spangler, OSU | 1982-85 | 294 |
| 3 | Tom Nichol, IOWA | 1981-84 | 277 |
| 4 | Chris White, ILL | 1983-85 | 262 |
| 5 | Morten Andersen, MSU | 1978-81 | 261 |
| 6 | Hans Nielsen, MSU | 1974-77 | 230 |
| 7 | Paul Rogind, MINN | 1976-79 | 218 |
| 8 | Mike Bass, ILL | 1980-82 | 212 |
| | Todd Gregoire, WIS | 1984- | 212 |
| 10 | Ali Haji-Shiekh, MICH | 1979-82 | 210 |
| 11 | John Duvic, NU | 1983-86 | 200 |
| 12 | Dan Beaver, ILL | 1973-76 | 198 |
| 13 | Rob Houghtlin, IOWA | 1985-86 | 181 |
| 14 | Vince Lamia, WIS | 1973-76 | 180 |
| 15 | Chip Lohmiller, MINN | 1984- | 179 |

## INTERCEPTIONS (Season)

| | | Year | No |
|---|---|---|---|
| 1 | Al Brosky, ILL | 1950 | 11 |
| | Al Brosky, ILL | 1951 | 11 |
| 3 | Tom Curtis, MICH | 1968 | 10 |
| | Mike Gow, ILL | 1973 | 10 |
| 5 | Chuck Lenz, MSU | 1949 | 9 |
| | Neovia Greyer, WIS | 1970 | 9 |
| | Mike Sensibaugh, OSU | 1969 | 9 |

## INTERCEPTIONS (Career)

| | | Years | No |
|---|---|---|---|
| 1 | Al Brosky, ILL | 1950-52 | 29 |
| 2 | Tom Curtis, MICH | 1967-69 | 25 |
| 3 | Mike Sensibaugh, OSU | 1968-70 | 22 |
| 4 | Lynn Chandnois, MSU | 1946-49 | 20 |
| 5 | Fred Bruney, OSU | 1950-52 | 19 |
| | Mike Gow, ILL | 1972-74 | 19 |
| | Tim Wilbur, IND | 1979,80-82 | 19 |
| 8 | Nile Kinnick, IOWA | 1937-39 | 18 |
| | Neovia Greyer, WIS | 1969-71 | 18 |
| | Devon Mitchell, IOWA | 1982-85 | 18 |
| 11 | Neal Colzie, OSU | 1972-74 | 17 |
| 12 | Ted Provost, OSU | 1967-69 | 16 |
| | Phil Parker, MSU | 1982-85 | 16 |

## TD RECEPTIONS (Career)

| | | Years | No |
|---|---|---|---|
| 1 | Anthony Carter, MICH | 1979-82 | 37 |
| 2 | Jade Butcher, IND | 1967-69 | 30 |
| 3 | Dave Young, PUR | 1977-80 | 27 |
| | Cris Carter, OSU | 1984- | 27 |
| 5 | Kirk Gibson, MSU | 1975-78 | 24 |
| | David Williams, ILL | 1983-85 | 24 |
| 7 | Al Toon, WIS | 1981-84 | 19 |
| 8 | Jim Bierne, PUR | 1965-67 | 17 |
| 9 | Dick Rifenberg, MICH | 1944-48 | 16 |
| | Gene Washington, MSU | 1964-66 | 16 |
| | Doug Donley, OSU | 1977-80 | 16 |
| | Gary Williams, OSU | 1979-82 | 16 |

| | | | |
|---|---|---|---|
| 13 | Trent Smock, IND | 1973-75 | 15 |
| | Eugene Byrd, MSU | 1975-79 | 15 |
| | Steve Bryant, PUR | 1980-81 | 15 |
| | Mike Martin, ILL | 1979-82 | 15 |

## CONSECUTIVE PAT (Career)

| | | Years | No |
|---|---|---|---|
| 1 | Ali Haji-Shiekh, MICH | 1979-82 | 76 |
| 2 | David Freud, IND | 1976-78 | 65 |

| | | | |
|---|---|---|---|
| 3 | Morten Andersen, MSU | 1976-80 | 62 |
| 4 | Paul Rogind, MINN | 1976-80 | 56 |
| 5 | Dana Coin, MICH | 1971 | 55 |
| | Chris White, ILL | 1984-85 | 55 |
| 7 | Vlade Janakievski, OSU | 1977-78 | 47 |
| 8 | Vlade Janakievski, OSU | 1979-80 | 46 |
| | Mike Gillette, MICH | 1985-86 | 46 |
| 10 | Rich Spangler, OSU | 1984-85 | 44 |
| 11 | Vlade Janakievski, OSU | 1978-79 | 42 |
| 12 | Rich Spangler, OSU | 1983 | 41 |

# (Home team in Caps) Individual Single Game Records

## SCORING

### MOST POINTS:
| | | |
|---|---|---|
| 30 | TB Keith Byars (5 TD), OSU vs Ill, 10-13-84 |
| 30 | HB Ron Johnson (5 TD), MICH vs Wis, 11-16-68 |
| 30 | HB Mike Northington (5 TD), PUR vs Iowa, 11-3-73 |
| 30 | HB Billy Marek (5 TD), WIS vs Minn, 11-23-74 |

### MOST TOUCHDOWNS:
| | |
|---|---|
| 5 | TB Keith Byars, OSU vs Ill, 10-13-84 |
| 5 | HB Ron Johnson, MICH vs Wis, 11-16-68 |
| 5 | HB Mike Northington, PUR vs Iowa, 11-3-73 |
| 5 | HB Billy Marek, WIS vs Minn, 11-23-74 |

### MOST PAT ATTEMPTS:
11   HB Vic Janowicz (10 made), OSU vs Iowa, 10-28-50

### MOST PAT MADE:
| | |
|---|---|
| 10 | HB Vic Janowicz (11 att), OSU vs Iowa, 10-28-50 |
| 10 | PK Ali Haji-Shiekh (10 att), MICH vs Ill, 11-7-81 |

### MOST FIELD GOALS:
| | |
|---|---|
| 5 | Chris White, ILL vs Wis (19, 48, 40, 37, 46), 10-6-84 |
| 5 | Dan Beaver, ILL vs Pur (52, 44, 35, 34, 32), 10-10-73 |
| 5 | Rick Anderson, PUR vs Mich St (37, 45, 36, 25, 28), 10-25-80 |
| 5 | Mike Bass, Ill vs WIS (19, 21, 30, 44, 46), 10-23-82 |
| 4 | Has been accomplished 19 times; in 1986 by Matt Frantz, Ohio St vs PUR, 10-18-86; Chip Lohmiller, MINN vs Ind, 10-18-86; and Jonathan Briggs, Pur vs ILL, 10-11-86 |

## LONGEST SCORING PLAYS

### RUN FROM SCRIMMAGE:
| | |
|---|---|
| 96 yds | HB Eddie Vincent, IOWA vs Pur, 11-6-54 |
| 94 yds | FB Mike Pruitt, Pur vs IOWA, 11-2-74 |
| 92 yds | TB Butch Woolfolk, MICH vs Wis, 11-3-79 |
| 92 yds | TB Royce Mix, IOWA vs Ill, 11-25-72 |

### PASS:
| | |
|---|---|
| 95 yds | QB Len Dawson to Erich Barnes, PUR vs North, 1955 |
| 94 yds | QB Mitch Anderson to Jim Lash, North vs MSU, 1972 |
| 93 yds | QB Mark Vlasic to Quinn Early, IOWA vs North, 1986 |

### FIELD GOAL:
| | |
|---|---|
| 63 yds | PK Morten Andersen, Mich St vs OSU, 9-19-81 |
| 62 yds | PK Chip Lohmiller, MINN vs Iowa, 11-22-86 |
| 61 yds | PK Ralf Mojsiejenko, Mich St vs ILL, 9-11-82 |

### PASS INTERCEPTION:
| | |
|---|---|
| 100 yds | DB David Brown, Ohio St vs PUR, 10-18-86 |
| 100 yds | DB Rod Woodson, Pur vs IOWA, 11-15-86 |

### KICKOFF RETURN:
100 yds   HB George Rice, Iowa vs PUR, 10-6-51; HB Bill Wentz, Ohio St vs ILL, 10-8-60; Rick Upchurch, Minn vs WIS, 11-23-74; Ira Matthews, WIS vs Iowa, 11-6-76; Bobby Weber, Minn vs OSU, 9-17-77; and Michael Jones, WIS vs North, 9-29-84

### PUNT RETURN:
| | |
|---|---|
| 95 yds | E Al Brenner, Mich St vs ILL, 10-1-66 |
| 95 yds | E Bill Happell, Iowa vs MINN, 11-17-84 |

### RECOVERED FUMBLE:
92 yds   Dale Keneipp, Ind vs MINN, 11-4-78

### BLOCKED KICK RETURN:
92 yds   Earl Falison, Ind vs MSU, 11-8-58 (FG att)

## RUSHING

### MOST RUSHES:
57   FB Kent Kitzmann (266 yds), Minn vs ILL, 11-12-77

### MOST YARDS GAINED:
| | |
|---|---|
| 350 yds | TB Eric Allen (29 rushes), Mich St vs PUR, 10-30-71 |
| 347 yds | HB Ron Johnson (31 rushes), MICH vs Wis, 11-16-68 |
| 316 yds | HB Mike Adamle (40 rushes), NU vs Wis, 10-18-69 |
| 306 yds | HB Billy Marek (43 rushes), WIS vs Minn, 11-23-74 |
| 286 yds | HB Ed Podolak (17 rushes), IOWA vs North, 11-9-68 |
| 286 yds | TB Lorenzo White (25 rushes), Mich St vs IND, 11-2-85 |

### MOST YARDS PER PLAY:
| | |
|---|---|
| 18.0 | FB Rob Lytle (10-180), MICH vs Mich St, 10-9-76 |
| 17.9 | FB Mike Pruitt (10-179), PUR vs Iowa, 11-2-74 |

## TOTAL OFFENSE

### MOST PLAYS:
| | |
|---|---|
| 76 | QB Dave Wilson (69 pass, 7 rush), Ill vs OSU, 11-8-80 |
| 76 | QB Sandy Schwab (71 pass, 5 rush), NU vs Mich, 10-23-82 |
| 75 | QB Mike Hohensee (67 pass, 8 rush), MINN vs Ohio St, 11-7-81 |

### MOST YARDS GAINED:
| | |
|---|---|
| 585 yds | QB Dave Wilson (7 − -36 rush, 69-43 − 621 pass), Ill vs OSU, 11-8-80 |
| 482 yds | QB Jim Everett (6 − 15 rush, 55-35 − 497 pass), Pur vs OSU, 10-19-85 |
| 480 yds | QB Tony Eason (7 − 1 rush, 51-37 − 479 pass), Ill vs WIS, 10-23-82 |
| 477 yds | QB Scott Campbell (10 − -39 rush, 52-31 − 516 pass), PUR vs Ohio St, 10-31-81 |
| 459 yds | QB Jim Everett (9 − -5 rush, 47-27 − 464 pass), PUR vs Ill, 10-12-85 |
| 450 yds | QB Tony Eason (6 − 41 rush, 48-27 − 409 pass), Ill vs NU, 11-21-81 |
| 405 yds | QB Chuck Long (1 − 6 rush, 26-19 − 399 pass), Iowa vs NU, 10-26-85 |

### YARDS PER PLAY:
18.0   FB Rob Lytle (10-180 rush), MICH vs Mich St, 10-9-76

## RECEIVING

**MOST CAUGHT:**

| | | |
|---|---|---|
| 17 | TE Jon Harvey (208 yds), NU vs Mich, 10-23-82 | |
| 16 | WR David Williams (164 yds, 3 TDs), Ill vs PUR, 10-12-85 | |
| 15 | E Todd Jenkins (189 yds, 2 TDs), North vs PUR, 10-18-82 | |
| 15 | RB Rodney Carter (190 yds, 1 TD), PUR vs Ill, 10-12-85 | |

**MOST YARDS GAINED:**

| | |
|---|---|
| 252 | Al Toon (8 catches), Wis vs PUR, 11-12-83 |
| 226 | Jim Lash (9 catches), NU vs Mich St, 11-25-72 |
| 226 | Todd Sheets (11 catches), NU vs Pur, 11-1-80 |

**MOST PASSES INTERCEPTED:**

| | |
|---|---|
| 4 | Clarence Bratt, WIS vs Minn, 11-20-54 |
| 4 | Paul Beery, Pur vs WIS, 10-9-76 |

## PASSING

**MOST ATTEMPTS:**

| | |
|---|---|
| 71 | QB Sandy Schwab (45 compl, 436 yds), NU vs Mich, 10-23-82 |
| 69 | QB Dave Wilson (43 compl, 621 yds), Ill vs OSU, 11-6-80 |

**MOST COMPLETED:**

| | |
|---|---|
| 45 | QB Sandy Schwab (71 att, 436 yds), NU vs Mich, 10-23-82 |
| 43 | QB Dave Wilson (69 att, 621 yds), Ill vs OSU, 11-6-80 |

**MOST YARDS GAINED:**

| | |
|---|---|
| 621 yds | QB Dave Wilson (43 of 69 att), Ill vs OSU, 11-8-80 |
| 516 yds | QB Campbell (31 of 52 att), PUR vs Ohio St, 10-31-81 |
| 497 yds | QB Jim Everett (35 of 55 att), Pur vs OSU, 10-19-85 |
| 479 yds | QB Tony Eason (37 of 51 att), Ill vs WIS, 10-23-82 |
| 464 yds | QB Jim Everett (27 of 47 att) PUR vs Ill, 10-12-85 |
| 444 yds | QB Hohensee (37 of 67 att), MINN vs Ohio St, 11-7-81 |
| 439 yds | QB Mark Herrmann (26 of 34 att), PUR vs Iowa, 11-8-80 |
| 436 yds | QB Sandy Schwab (45 of 71 att), NU vs Mich, 10-23-82 |
| 425 yds | QB Dave Wilson (35 of 58 att), ILL vs Pur, 10-18-80 |
| 420 yds | QB Chuck Long (23 of 33 att), IOWA vs North, 10-8-83 |
| 413 yds | QB Jack Trudeau (39 of 66 att), Ill vs PUR, 10-12-85 |
| 409 yds | QB Tony Eason (27 of 48 att), Ill vs NU, 11-21-81 |
| 403 yds | QB Dave Wilson (24 of 42 att), Ill vs IND, 11-15-80 |

**BEST COMPLETION PERCENTAGE (10 or more att):**

| | |
|---|---|
| .923 | QB Jim Harbaugh, MICH vs Pur (12 of 13), 11-9-85 |
| .917 | QB Dave Yarema, MSU vs North (11 of 12), 11-6-82 |
| .867 | QB Chuck Long, Iowa vs IND (26 of 30), 10-20-84 |

**MOST CONSECUTIVE COMPLETIONS:**

| | |
|---|---|
| 22 | QB Chuck Long, Iowa vs IND, 10-20-84 |
| 14 | QB Tony Eason, Ill vs IOWA, 10-30-82 |

**MOST HAD INTERCEPTED:**

| | |
|---|---|
| 6 | Tom O'Connell (34 att, 22 compl), Ill vs IOWA, 11-8-52 |
| 6 | Don Swanson (17 att, 6 compl), Minn vs WIS, 11-20-54 |

**MOST TD PASSES:**

| | |
|---|---|
| 6 | QB Dave Wilson (69 att, 43 compl, 621 yds), Ill vs OSU, 11-8-81 |
| | (TD passes of 24, 38, 8, 13, 2 and 1 yds) |
| 6 | QB Chuck Long (26 att, 19 compl, 399 yds), Iowa vs NU, 10-26-85 |
| | (TD passes of 28, 44, 89, 35, 25 and 4 yds) |
| 5 | QB Fred Riddle (16 att, 10 compl, 155 yds), IOWA vs Ind, 10-12-63 |
| | (TD passes of 5, 5, 3, 76 and 4 yds) |
| 5 | QB Mitch Anderson (41 att, 22 compl, 315 yds), NU vs Minn, 11-3-73 |
| | (TD passes of 18, 19, 21, 13 and 20 yds) |
| 5 | QB Mike Hohensee (67 att, 37 compl, 444 yds), MINN vs Ohio St, 11-7-81 |
| | (TD passes of 1, 27, 17, 18 and 28 yds) |

**MOST YARDS INTERCEPTION RETURNS:**

| | |
|---|---|
| 140 | DB Walt Bowser (34 interc), Minn vs MSU, 11-14-70 |

**MOST TD PASSES:**

| | |
|---|---|
| 4 | Reggie Arnold, PUR vs Iowa, 10-22-77 |

## PUNTING

**MOST KICKED:**

| | |
|---|---|
| 24 | HB Chuck Ortmann (723 yds), Mich vs OSU, 11-25-50 |

**MOST YARDS KICKED:**

| | |
|---|---|
| 723 yds | HB Chuck Ortmann (24 punts), Mich vs OSU, 11-25-50 |
| 685 yds | FB Vic Janowicz (21 punts), OSU vs Mich, 11-25-50 |

**BEST AVERAGE:**

| | |
|---|---|
| 57.3 | FB Fred Morrison (4 punts, 229 yds), Ohio St vs WIS, 10-22-49 |

**LONGEST PUNT:**

| | |
|---|---|
| 96 yds | George O'Brien, Wis vs IOWA, 10-18-52 |
| 87 yds | Karl Edwards, Ohio St vs ILL, 10-15-83 |
| 86 yds | Greg Montgomery, Mich St vs MICH, 10-11-86 |

**MOST PUNTS RETURNED:**

| | |
|---|---|
| 10 | William Lane (83 yds), WIS vs Ind, 11-3-51 |

**MOST YARDS RETURNED:**

| | |
|---|---|
| 201 | Nile Kinnick, IOWA vs Ind, 10-7-39 |

**MOST BLOCKED:**

| | |
|---|---|
| 2 | Mike Enich, Iowa vs PUR, 11-4-39 |
| 2 | Lonnie Young, MSU vs Minn, 10-29-83 |

## KICKOFFS

**MOST RETURNED:**

| | |
|---|---|
| 8 | Craig Clemons (165 yds), Iowa vs MICH, 11-6-71 |

**MOST YARDS RETURNED:**

| | |
|---|---|
| 203 | Ron Engel (7 ret), Minn vs MICH, 10-27-51 |

# Team Single Game Records

## SCORING

**MOST POINTS:**

| | |
|---|---|
| 85 | Mich vs CHICAGO, 10-21-39 |
| 83 | OSU vs Iowa, 10-28-50 |

**MOST TOUCHDOWNS:**

| | |
|---|---|
| 12 | Mich vs CHICAGO, 10-21-39 |
| 12 | OSU vs Iowa, 10-28-50 |

**MOST SAFETIES:**

| | |
|---|---|
| 2 | Iowa vs PUR (11-4-39); Pur vs IND (11-19-55); Wis vs PUR (10-20-51); Minn vs IND (10-17-81) |

**MOST PAT MADE:**

| | |
|---|---|
| 11 | OSU vs Iowa (12 att), 10-28-50 |
| 10 | Mich vs CHICAGO (12 att), 10-21-39 |
| 10 | MICH vs Ill (10 att), 11-7-81 |

**MOST FIELD GOALS:**

| | |
|---|---|
| 5 | Ill vs Wis, 10-6-84 |
| 5 | PUR vs Mich St, 10-25-80 |
| 5 | Ill vs Pur, 10-10-73 |
| 5 | Ill vs WIS, 10-23-82 |
| 4 | Has been accomplished 19 times |

## RUSHING

**MOST RUSHES:**

| | |
|---|---|
| 92 | PUR vs Iowa (483 yds), 10-26-68 |

**MOST YARDS GAINED:**

| | |
|---|---|
| 573 | Mich St vs PUR (70 rushes), 10-30-71 |
| 573 | MICH vs North (69 rushes), 10-8-75 |
| 551 | Wis vs NU (79 rushes), 11-16-74 |
| 524 | MICH vs Iowa (77 rushes), 11-15-69 |

**BEST AVERAGE PER RUSH:**

| | |
|---|---|
| 10.33 | PUR vs Ill (39 rushes, 403 yds), 10-2-43 |

## PASSING

**MOST ATTEMPTS:**

| | |
|---|---|
| 71 | NU vs Mich (45 compl, 436 yds), 10-23-82 |
| 69 | Ill vs OSU (43 compl, 621 yds), 11-8-80 |
| 67 | MINN vs Ohio St (37 compl, 444 yds), 11-7-81 |

**MOST COMPLETED:**

| | |
|---|---|
| 45 | NU vs Mich (71 att), 10-23-82 |
| 43 | Ill vs OSU (69 att), 11-8-80 |

**MOST YARDS GAINED:**

| | |
|---|---|
| 621 | Ill vs OSU (60 att, 43 compl), 11-8-80 |

**BEST COMPLETION AVERAGE:**

| | |
|---|---|
| 1.000 | OSU vs Iowa (8-8, 117 yds), 10-11-75 |

**BEST COMPLETION AVERAGE (more than 8 attempts):**

| | |
|---|---|
| .923 | MICH vs Pur (12-13, 230 yds), 11-9-85 |
| .889 | MICH vs Minn (8-9, 203 yds), 10-27-51 |
| .857 | MICH vs Ill (12-14, 265 yds), 11-1-86 |

**MOST TD PASSES**

| | |
|---|---|
| 6 | Ill vs OSU, 11-8-80 |
| 6 | Iowa vs NU, 10-26-85 |
| 5 | OSU vs Iowa, 10-25-50; IOWA vs Ind, 10-12-63; NU vs Minn, 11-3-73; and MINN vs Ohio St, 11-7-81 |

**MOST HAD INTERCEPTED:**

| | |
|---|---|
| 7 | Minn vs WIS, 11-20-54 |

## TOTAL OFFENSE

**MOST PLAYS:**

| | |
|---|---|
| 109 | Ind vs MINN (68 rushes, 41 passes, 557 yds), 11-4-78 |
| 107 | MICH vs Minn (77 rushes, 30 passes, 453 yds), 10-26-68 |
| 103 | PUR vs Mich St (57 rushes, 46 passes, 586 yds), 10-25-80 |

**MOST YARDS GAINED:**

| | |
|---|---|
| 713 | IOWA vs North (138 rush, 575 pass), 10-8-83 |
| 698 | Mich St vs PUR (573 rush, 125 pass), 10-30-71 |
| 673 | Mich vs IOWA (524 rush, 149 pass), 11-15-69 |
| 662 | Ill vs NU (281 rush, 381 pass), 11-19-83 |
| 660 | MSU vs Iowa (489 rush, 171 pass), 11-23-74 |
| 659 | Ill vs OSU (38 rush, 621 pass), 11-8-80 |
| 658 | IOWA vs Ind (249 rush, 409 pass), 10-29-83 |
| 656 | IOWA vs Minn (517 rush, 139 pass), 11-19-83 |
| 655 | OSU vs Ill (517 rush, 127 pass), 11-2-75 |
| 645 | MSU vs Wis (295 rush, 350 pass), 10-28-78 |
| 645 | MICH vs Ill (373 rush, 272 pass), 11-7-81 |

## PUNTING

**MOST PUNTS:**

| | |
|---|---|
| 24 | Mich vs OSU (723 yds), 11-25-50 |

**MOST YARDS KICKED:**

| | |
|---|---|
| 723 | Mich vs OSU (24 punts), 11-25-50 |
| 685 | OSU vs Mich (21 punts), 11-25-50 |
| 531 | ILL vs North (14 punts), 10-28-39 |

**BEST AVERAGE:**

| | |
|---|---|
| 56.5 | Ohio St vs ILL (226 yds), 11-8-75 |

## FIRST DOWNS

**MOST BY RUSHING:**

| | |
|---|---|
| 32 | Wis vs NU, 11-16-74 |
| 31 | PUR vs Iowa, 10-26-68 |

**MOST BY PASSING:**

| | |
|---|---|
| 26 | Ill vs OSU, 11-8-80 |
| 23 | NU vs Mich, 10-23-82 |

**MOST TOTAL FIRST DOWNS:**

| | |
|---|---|
| 37 | Wis vs NU, 11-16-74 |
| 36 | Ill vs OSU, 11-8-80 |
| 34 | Ohio St vs NU, 11-1-69 |
| 34 | Mich vs IOWA, 11-15-69 |
| 34 | MINN vs Ind, 11-4-78 |
| 34 | Mich St vs NU, 11-18-78 |
| 34 | PUR vs Mich St, 10-25-80 |
| 34 | ILL vs Mich, 11-6-82 |
| 34 | Wis vs NU, 10-1-83 |

## FUMBLES:

**MOST:**

| | |
|---|---|
| 14 | MSU vs Iowa (3 lost), 10-23-71 |
| 12 | Wis vs MICH (5 lost), 11-8-44 |
| 11 | Ill vs WIS (8 lost), 10-20-45 |

**MOST LOST:**

| | |
|---|---|
| 8 | Ill vs WIS (11 fumbles), 10-20-45 |

## PENALTIES:

**MOST:**

| | |
|---|---|
| 17 | Mich St vs IND, 9-28-57 |

**MOST YARDS:**

| | |
|---|---|
| 171 | PUR vs North, 10-25-69 |

ACKNOWLEDGMENTS
The publisher would like to thank the following people who helped in the preparation of this book: Mike Rose, who designed it; Donna Cornell Muntz and Lynn Leedy, who did the picture research; and Cynthia Klein, who prepared the index.

PICTURE CREDITS
The Bettmann Archive, Inc: pages 22 (top left), 40 (top), 176 (bottom)
Big Ten Conference: page 55 (right)
Chance Brockway: pages 1, 2-3, 6 (bottom right), 7 (top right and bottom right), 33 (bottom left and right), 34 (bottom left and right), 35 (top), 69 (top), 70-71 (top and bottom), 99 (top), 114-15, 127 (top and bottom left), 128, 137 (top left), 138-39, 158 (left and top right), 159 (bottom right), 170 (top), 172-73, 182 (center right)
Jonathan Daniel/Northwestern University Sports Information Office: page 136 (top)
Malcolm W Emmons: pages 6 (bottom left), 7 (center left and right, bottom left), 18, 32, 33 (top left), 34 (top left), 35 (bottom left and right), 37 (bottom right), 47 (top), 49 (top left and bottom left), 50 (left), 51 (bottom left and right), 52, 72, 92-93, 93 (left), 94 (top), 96, 97 (both), 98, 99 (bottom left), 102, 107 (top), 109 (top), 110, 111 (both), 112 (both), 113, 124 (top), 125 (both), 126, 127 (center left and right), 137 (top right), 154 (both), 155, 157 (both), 158 (bottom right), 160, 168, 169 (all three), 170 (bottom left and right), 171 (both), 181 (both), 182 (left, top and bottom right)
Gerald R Ford Library: page 83 (bottom)
Indiana University Athletic Department, Photo Lab: pages 6 (logo), 38-39, 40 (bottom), 41 (right), 42 (both), 43, 44 (both), 45, 46 (both), 47 (bottom), 48, 49 (top right and bottom right), 50-51
Iowa State Historical Society: page 63
Per H Kjeldsen, University of Michigan: pages 7 (top left), 95, 100 (bottom), 100-01, 101 (top right and bottom right)
Michigan State University, University Relations: pages 6 (logo), 105 (top), 106 (both), 107 (bottom), 108-09, 109 (bottom)
Northwestern Sports Information Office: pages 6 (logo), 130 (center), 130-31, 131 (top), 132 (both), 133, 134 (bottom), 136 (bottom), 137 (bottom)
Northwestern University Archives: pages 4-5, 130 (top), 134 (top), 135 (top)
Ohio State University Photo Archives: pages 140, 141 (both), 142 (both), 143, 144 (both), 145 (left), 146, 149, 150, 151 (both), 152, 153, 156, 159 (bottom left)
Pasadena Tournament of Roses Association: pages 29 (both), 30 (top), 37 (top and bottom left), 135 (bottom)
Pro-Football Hall of Fame: page 75 (left)
Purdue University Athletic Public Relations Office: pages 6 (logo), 8, 9 (left), 162 (both), 163, 164 (both), 165, 166 (top left, bottom left and right), 167
Mike Smeltzer/University of Illinois: page 36
Stanford Sports Information, Stanford University: page 15 (bottom)
University of Chicago: pages 6 (logo), 13 (right), 14 (both), 16, 17
University of Illinois: pages 6 (logo), 21, 22 (top right), 23 (top right and bottom), 27, 28 (bottom)
University of Illinois Archives, Record Series 39/2/20: pages 20 (both), 24 (bottom), 26 (center), 28 (top)
University of Iowa Photo Service: pages 6 (logo), 54, 56 (both), 57 (both), 58, 59 (both), 60, 61 (both), 62 (all three), 64, 65 (top left and right, bottom left), 66 (both), 67 (top), 68, 69 (bottom), 70 (top left and bottom left)
University of Michigan Athletic Department: pages 6 (logo), 74, 75 (top right and bottom right), 76, 77 (both), 78, 80, 82 (both), 83 (top), 84 (top left and bottom left), 86, 87 (bottom left), 88 (bottom), 90, 91 (top right and bottom), 92 (bottom left), 94 (bottom)
University of Minnesota Archives: pages 9 (right), 116, 117 (both), 118, 119, 120 (both), 121 (both), 122 (both), 123 (both)
University of Minnesota Department of Men's Athletics: pages 6 (logo), 124 (bottom)
University of Wisconsin-Madison Archives: pages 6 (logo), 174 (both), 175, 176 (top), 178 (both), 179, 180 (bottom)
UPI/Bettmann Newsphotos: pages 10-11, 12, 13 (left), 15 (top), 24-25, 26 (top), 30 (bottom), 31 (both), 41 (left), 55 (left), 59 (top), 65 (bottom right), 67 (bottom), 79, 81, 84 (top and bottom right), 85, 87 (top and bottom right), 88 (top), 89 (both), 91 (top left), 92 (bottom right), 99 (bottom right), 101 (bottom right), 104 (both), 105 (bottom), 145 (right), 147, 148, 159 (top), 166 (top right), 177, 180 (top)
Urbana Free Library: pages 22 (bottom), 23 (top left)